CECIL ROTH

A HISTORY OF
THE JEWS

From Earliest Times
Through the Six Day War

Revised Edition

SCHOCKEN BOOKS · NEW YORK

First SCHOCKEN PAPERBACK edition 1961
Revised Edition 1970
15 14 13 12 11 10 9 8   79 80 81 82

IN MEMORY OF

MY FATHER

JOSEPH ROTH

1866–1924

PREFACE

Thank God that I have been privileged to witness and to record the crowning mercies inadequately described in the new pages now appended to this work.

Jerusalem　　　　　　　　　　　　　　　C.R.
June 1967

TABLE OF CONTENTS

Table of Contents

BOOK FOUR

THE BREAK OF DAWN 1492 - 1815

BOOK FIVE

THE NEW AGE 1815 - 1935

BOOK SIX

CATASTROPHE AND RESURRECTION

BOOK ONE

ISRAEL
(circa 1600-586 B.C.E.)

I.

THE BIRTH OF THE HEBREW PEOPLE

1.   In the sixteenth century before the Christian Era began, the land which we now call Palestine, a fertile fringe between the Mediterranean Sea and the Arabian Desert, was occupied by a medley of races. There was still some remnant of the primitive "neolithic" stock of cave-dwellers, whose gigantic stature later became proverbial. They had been dispossessed by a Semitic people known as Amorites, who had emigrated not long ago from the wilds of Arabia, and, abandoning their nomadic life, had settled on the soil. In the lowlands to the north, especially along the coast beyond Mount Carmel, were the trading Canaanites, who gave their name to the country (the Land of Canaan, it was generally called). The all-powerful Egyptian Empire was making sporadic attempts to spread its influence northward, with a considerable degree of success; and its garrisons or fortified posts were dotted throughout the country. The mysterious Hittite had made his appearance not only as conqueror, but also as colonist. Assyrian rulers marched and countermarched through the land in campaigns against Egypt, or in efforts to subdue the local chieftains. And, in their wake, came numbers of Aramean immigrants from the crowded plains of Mesopotamia, desirous of establishing themselves in this exuberant land. *Ibrim,* or Hebrews, they were called, either because of their legendary descent from one Eber, or

else from the fact that they came from "Beyond the Great River" (*Eber ha-Nahar*), the Euphrates.

One of these Aramean immigrants stands out from the rest, a certain Abram, or Abraham, a native of Ur of the Chaldees. His home city, as recent excavations have shown, was already at that time the seat of an ancient and highly polished culture. Its religious life, on the other hand, was based upon a system of polytheism, revolving about stately temples in which a gross ceremonial was carried on by a hierarchy of priests. It was with the glimmering at least of something higher, and in the hopes of attaining a more complete spiritual fulfilment, that Abraham is said to have left his country. In this sense, he is rightly considered the founder of the Jewish people; and it is significant that converts to Judaism even today are termed "children of Abraham, our Father."

We have the picture of a stately sheik-like figure moving about Palestine from north to south, with his wife and his concubines and his flocks and his herds and his tents. On one occasion he was driven by famine to seek refuge in Egypt. The "land of the Canaanite" had already established its hold upon him, and he took an early opportunity to return. Yet he considered that he belonged to a higher civilization than did the other inhabitants of the country; and it was to his own kinsfolk in his native Mesopotamia that he sent for a wife for his son, Isaac.*

The latter is the next leader of the group. He stands out less distinctly, and with less grandeur than the majestic Abraham. It is only with the next generation that the

See additional note at the end of this chapter.

family became a tribe. In the evening of his days, Isaac's children, Esau and Jacob, quarreled violently among themselves. Jacob, or Israel, has twelve sons; and, by the time of his old age, his descendants number some seventy souls. His had been an adventurous, troubled career. In youth, driven out of his home through his brother's jealousy, he returned to his mother's kinsfolk in Mesopotamia. Many years later he came back to Palestine with his growing family, and lived the life of a wandering sheik, as his father and grandfather had done. Another famine drove the household (to be known in the future as Israelites) down into Egypt. Here, one of the family, a certain Joseph, had preceded him. It was the period of Shepherd, or "Hyksos," Kings who were of Semitic origin; and it may have been because of this fact that Joseph had been able to obtain for himself a position at Court. In consequence, his father and brothers received a warm welcome, and were permitted to settle in the province of Goshen.

Not long afterwards the Hyksos monarchy fell (c. 1600 B.C.E.)—an event which must have affected the position of the Israelites adversely. Under succeeding rulers or Pharaohs, their position deteriorated more and more, until at last they were reduced to unqualified serfdom. Their individuality was preserved, not only by their common origin, but also by the fact of the survival of their ancestors' spiritual ideals. Their faith stood out in acute contrast to the fantastic polytheism of their masters. It is significant that their revolt and deliverance came about under the inspiration of a leader who was at once a political and a religious reformer.

2.   A certain Israelite named Moses, who had been brought up in the royal court, placed himself at the head of a movement for the regeneration and liberation of his people. After many vicissitudes (recounted with a wealth of detail in the traditional lore of his race), he succeeded in leading his fellow-tribesmen out of the country, in the direction of the land in which their fathers had settled.* We read of a disaster which overtook the pursuing Egyptian forces in the Red Sea, where they were caught by the advancing tide. The Feast of Passover, which the fugitives instituted in celebration of their deliverance, is observed by their descendants to the present day. With the Israelites, there went out also a medley of other races, belonging mainly, in all probability, to the Hyksos and other depressed elements. The latter became absorbed in the twelve families or tribes, into which the descendants of Jacob's twelve sons had by now become divided.

The entrance to Palestine, where the Egyptian authority was still strong, could not be achieved immediately. For a prolonged period (traditionally reckoned at forty years) the Israelites remained in the wilderness of Sinai, between the two lands. It was a stern period of probation. Moses, a stupendous figure, welded the jealous tribes into a people. He inculcated a purer idea of monotheism. He laid down the basis of an advanced moral and ethical system. He promulgated a code of laws, which has formed the foundation of Jewish practice and jurisprudence to our own day, as well as of much of the humanitarian idealism of modern

* According to some authorities the date was about 1445 B.C.E., but the majority of scholars favor about 1227 B.C.E.

times. It is said that not a shred of evidence for the historicity of Moses exists. That may be so, if we are to regard potsherds as being more significant and more reliable than the memory of a whole people, or written records of immemorial antiquity. But the influence which the figure of the great lawgiver had on the Hebrew mind is traceable from the earliest period; and it is so profound that it can hardly fail to depend in the last resort upon a personality which made an indelible impression upon contemporaries. If we had no account of Moses at all, it would be necessary to assume the existence of a person such as he is said to have been, in order to explain the being of the Hebrew people, with its distinctive literature, law, ethics, and religious code.

3.   The story of the Hebrew race, as it has been told thus far, follows in its general lines the traditional account, embodied in the historical books of the Jewish Scriptures, which have become part of the fibre of the Jewish being. It is proper to append the outline of the same events as they appear from the angle of modern biblical criticism; not, indeed, from that of radicals who question the veracity of the traditional story in almost every detail, but of the more moderate school who accept at least its outline.

According to the latter, the so-called *Israelites* did not possess any common origin in the immediate past, nor did they have any common history down to a period subsequent to their settlement in Palestine. They were made up of a number of different elements, allied only by language, and possibly by their ultimate descent from an

Aramean stock. Each element had its own history and folk-lore; and only at a comparatively late date did the various traditions become fused into the familiar account which we know today.

If Abraham existed (and many would question even this), it was simply as an outstanding personality, to whom many of the shrines of Palestine traditionally owed their foundation; he was not in any sense the ancestor of the Hebrew people. Isaac and Jacob are regarded as semi-symbolic figures, perhaps representing a tribal motif. The latter, indeed (who seems to preserve the name of some ancient Palestinian deity), was personified in order to provide a common progenitor for the Twelve Tribes, named, not after their ancestors, but for the most part after their respective totems. Not all of these (perhaps only the "Joseph" clan, Menasseh and Ephraim) were in Egypt; while if Joseph himself was an historic figure, he probably was nothing more than a prominent tribal leader.

Moses himself was a Hebrew, or Israelite, with some Egyptian affiliations; in all probability belonging to the tribe of Ephraim rather than to that of Levi, to which he is assigned by tradition. During a period of exile or of travel, he was brought into contact with a deity YHWH, formerly known only amongst the Kenites, whom he induced the various Hebrew tribes to accept as the object of their worship. It was only now that the Israelites (or a portion of them) became united by the bonds of a common faith. However, though the new cult was exclusive, and implied the abandonment of polytheism, and though Moses insisted upon a moral code sterner and purer than the ordinary, YHWH was, in effect, a deity of the same type as any other, represented at various times by a bull, or a snake, or a sacred stone. It was only very much later, under the Hebrew monarchy, that this "monolatry" (as it is best termed), became reformed, purified, and spiritualized, developing into a "monotheism" in the proper sense of the word.

Palestine was entered in a number of distinct nomadic waves, the most important of these being that of the so-called "Joseph" clan from the south. At least some of the tribes, however, had participated neither in the Egyptian bondage, nor in the Exodus. This was particularly the case as regards the tribe of Judah, who seem to have been a settled Canaanite strain rather than nomadic Arameans. The tribe of Judah entered the Israelitish polity, absorbing its national outlook at a very late date. Only during the long period of warfare and of travail which succeeded the entry of the Hebrews into Palestine did these various groups, with different origins and different traditions, acquire a rudimentary sense of unity, and develop their common faith.

The new conception of early Israel thus presents the monotheistic principle, which has been the basis of Jewish history, as a slow and gradual evolution, rather than a sudden emergence. It is a theory which does credit to the national genius no less than the traditional story, though it may rob the latter of much of its personal interest and charm. It is a record, not of the cataclysmic revelation of the Deity to man, but of the gradual discovery by humanity of the Divine.

4.   Even before Moses' death, the tribes that he controlled had begun to establish themselves in the narrow fertile strip on the eastern side of the Jordan, between the river and the wilderness. The great leader, "who had known God face to face," passed away before anything more could be done under his immediate direction. It was under a certain Joshua, of the powerful tribe of Ephraim (unlike Moses, a military commander rather than an essentially spiritual force), that the penetration of Palestine began. The Jordan was crossed at a point near the mouth of the Jabok, some twenty-five miles north of the Dead Sea. Jericho, a strong city which appears to have continued faithful to the Egyptian suzerainty, was stormed. A confederation of local petty rulers was defeated in the historic pass of Beth Horon. The Israelites were now in control of the hill-country in the center of Palestine. Hence they spread by slow degrees northwards, until their progress was checked by the chain of strong positions which protected the plain of Jezreel (Esdraelon). Thus began the settlement of the Israelites in the land with which they were to be associated, more or less closely, in all subsequent history.

The conquest was a slow, laborious process. The invaders were unable to reach the coast for many generations to come. Several of the principal cities continued to owe allegiance to the Pharaohs or to be occupied by Egyptian garrisons. The original inhabitants retained many a mountain fastness long after the surrounding countryside had fallen. Often, the invaders in their turn found themselves so hard pressed that their own existence was threatened.

The various sections were isolated from one another by long strips of enemy territory—Judah, Simeon, and Reuben to the extreme south; Naphtali and Zebulun to the north, cut off from the center by the fortresses which stretched from Beth Shean to Megiddo; the all-powerful Menasseh and Ephraim in the central hill-country, with an off-shoot on the other side of the Jordan. Intense local jealousies made themselves felt. Thus, foreign incursions were facilitated, and sometimes invited. Ancient records have preserved the names of no fewer than six foreign powers who oppressed all or part of the Hebrew race in the course of the generations which immediately succeeded the death of Joshua. It was only on very few occasions, as, for example, when a coalition was formed against them by the northern principalities, inspired by the Canaanite king of Hazor, that the Hebrews were able to sink their internal jealousies and make common cause against the foe. But, in spite of all obstacles, the work of conquest slowly continued.

By the twelfth century before the Christian Era, the population of Palestine, within its historic borders, was fairly homogeneous. There were numerous relics of heathenism and sometimes lapses which were even more regrettable, but the old monotheistic ideals of Israel retained a general hold. The former wandering shepherds had renounced their nomadic, pastoral life and settled down as farmers and peasants, tilling the soil. The countryside was dotted with small towns and villages, crowning every fertile eminence. The constitution was rudimentary. There was a certain vague national feeling, expressed in and consolidated by the common religious cult; and the tribes

might come to one another's aid in time of danger. Even
the section beyond the Jordan was regarded as part of the
same body politic, notwithstanding its isolated position and
its specific interests.

The tribal organization itself was very weak. Each town
and village was, in effect, an independent unit, ruled and
judged by its elders. Occasionally, some outstanding figure
might attain a wider recognition, generally by reason of
a military achievement against the national enemies. By
virtue of this, he would be in a position to "judge" his people, or a portion of it, for some time to come. We read of a
number of these judges in the obscure period which succeeded the death of Joshua: a woman, Deborah, who
effected a temporary coalition of almost all the tribes
against the Canaanite menace in the north under the King
of Hazor and his powerful general (or ally) Sisera; Ehud,
who assassinated the marauding king of Moab and thereby
secured an interlude of peace; Gideon, who, with a picked
force, overwhelmed the Midianite raiders by a stratagem;
Jephtha, a famous outlaw of Gilead, whose aid was enlisted
to crush the Ammonites; and a number of other more
shadowy figures.

Excepting in the first mentioned case, when Deborah
was judge, the enemy were seldom Canaanites. Generally
they were invaders from beyond the Jordan, seeking to
repeat what Israel had already performed; and the struggle
assisted in welding the whole population into a unity.
Egypt, looming vaguely in the background, continued to
maintain a nominal suzerainty over the whole country; and
the land "had rest" (in the biblical phrase) in those rare

interludes when she was powerful enough to assert her influence and put down disorder.

At times, there was internecine warfare among the tribes; as, on one occasion, when the tribe of Benjamin was almost annihilated in consequence of a lawless accident which had taken place within its boundaries. Once, at least, an attempt was made (by Abimelech, son of the Gideon mentioned above) to set up a monarchy, with its capital at Shechem. But the sentimental center of the country was Shiloh, where the national Palladium, the "Ark of the Lord" (constructed, according to tradition, during the forty years of wandering in the wilderness), had found its home, and where the religious worship of the whole people had its focus. Thus, under conditions which are to us today wrapped for the most part in obscurity, the Hebrew people passed three of the most crucial centuries of its existence.

NOTE TO CHAPTER I

In dealing with the biblical age, the author has made what must nowadays be considered the innovation of adhering in general outline to the traditional account; though presenting it as far as possible in a coherent fashion, neglecting the miraculous element, and using a vocabulary such as one would in dealing with any other people. This has not been due to any inherent obscurantism on his part, nor to any ignorance of the conclusions of Higher Criticism, with which he has done his best to familiarize himself. The critical attitude, however (contrary to the popular belief), is by no means unimpeachable in every detail. Moreover, its conclusions are constantly changing, from generation to generation, almost from year to year. Penetrating though its destructive criticism has been, it has failed thus far to provide any alternative account which commands universal acceptance. A majority of histories thus resolve themselves, in point of fact, into a highly unimpressive discussion of the sources. On the other hand, an unmistakable reaction has set in against the radical school of the last century.

It is a somewhat ironic consideration that, as usual, the popularization of these conceptions lags behind, so that the hypothetical "man in the street" has just managed to absorb the advanced views which were abandoned in the better-informed scientific circles some time ago.

It is thus impossible to formulate an account of the origins of the Jewish people which will, firstly, command universal agreement even among the Higher Critics of today; and secondly, is likely to remain valid in ten or twenty years' time. The traditional story, on the other hand, is always likely to retain the same validity, much or little, which it now possesses.

There is one further consideration, perhaps more fundamental. There is a subjective as well as an objective historicity. A personality which a people has cherished in its heart for a score of centuries, whether he existed or no, attains an importance of his own in sentimental reality. The incidents legendarily connected with his name crystallize, in some measure, the national idea of conduct. The mere fact that they were believed to have taken place may itself exercise a profound influence upon the course of events. The lives of the Patriarchs and the subsequent episodes, whether story or history, thus constitute an essential part of the background of the Jewish people; and it is out of the question to neglect them.

II.
THE E STABLISHMENT *of the* MONARCHY

1.   The condition of the Hebrews in Palestine, at the
close of what is known as the Age of the Judges, was very
similar in many respects to that of the Anglo-Saxons in England two thousand years later. In each case, the country
was occupied by the descendants of invaders of some generations earlier. They had settled down; they had intermarried with and assimilated the original inhabitants, losing in the process something of their martial qualities; and
they were now divided into a number of independent units.
There was in each case a rudimentary sense of solidarity,
fostered by a common blood and a common faith. The
stimulus and the agonies of a universal danger were necessary to weld the scattered tribes into a people. In the
case of England the stimulus was provided by the incursions of the Danes. In the case of the Hebrews, it came
from a maritime people similar in many respects to the
latter, the Philistines.

At the beginning of the twelfth century B.C.E., some
local upheaval, or the magnet of loot, seems to have caused
a wholesale migration southwards from Crete and the
coast-lands of Asia Minor. The strangers, repulsed from
Egypt in 1194, fell back upon the rich coastal plain to the
north. Here they had little difficulty in establishing themselves. Their confederation of five city-states, each under its
own *Seren,* or Tyrant, commanded the high road between

15

Asia and Africa. Such was the impression which they made upon the ancient world that ultimately their name was given to the whole of the country, which is still known after them, as Palestine (*Philistina*).

Once they were firmly established on the coastal plain, the restless invaders pushed inland. The Israelites of the lowlands began to live in constant fear of their raids. It was the neighboring tribe of Dan which first felt the brunt of the attack. A single individual, Samson, a man of gigantic strength and quickness of resource, who remained long afterward the hero of many a Hebrew saga, helped to stem the attack for a time. Ultimately, he was captured and blinded; though, the story recounts, he did more execution in his death than in his life. The Philistine attacks redoubled in intensity. In the end, the tribe of Dan, now reduced to no more than 600 fighting men, was forced to evacuate its territory and to look for another home in the extreme north, where they, in turn, displaced the earlier inhabitants. Henceforth, "from Dan to Beersheba" was considered to comprise the full extent of the Israelitish territory.

The Philistine raids had by now assumed the character of a systematic war of conquest. In the face of common danger, the tribes were compelled to patch up their internal differences and to present a united front. Nevertheless, they were overwhelmed in a double encounter near Aphek, losing in addition the portable shrine, long since established in the sanctuary at Shiloh, which they had carried into battle with them. For many years to come Israel lay under the Philistine heel.

2.   One important consequence in the internal affairs of the nation had resulted from the disaster at Aphek. The two priests who had accompanied the Ark into the field had both fallen; their father, Eli, had died on hearing the news. This, coupled with the capture of the object about which their functions had hitherto centered, broke the power of the corrupt priesthood—legendarily descended from Aaron, the brother of Moses—which had been the principal unifying bond in national life for some generations past. A certain Samuel, who had been brought up in the sanctuary at Shiloh but who did not belong to the priestly line, henceforth received, by virtue of his commanding personality, much of the consideration previously paid to them; and his home, at Ramah in the hill-country of Ephraim, became in a sense the national center.

The new leader realized that the country required a strong unified government if it was to make headway against the enemies who were threatening its independence. Only a king could command the obedience of the whole people, and thus stem the Philistine peril.

At this period, as it happened, the Ammonites made one of their intermittent attacks upon the trans-Jordanic tribes, who appealed to their kinsfolk for help. The whole people was so disheartened that the summons fell on deaf ears. However, a courageous Benjaminite farmer, named Saul, took it upon himself to assume the leadership. There was a sudden counter-raid across the Jordan, and the enemy was repulsed. The effect on the Hebrews was magnetic. Saul seemed to be predestined as the national leader; and, with Samuel's approval, he was proclaimed king by the people.

It was not long before the War of Liberation began. It was a guerilla campaign. Saul and his followers, familiar with every inch of the country, were able to fall upon enemy detachments in surprise attacks. The fortunes of war varied. At times, the patriot forces were reduced to no more than a few hundred men. But a spectacular victory at Michmash led to the expulsion of the enemy from the central range and from a portion of the south of the country, including the territory of Judah and Benjamin. Punitive or retaliatory raids were executed against several neighboring tribes, the Moabites, Ammonites, and Arameans to the east and southeast; and, on a somewhat larger scale, against the Amalekites to the south. Under the stimulus of this series of victories, following upon the stress of a common oppression, the Israelites gradually acquired a sense of cohesion. Eventually, the country was cleared almost entirely of the Philistine forces. The peril remained, however, one of the dominating factors in national affairs for a full generation to come.

As time went on, it became evident that the national choice had been unwise. Saul was a gifted and undaunted military commander, but nothing more. His court was always a camp. He was capable of sudden, irresponsible outbreaks of barbarity, for which not even the interest of the state served as a palliating circumstance. Moreover, though the central and northern tribes, possibly because of their distance from the seat of authority, were disposed to favor, or at least to tolerate his rule, the powerful tribe of Judah found its eclipse by that of Benjamin insupportable.

David, son of Jesse, a Judaean farmer, enjoyed great con-

sideration in Saul's rough military household. He had come
into prominence while still a boy, by defeating a gigantic
Philistine champion in single combat. Since then, he had
been a popular darling. He had married the King's
daughter; he was the bosom friend of the King's son, Jonathan; and his daring raids on the enemy were the burden
of popular ballads. At length, Saul's jealousy became
aroused. Finding his life in danger, David escaped to his
native district, the hill-country of Judah. For the next few
years he lived as an outlaw, at the head of a band of devoted followers. Saul made sporadic attempts to hunt him
down and showed little mercy to any of his sympathizers.
At last, the rebel chieftain was forced to take refuge
among the Philistines, in the campaigns against whom he
had made his name. He was living at Ziklag, under the
protection of the King of Gath when Saul, together with
Jonathan and two of his other sons, fell in battle on the
slopes of Mount Gilboa, in an ineffectual effort to stem a
further Philistine incursion into the heart of the country.

3.   The dead king was succeeded (thanks to the devotion of his kinsman, Abner) by one of his surviving sons,
Ishbaal. As a consequence of the recent disaster, the majority of the country was once again under the Philistine
yoke. The royal residence, together with the seat of administration, was accordingly removed to Mahanaim, on
the other side of the Jordan, where the memory of Saul's
courageous exploit many years previous was still strong.
David, on the other hand, though he had bewailed Saul's
death in one of the most touching elegies in all literature,

lost no time in availing himself of the opportunities it afforded him. He immediately reentered the country with his seasoned veterans and seized Hebron—very probably with the aid of the Philistines, who were not averse to seeing their enemies weakened by internal divisions. The Judaean tribesmen looked up to him as their leader. It did not need much persuasion for them to accept him as their king (1013 B.C.E.).

David's ambition was too great to be satisfied by the exiguous area in the extreme south which recognized his authority. He looked with longing eyes to the north, restive under Ishbaal's weak rule. Clashes between the two factions followed as a matter of course, ending in Ishbaal's assassination. Tardily, and somewhat unwillingly, the northern tribes now transferred their allegiance to David, who was thus recognized as ruler over all Israel (1006 B.C.E.).

The great event of his reign, in the political sphere, was the shattering of the Philistine power. Another incursion had threatened to engulf the whole country, and David had been driven out of his capital. Unlike Saul, however, he did not rely entirely on force of arms, or on his own personal following. He countered attacks by alliances, and enlisted mercenaries to pit against the trained Philistine troops. After two victories in the Vale of Rephaim, the country was freed from the invader, and the war was carried back into their own territory. The capture of the city of Gath, one of the federation of five which had overawed Israel for the past century, ended the campaign. Henceforth, the Philistine menace belonged to the past.

A succession of foreign expeditions followed this triumph. David took advantage of the temporary weakness of Egypt to the south, and of Assyria to the north, to build up a powerful border kingdom. His veterans swept all before them. He secured his frontiers by a succession of wars against neighboring states. The insulting treatment of an embassy sent to the Ammonites was the pretext for a punitive expedition, which achieved a decisive victory. An Aramean coalition, comprising a number of petty principalities stretching northward as far as the Euphrates, was overwhelmed in an attempt to relieve Rabbah, the besieged Ammonite capital. A Hebrew garrison was placed in Damascus. Moab and Amalek were subdued (in the latter case, finally), and the land of Edom was annexed. One or two enclaves of non-Israelitish settlement, which remained from a former age to disturb the homogeneity of the country, were conquered, the last relic of the Jebusite strip which cut Judah off from the northern tribes thus becoming absorbed. Alliances were entered into with powerful neighbors, such as Hamath and Tyre. The authority of David was recognized from the borders of Egypt and the Gulf of Akabah on the south to the banks of the Euphrates on the north.

Within the historic frontiers of the country, the administration was revolutionized. The military camp which had served Saul as the seat of government developed into a court, with all its defects as well as its advantages. The long roll of officers of state testifies to the elaboration, if not necessarily to the efficiency, of the new regime. The system of military service was revised around the nucleus of a standing force of foreign mercenaries. The civil service was remodeled and elaborated. Even the priesthood was drastically reorganized. The loose confederation of clans was becoming converted into a strongly centralized kingdom.

Yet the monarchy established by David was, in spirit, what we would today call a constitutional one. The democratic feeling of the nomadic Aramaean tribes to which the Hebrew race owed its origin was still strong. The rights of the sovereign were limited by public opinion, which was fearlessly voiced. There was the basic idea of a "covenant" between the King and his people, executed under the auspices of a Deity who hated oppression and who would not tolerate injustice. We find none of the unbridled absolutism traditionally associated with the Oriental ruler. The King might covet the wife of one of his subjects, but he did not dare to seize her from her husband. He had the latter put out of the way by a subterfuge, which fact itself demonstrates his recognition of the limitations imposed upon his rights. When a popular representative arraigned him for his conduct, he did not manifest his resentment, though he could find no answer. It is obvious from this episode and others like it that he considered his prerogatives strictly limited. Under his successors, we find the same state of affairs.

This conception, of a monarchy based in the last instance upon an agreement between the ruler and his subjects, and with the rights of the former narrowed down by popular opinion and moral restrictions, is one of the utmost significance in the history of human ideas; for, studied, revived, and imitated in the seventeenth and eighteenth centuries, it led to the growth of the constitutional idea in modern Europe and America, and thus played a part of immeasurable importance in shaping the destinies of mankind.

The newborn nation still lacked its center. Among the cities captured by David within the natural borders of the country there was one, Jerusalem, which seemed ideally suited for the purpose. It was centrally situated. It was historically associated with no single tribe. The site was almost impregnable, by reason of the precipices which surrounded it on three sides. It lay close to important highways of communication and commerce. Above all, it was a conquest, almost a creation of David's. He lavished upon his new capital all his energies. He enlarged the fortifications to comprise the hill of Zion, calling the part thus included within the walls "The City of David." He constructed a sumptuous royal palace. He transferred thither the ancient shrine of the God of Israel; and he made preparations for the construction of a magnificent Temple to house it. From the reign of David, to this day, Jerusalem and Mount Zion have remained the sentimental, if not always the political, center of allegiance for the most vital portion of the Hebrew people.

The later years of the reign were troubled and disturbed. The royal household, which conformed both to Oriental tradition and to the King's deeply sensuous nature, bore its usual fruit of cruelty, jealousy, and household dissension. David, himself, worn out by a life of constant struggles and hardship, became prematurely aged. His sons by various wives quarrelled fiercely amongst themselves, so that the

royal house itself was stained by bloodshed. Ultimately his
own son, Absalom, broke into open revolt. The pace of the
recent reforms had been too rapid for a large proportion
of the population. The whole country, accordingly, flocked
to his standard. The new capital was occupied. David, himself, was driven to seek refuge beyond the Jordan; and he
was saved from utter ruin only by the fidelity of his bodyguard. Absalom's death, in the campaign that followed,
robbed the victory of its glory.

Not long afterwards, David died. Forty years had passed
since he had returned from exile to become King of Judah,
and thirty-three since his authority had been recognized by
the rest of Israel. There are few characters of ancient history whom we know more intimately. We see an intrepid
youth develop into a passionate manhood and a cold, calculating old age. We see the gifted lyric poet who won the
name of "the sweet singer of Israel" sinking to some of the
lowest depths of depravity. But there is about it all an en-
gaging honesty, a faculty for admitting himself at fault, a
final recognition of moral standards, which did something
to palliate even his most shameless wrong-doing. David's
personal ability, moreover, was exceptional. It was not
simply as the founder of the royal line, nor as reputed
writer of many lyrics, that his people had chosen to en-
shrine him in their hearts with peculiar affection. If
Hebrew history before his day is an indistinct labyrinth,
but with him begins to acquire consistency and cohesion,
the reason lies, above all, in his energy and genius. He
found Israel a collection of warring tribes. He left it a
strong and, as it seemed for the moment, united people.

4.   On his death-bed, David ordered his youngest
son, Solomon, as yet hardly out of childhood, to be anointed
his successor. The new ruler was faced at the opening of
his reign with a wave of discontent, which he put down
with a heavy hand. Thereafter, his rule was predominantly
pacific. Legend has chosen to remember Solomon as the
type of human wisdom. This is perhaps based on the appreciation of the fact that he forwarded the interests of his
realm primarily by statecraft, while his father employed
force of arms. It was a period of profound peace. The position of Palestine as the highway between Africa and Asia,
and, ultimately, Europe as well, was thus realized more
acutely than ever before. David, in the course of his campaigns, had succeeded in occupying Ezion-Geber on the
Gulf of Akabah. Solomon realized fully the value of this
possession. There was, in those days, no Suez Canal to join
the Mediterranean Sea and the Indian Ocean. But Ezion-
Geber, or the neighboring port of Elath, was the point of
embarkation for India and the Far East; and he who possessed it and Palestine at the same time, commanded the
bridge which joined three continents.

The Israelitish sovereign consolidated his position on the
south by an alliance with Egypt, through whose aid he
added to his territories Gezer, the last remaining Canaanite
fortress, and one of the great trading emporia of the
Near East. Thus, at last, the Hebrew kingdom obtained a
foothold on the Mediterranean. He fortified the positions
which commanded the various great trade routes passing
through his territory, from Egypt to Babylonia on the one
hand, and from the Mediterranean Sea to India on the

other. Linen-yarn and trained chariot horses were imported from Egypt, to be exchanged for the precious woods of the Lebanon, and the spices of Arabia. Solomon continued the intimate relations established by his father with the Phoenicians. The latter, happy with the use of the ports on the Gulf of Akabah for their expeditions to the Far East, permitted Hebrew sailors to join them, and assisted their ruler in his various enterprises. The trade from north to south, and from east to west, flowed through Palestine.

In return for the security which his policy gave, Solomon exacted a tribute from the merchant caravans. He, himself, did not disdain to participate in various trading expeditions. His treasury became filled to overflowing; and the rare beasts and commodities of the Orient became familiar in Jerusalem as they had never been before. The court was resplendent with its elaborate organization and its numerous functionaries. The size of the royal harem became proverbial. Distant princes came to visit the wisest of the monarchs. The capital was enlarged and transformed. Supplies of material and skilled artificers were obtained from Phoenicia, while labor was provided by forced native levies. Tyrian workmen assisted in constructing a series of magnificent royal palaces. For financial and administrative purposes, the country was divided into twelve districts, which neglected the old tribal boundaries; though, as events were to show, the centrifugal tendency was too strong to be submerged. The defenses of the realm were strengthened by the fortification of several border towns; while here and there forces of chariotry were established.

A literary renaissance followed this sudden enlargement

of the horizons of the country and the rapid increase in its wealth, as has generally been the case under similar circumstances throughout history. The name of the King himself was associated with vast numbers of polished epigrams, of a style similar to those found in the biblical *Book of Proverbs,* itself traditionally ascribed to his authorship. The contrast with his father's spontaneous lyrical outbursts is characteristic of the change that had taken place in the condition of the nation and of the royal house.

The climax of the reign came with the erection on Mount Zion of a magnificent Temple, to house the shrine transferred thither by David. This was dedicated with immense pomp at the Feast of Tabernacles, c. 953 B.C.E.; Jerusalem thus became the religious, as well as the political capital of the country. The three pilgrim feasts, especially the Passover, when every male was supposed to appear before the common Deity, served to enrich the city, and to make it, in a very real sense, the center of national life. In order to accentuate the importance of the Temple, there was an increasing tendency to prohibit animal sacrifices at any other spot. In origin this may have been a political move, intended to enhance the importance of the national sanctuary and of the priests who officiated in it. However, in the long run, it added to the spiritual potentialities of Hebraic monotheism, showing its followers that religion was possible without sacrifice, and enabling them to maintain their characteristic beliefs even when the Temple was no more.

The magnificence of Solomon's reign was not achieved without recourse to heavy taxation, from which, as it seems,

Judah was partially exempted. Even had this not been the case, the southern part of the country was tied to the dynasty not only by blood, but more especially by the economic prosperity which resulted from the royal policy and from the presence of the new capital. It found ample compensation in these facts. In the north, however, discontent was general. Even before the death of the Jewish *roi soleil,* the Empire which his father had founded showed signs of breaking up. The Aramaeans to the northeast had recovered their independence, setting up a new state with its center in Damascus. The Edomites had revolted. Unrest had made its appearance among the northern tribes. On the accession of Solomon's untried young son, Rehoboam, in 933 B.C.E., a petition was presented for the revision of taxation; and on its rejection, a general revolt broke out. The North rose in rebellion; and a certain Jeroboam ben Nebat, who had been at the head of a similar conspiracy during the previous reign, was acclaimed King.

It spoke well for the statesmanlike qualities of David and his son, that the tribe of Benjamin, which had formerly been the most unrelenting opponents of the dynasty, now threw in their lot with the tribe of Judah. David's Empire, with all its magnificent potentialities, fell to pieces. The outlying dependencies broke away. Henceforth, for a period of two centuries, Hebrew history has to divide its attention between two neighboring states, akin in blood, but always intense in rivalry, and at times engaged in war. There was the kingdom of Judah, with its capital in Jerusalem; and that of Israel, centering about Shechem. It is noteworthy that the ties of a common origin, language, and tradition were frequently able to nullify political separation. The literature of the period consistently represents the people as one, notwithstanding the political fissure. Intercourse between the northern kingdom and the southern remained intimate down to the end. Prisoners of war, captured in the not infrequent campaigns, could expect more humane treatment than would have been the lot of a stranger. Yet the strength of the country was wasted in internecine warfare; and the development of Palestine into the center of a great Empire, such as its geographical position justified and David's work might have led contemporaries to expect, was henceforth impossible. Palestine's might was not to be in the political sphere.

III. THE KINGDOM OF SAMARIA

1.   It was in the southern kingdom, that of Judah,
that the Hebraic tradition perpetuated itself, and thereby
has been transmitted to our own day. By the inclusion in
the Hebrew Bible of a detailed history of the northern
tribes, this fact tends to be obscured. For the sake of clarity,
it is better to pursue the barren record of the so-called
"Kingdom of Israel" to its end before returning to follow
the main stream on its majestic course.

In contrast to the comparative tranquility of the kingdom
of Judah, where the Davidic dynasty had already established a strong hold on the popular imagination, the Kingdom of Israel was in a state of continual unrest. There was
perpetual jealousy of tribe against tribe. Any successful
general was a menace to the stability of the throne. In the
course of its two centuries of existence, nineteen sovereigns
ruled over the northern monarchy (half as many again as
was the case in the southern part of the country). Many
reigned for only a couple of years; some, for no more than
a few months, and one for only seven days. At least half of
them died violent deaths, in most instances at the hands
of their successors. It was in a minority of cases that a ruler
was succeeded by his own son; and only two dynasties
lasted for more than as many generations.

Jeroboam had noted, with foreboding, the dominant role
which Jerusalem had come to play during the past two

reigns, a consequence not only of its dignity as capital, but also of the fact that it was the seat of the national shrine. With considerable insight, he set about undermining the esteem which it enjoyed on the latter account. At the two extremes of his realm, at Dan and at Bethel, he erected rival sanctuaries which would deflect the pilgrims who had formerly gone up to Jerusalem, and attract something of that allegiance which the Judaean capital had previously possessed. At the same time, the secessionist King made, or perpetuated, a concession to popular weakness. He set up in these shrines images of bulls overlaid with gold. It was not, in fact, an attempt to reintroduce idolatry. The figures were intended to represent in a concrete form the God of Israel—"These are your Gods, O Israel, who brought you forth from the Land of Egypt." Yet the inevitable effect was to lessen the sternness of the monotheistic conception and to modify the national distinctiveness. The consequences were to become manifest in later years.

2.   After Jeroboam (who died in 912, after a reign of twenty-one years), one or two outstanding rulers only are encountered. Omri (887-876), who mounted the throne in 887 after a civil war, proved himself a vigorous and far-seeing monarch. He transferred his capital from the ancient Shechem, which had been ill-fated for so many of his predecessors, to a new site six miles to the northwest, called Samaria. Henceforth, the kingdom as a whole is often known by this name. In order to develop the commerce of his realm, as well as to safeguard himself from the advancing power of the kingdom of Damascus, he entered

into an alliance with the Phoenicians, cemented by a marriage between Jezebel, daughter of the King of Tyre, and his son, Ahab.

It was in the latter's reign (876-853) that the policy of Omri bore fruit. The extraneous influences resulting from the King's foreign alliance culminated in the importation from Tyre of the Baal (or Melkart) worship in its grossest forms, with the accompaniment of human sacrifice. Queen Jezebel introduced ideas of absolutism completely alien to the traditional Hebraic conception of the monarchy. Justice was corrupted; and the story of how the King's ill-fated neighbor, Naboth, was deprived simultaneously of his vineyard and his life, made an indelible impression upon the popular mind.

From the political and military points of view, Ahab's reign was predominantly successful until its close. Notwithstanding the advance of the Assyrian power, bickering with the kingdom of Damascus continued, with varying fortune. There was a continual succession of border-raids; and at intervals, the Syrian bands penetrated far into the country. At length, open war broke out. After two serious defeats, King Benhadad sued for peace. But hostilities were eventually renewed; and, in the year 853, Ahab fell in an attempt to recover Ramoth-Gilead. He was succeeded in turn by his two sons, Ahaziah (853-2) and Jehoram (852-843). The Queen-Mother Jezebel remained, however, all-powerful in Samaria; and the conservative party continued to be antagonized by the pervasion of foreign influence, as well as the palpable injustice of the court. In the end, they instigated Jehu, the most dashing of Jehoram's gen-

erals, to make a bid for the throne (843). It was a religious
as well as a political revolution. The dynasty of Omri was
entirely wiped out; and the followers of Baal Worship were
relentlessly exterminated.

3.   The dynasty of Jehu lasted for precisely one century (843-744), father and son succeeding each other for
five generations—a record unprecedented in the history of
the northern monarchy. The new royal house abandoned
the idea of maintaining a *bloc* of the Syrian border-states
against the advancing power of Assyria, and entered into
friendly relations with the Great King. The hostility of the
new dynasty which had risen to power simultaneously in
Syria was thus a foregone conclusion. Profiting by the momentary diversion of the attention of Assyria in a different
direction, Hazael of Damascus turned his fury against his
southern neighbor. Defeat followed defeat. Eventually, during the reign of Jehu's son, Jehoahaz (816-800), Samaria
was itself blockaded, and saved from capture only by a
sudden panic in the enemy camp.

Under Jeroboam II (785-745), Jehu's great-grandson, there
was a brief return of the halcyon days of a former age. By
reason of internal weakness, the Assyrian advance was momentarily halted. Damascus was no longer a serious rival.
Israel was the most powerful of the minor Syrian states,
and, as under David and Solomon, her authority extended
over the neighboring territories from the Orontes down to
the Red Sea. Once more, the great caravan routes on either
side of the Jordan were under Israelitish control. Trade and
industry revived. There was a considerable influx of wealth

into the country, and a corresponding growth of luxury. This, in turn, produced moral and religious evils that were denounced by the prophets Amos and Hosea, whose activities will be referred to later.

Yet the dynasty of Jehu ended, as it had begun, in blood. When Jeroboam's son, Zechariah, was assassinated in 744, the country lapsed into semi-anarchy. During the course of the next ten years, five rulers succeeded one another on the throne; only one of whom died a natural death. Egypt to the south, and Assyria to the north, maintained their parties in the state, and fostered palace intrigues. Under Pekah ben Remaliah, who mounted the throne in 736 as the result of an insurrectionary movement, fostered by the Egyptian interest, Damascus and Israel, with some Philistine and Phoenician cities, formed a coalition against Assyria. They were overwhelmed, in a lightning campaign. Israel was stripped of Gilead and its northern provinces, the population of which was deported. Pekah, himself, was deposed and murdered by the opposition party (734), his assassin, Hoshea, being raised to the throne in his place. It was no comfort that the rivalry of Damascus was now finally ended, by its capture after a two years' siege (732); for nothing now stood between Israel and the northern fury.

4.   A change of ruler, and the momentary diversion of Assyrian interests northward, were enough to embolden Hoshea, hopeful of establishing complete independence, to listen to the tempting suggestions put forward by Egypt. An understanding was reached with the reigning Pharaoh,

and the heavy tribute annually exacted by Assyria was provocatively withheld. Punishment was prompt and terrible. Shalmaneser V thundered south with an army. As so often, the promised Egyptian aid failed to materialize. Hoshea was captured and imprisoned, and in the end, no doubt, put to death. Samaria itself was besieged. Month after month, the city managed to hold out, a tribute to the strength of its position and the massiveness of its fortifications. After a three years' siege, it was captured by Sargon, Shalmaneser's successor, and razed to the ground (721). In accordance with the ruthless, but invariable, Assyrian policy, the more valuable elements in the population, including the nobility and the wealthier citizens, were deported to distant parts of the Empire. Here, divorced from their ancestral soil, and intermingled with other races, their fidelity would be assured.

A few years later (715), in consequence of a further local revolt, the process was repeated on perhaps a larger scale. Samaria was reorganized in Assyrian provinces, each under its own governor; and the military garrison now installed was reinforced by foreign settlers from the central districts, who performed the same function in Palestine as the Palestinian exiles were expected to fulfill elsewhere.

Ultimately, these intermarried with the native population and partially absorbed its traditions. Thus a new race arose, later to be known after their capital, Samaria, as the Samaritans. They were akin to their Judaean neighbors in blood and in culture, but cut off from them by political interests, and not quite to be identified either spiritually or physically with the Hebrews whose place they had taken. Those deported eventually lost their identity, becoming merged either in the races amongst whom they were settled, or else in their Judaean kinsmen with whom they came into contact. For many generations to come, indeed, many individuals were able to trace their descent from one or the other of the old Israelitish tribes. But the political independence and the spiritual identity of the Northern Kingdom belonged to the past. It was in the Kingdom of Judah that all that was most characteristic and most vital in the national consciousness was henceforth concentrated.

IV. THE KINGDOM OF JUDAH

1.   The record of the sister Kingdom of Judah was very different from that of Israel. It was, on the whole, quiet and unadventurous, generally remaining undisturbed by internal dissension at least. The house of David never lacked an heir to occupy the throne of their great ancestor; and, until its last days, a disputed succession, so common in the northern kingdom, was exceptional.

Thus, the royal dynasty acquired a hold upon the sentiment of the people which could never be wholly eradicated. On the other hand, the history of the southern kingdom was politically undistinguished. Yet this political insignificance is more than outweighed by its crucial importance in the history of the human race. The whole of Palestine is only about the size of New Hampshire, Judah comprising an area not much greater than a couple of its counties. But that tiny territory was the nursery of the Jewish race and the Jewish religion; and from it there issued conceptions which, together with those of Athens and of Rome, have been all-powerful in moulding human civilization. Even if some of the literature in which these conceptions are enshrined owed its origin to the kingdom of Samaria, it was by that of Judah that they were preserved and developed, to become the common heritage of mankind.

The reigns of Rehoboam of Judah (933-917), and his

immediate successors, were largely concerned with a contest against the secessionists, a contest which alternated,
according to the fortunes of the campaign, between a war
of conquest and a struggle for independence. At the outset, indeed, it seemed as though the revolt of the North
would collapse. Jeroboam, compelled to move his capital
beyond the Jordan, appealed for help to Egypt, where he
was well-known because of his residence there as an exile.
Shishak (Sheshonk), the first Pharaoh of the Twenty-
Second or Lybian dynasty, appeared before the gates of
Jerusalem, and had to be bought off by a heavy bribe.

Under Rehoboam's successors, the struggle continued.
To secure his country's military position, his son, Abijah
(917-915), concluded an alliance with the Kingdom of Damascus. For the moment, the policy was successful; and
in the long reign of Abijah's son and successor, Asa (915-
875), the independence of Judah was at last assured.

2.   Under Asa's son, Jehoshaphat (875-851), relations
between the two neighboring states became more cordial,
though the subordination of the southern power to the
northern remained very marked. The heir-apparent, Jehoram, married Athaliah, daughter of Ahab and Jezebel. It
was not surprising, under those circumstances, that the
political and religious revolution led by Jehu implicated
Judah as well. At the time, Ahaziah (844-843), Jehoram's
son, had led his forces to assist in a further attack on
Ramoth-Gilead. He fled for his life, but was overtaken on
the road by the rebel general and mortally wounded.

When the news reached Jerusalem, the reins of government were seized by Athaliah, the Queen-Mother. She proved a true daughter of Jezebel, energetic, unscrupulous, and devoted to the interests of her foreign kinsfolk. To secure her personal position, she made away with all members of the royal seed, including even her own grandchildren. After six years of rule, however, a reaction took place. The chief priest, Jehoiada, who was allied by marriage to the royal house, planned the revolt. Athaliah was put to death, and the youthful Jehoash (Joash), the seven-year old son of Ahaziah, was placed on the throne.

Under the circumstances, it was a foregone conclusion that the long reign of the new king (837 798) should have witnessed, in its early stages at least, a triumph of priestly influence, and a revival of traditional religious values. The Baal-worship introduced by Athaliah was suppressed. The Temple buildings were restored by public subscription. In foreign affairs, the country suffered by reason of the temporary decline of the northern kingdom, to which it continued subservient. On one expedition, Hazael of Damascus, who had become all-powerful in Palestinian politics, captured Gath, and prepared to march on Jerusalem; and he consented to withdraw only on the payment of a heavy indemnity. This misfortune was perhaps responsible for Jehoash's assassination which took place not long after. His son, Amaziah (798-780 B.C.E.), attempted to initiate a more vigorous policy. A successful expedition against Edom emboldened him to throw off his allegiance to Samaria. However, he was heavily defeated, and his capital captured and despoiled. The political subordination of Judah to Samaria, hitherto a matter of surmise, is from now on an indubitable fact. It is no wonder that Amaziah's reign was ended by a palace revolution, which cost him his life.

The reign of Amaziah's successor, Uzziah, or Azariah (780-740 B.C.E.), coincided over a number of years with that of Jeroboam II of Israel (785-745 B.C.E.). Towards the close of the reign, there was a violent quarrel with the priesthood, occasioned by an attempt of the King, in his restless passion for reform, to usurp the sacerdotal functions. Excepting in this respect, Uzziah's policy was faithfully followed by his energetic son and successor, Jotham (740-736 B.C.E.), who had acted as regent during his father's last years.

On Jeroboam's death in 745 B.C.E., and the violent close of the dynasty of Jehu in the following year, Judah seems to have broken away from its allegiance to its neighbor. The country did not adhere to the anti-Assyrian bloc formed between Samaria and Damascus with such fatal results. To punish the new ruler, Ahaz (735-720 B.C.E.), an expedition was undertaken by the two northern monarchs against Jerusalem, where they intended to set up their own puppet king. Ahaz, terrified in spite of the calm confidence of some of the wisest among his advisors, appealed to Assyria for help. The pretext was barely necessary to provoke intervention. The invaders were drawn off by an onslaught from the north. Damascus, as we have seen, was attacked, and ultimately captured; and Samaria was stripped of her northern provinces. Judah itself, one of the few border-states which preserved nominal independence, was henceforth considered a tributary kingdom.

3.   Ahaz lived long enough to see the fall of Samaria
(722 B.C.E.), dying two years later. Any feeling of exultation which might normally have been occasioned by the
downfall of the rival kingdom was qualified by the fact
that Judah herself was now face to face with the Assyrian
power, being the solitary buffer state which henceforth divided the latter from Egypt, on which its eyes were turned
longingly. The road between the two lay through Palestine,
which thus became the cockpit for the ensuing conflict.
Year after year, the great armies of the Assyrian war-lords
devastated the country. It was in the troubled but not in-
glorious reign of the Judaean ruler, Hezekiah (720-692
B.C.E.), that the principal features of the struggle were
staged. For a long time he steadily resisted the temptation
to join a coalition which was formed by the southern
states with Egyptian support. But the general revolt which
broke out throughout the Assyrian Empire, from Babylon
almost to the Nile, on the accession of Sennacherib in 705,
ultimately emboldened him to alter his policy; and he became one of the principal members of a combination formed
by the various Palestinian rulers.

His punishment was not long delayed. This was the
famous occasion when the Assyrian swept down "like a
wolf on the fold." He subdued the Phoenician cities of
the coast one by one, defeated an Egyptian army at Eltekeh,
received the submission of some of the minor rulers, and
penetrated into Judah. One fortress after another opened
its gates. An impossible indemnity was demanded. A force
under the King's principal lieutenant, Rabshakeh, was sent
to besiege the capital. It appeared that Jerusalem was

about to share the fate of Samaria. But some unexplained cause led to a change of policy. Peace was hastily concluded with Egypt, and the army entrenched before Jerusalem was withdrawn. The capital and the state were saved; and though in a subsequent campaign Sennacherib subjugated southern Palestine, and even stripped Hezekiah of some of his territory, Jerusalem was never again threatened. Later generations could ascribe this deliverance to nothing less than a supernatural intervention, second only to that which had secured the freedom of the Israelites from the Egyptian captivity.

The Assyrian suzerainty remained a fact during the long reign of Hezekiah's son, Menasseh (692-638 B.C.E.), which at last witnessed the occupation of Egypt by the Assyrian military machine under Esarhaddon. Political dependence was reflected in the intellectual sphere. Foreign social and religious influences, profoundly distasteful to the conservative body of the people, acquired an ever-tightening hold. Old local sanctuaries were restored; human sacrifice was practiced; and fashionable alien cults were introduced into the Temple itself at Jerusalem.

The conflict of parties and policies within the country now became more intense. Menasseh's successor, Amon (638-7 B.C.E.), was assassinated by his own servants in the second year of his reign. The revolutionaries were soon suppressed by the "people of the land," or landed nobility, who placed on the throne the dead king's young son, Josiah (637-609 B.C.E.), then only eight years of age. During the regency, the *status quo* was maintained. When he reached manhood, however, a patriotic reaction took place.

The Temple was repaired and purged of the foreign influences which had trespassed upon its ritual during past reigns. In the course of the repairs, a "Book of the Law" was found (*see* p. 53), stressing the view that the only legitimate sanctuary was at Jerusalem and this was once again promulgated. In the rest of the kingdom, the local shrines in the "high places" were suppressed. The Feast of Passover, commemorating the deliverance from Egypt, was celebrated with a patriotic fervor never before equalled.

Following this, a determined attempt was made to reassert the independence of the country, which had been in eclipse during the past four reigns. Political conditions were propitious. The Assyrian Empire had received a fatal blow at the hands of the raiding Scythian and Cimmerian hordes from the north. A Babylonian prince, Nabopolassar, had made common cause with the Medes, and raised the standard of revolt. Ashur fell before them in 614 B.C.E. and Nineveh itself, amid that frenzied exultation of the Hebrew prophets, in 612. It was upon the new distribution of power that Josiah's hopes were pinned; and when in 609 the Egyptians under Necho joined with Assyria against the rebels, who had long since opened up diplomatic relations with Judah, Josiah attempted to interrupt their march. In a battle at Megiddo he was defeated and mortally wounded. The clouds were now to gather ever more thickly.

4.   Josiah's family were made to pay dearly for their father's unfortunate, though far-seeing, policy. The popular voice had placed upon the throne his second son, Jehoahaz (a striking commentary upon the essentially democratic

character of the Hebrew monarchy). The latter, who attempted to continue his father's line of conduct, was dethroned after a few months by the Assiro-Egyptian alliance, and sent in chains to Egypt, where he died. In his place, his unscrupulous brother, Jehoiakim, upon whose sympathies full reliance could be placed, was raised to the throne (608-598). Once again an anti-national policy was followed; and patriotic spokesmen, who denounced corruption in the state, were in peril of their lives. However, Necho's assistance had proved powerless to save his allies. The Egyptian military power was finally overthrown at Carchemish, in an attempt to cross the Euphrates (605). Within a few months, Assyria collapsed; and Nebuchadnezzar, heir-apparent and before long King of the new Babylonian Empire, came to the fore as the military colossus who bestrode the Middle East.

Under the force of circumstances, Jehoiakim recognized the suzerainty of the power, to oppose which he had been raised to the throne. Three years later, however, he threw off his allegiance. During the disorders which followed the approach of Nebuchadnezzar's armies, preceded by undisciplined bands of auxiliaries, the king perished. His son, Jehoiachin (598-7), a youth of eighteen, was made king in his place. Seeing that resistance was useless, the latter decided to throw himself on the enemy's mercy. He was despatched in triumph to Babylon, together with thousands of the nobility, the priesthood, and the middle-class population, accompanied by the treasures both of the Temple and of the royal palace.

The Babylonian ruler tempered justice with moderation.

For some years he did his best to maintain Judah in existence as a semi-independent, though subordinate monarchy. Jehoiachin's throne was filled by his uncle, Zedekiah
(Mattaniah), another son of Josiah; a well-meaning weak-
ling, whose treachery did not have even the palliation of
success. Though bound by solemn oath to maintain allegiance to Babylon, he began to toy with the idea of an
Egyptian alliance, and ultimately threw in his lot with a
fresh southern coalition formed to oppose the Babylonian
domination. In the winter of 588-7 B.C.E., Nebuchadnezzar
appeared once more before the walls of Jerusalem. The
advance of an Egyptian force saved it for the moment.
The siege was suspended; and the hopes of the war-party
were raised to dizzy heights. But the trained Babylonian
forces had little difficulty in defeating the Egyptians, and
in the winter of 587-6 B.C.E., on the Tenth of Tebeth, the
blockade was recommenced. Six months later, on 17th
Tammuz (a date henceforth to be observed, like the former, as a public fast), a breach was made in the walls.
Zedekiah, seeing that there was no further hope in resistance, attempted to flee. He was captured at Jericho, and
forced to witness the butchery of all his family and courtiers; after which his eyes were put out, and he was sent
in chains to Babylon. In the following month, a Babylonian
general, Nebuzaradan, was sent to complete the work of
destroying Jerusalem. The city was looted; the principal
buildings destroyed by fire; and the fortifications entirely
dismantled. A large proportion of the population was led
captive to Babylonia in pursuance of the deliberate policy
which the new Empire had inherited from its Assyrian

precursor. Only the rural population, or some of it, was allowed to remain. It was plainly the Chaldean intention to make Judah and its capital utterly impotent, so that it should never serve again as a focus of rebellion.

Even now the existence of the state was not completely ended. The seat of government was transferred to Mizpah, some five miles from Jerusalem, and the administration entrusted to a certain Gedaliah, a nobleman belonging to the conservative family of Shaphan, and grandson of Josiah's chancellor. For a short period he did what was possible to nurse the country back into a healthy state, and to repair the ravages of war. But, even at this stage, the old factions were not stilled. One Ishmael ben Nethaniah, a member of the former royal house, enlisting Ammonite support, murdered the governor and exterminated the garrison. No attempt was made to set up an alternative government. The surviving leaders and nobility, fearing fresh Babylonian reprisals, fled to Egypt taking with them all who cared to follow. The land of Judah was left without any settled government, deserted by all its former children, excepting for a handful of refugees lurking in the ruined towns and the hill-side caverns. It was not without reason that Jewish tradition prescribed, in perpetual remembrance, an annual fast, which still commemorates the death of Gedaliah as a major national disaster.

V. THE PROPHETS OF ISRAEL

1.   The story of the Hebrew kingdoms, as recorded down to this point, is not materially different from that of half a dozen neighboring countries, with nothing in it to deserve study after an interval of three thousand years, or to secure racial perpetuity long after great empires had been forgotten. If this has not been the lot of the Kingdoms of Judah and Samaria, alone among all the lesser states of the Asiatic world of that far-off age, the reason is to be sought in one factor only: the Hebrew prophets.

The *nabi* or prophet, as the mouthpiece of the moral consciousness of the people, is encountered at an early date. Moses himself was considered the prototype. There was no limitation as to sex; and, in the age of the Judges, Deborah the Prophetess was recognized a foremost national figure. By virtue of sheer moral force, he or she might receive local or, as in the case of Samuel, general recognition. From the beginning of the period of the monarchy, bands of prophets became a familiar feature in national life; younger men, who followed as closely as possible the example of better-known leaders, and like them endeavored to stir the feelings of their neighbors at times of emergency. At every hour of crisis, a "prophet" was likely to come forward to chide the people for its backsliding, to stir it up against a common enemy, to rebuke the King himself for some misdeed, or to advise how to counteract

47

an imminent danger. Not all were necessarily genuine or sincere. Many were demonstrably self-seeking hypocrites. But there was a considerable proportion whose character and sincerity were above suspicion. There was always amongst the prophets a residuum who refused to bow the knee to Baal, either literally or metaphorically. They represented the cause of the Lord against His rivals; but at the same time they represented the cause of the Hebrew against his enemies, of the poor man against his oppressor. Their function was indeed religious; but only in the sense in which religion embraces the whole of life, and is not confined to questions of theology.

They might be drawn from all ranks of society, from the highest to the lowest. There were courtiers, priests, shepherds, and ploughmen. When, in the reign of Ahab, Samaria reached the apex of its luxury, its corruption, its idolatry, and its vice, Elijah the Tishbite led the spirit of protest; a rough countryman, clad only in skins, who could appear out of nowhere to upbraid the sovereign or his consort, and disappear into nowhere afterwards. His personality made an indelible impression on the popular imagination. Marvelous stories were recounted about his achievements; and, to the present day, the fantasy of the Hebrew race regards him as alive and active among the people to whom he dedicated his life. Elijah was succeeded by Elisha, a more spectacular figure, who was at home in the court as well as in the fields, and in constant intercourse with members of the upper classes. His influence was hardly less in Damascus than it was in Samaria; and he looms behind the scenes as instigator of the revolution which replaced the house of Omri by that of Jehu.

Neither of these towering characters left behind him any written record, which could remind succeeding generations of the exact purport of his teaching. It was from the reign of Jeroboam II, that the messages of the prophets began to be preserved in written form. The names of many of these early God-intoxicated reformers are no doubt lost; and it is probable that of the "prophecies" of those whose names are remembered, only a very small proportion survives. They are sufficient, however, to have had a lasting influence on the life of mankind, and of the Hebrew race in particular. They embody the ideals of righteousness which dreamers and reformers, of all races and in all countries, have continually had before them from that day to this. English history and American, in particular, would have been very different but for the influence of this handful of Hebrew writers, fragments of whose rhapsodies are preserved in the so-called "Prophetical" books of the Bible. Not a small degree of the effectiveness of these utterances is due, not merely to the moral indignation which burns within them, but also to the inimitable style in which they are composed—alternating between prose and poetry, vivified by graphic similes, and turning aside at intervals to include lyrics, dirges, or satires, which are still reckoned among the masterpieces of world literature.

2.   About the year 765 B.C.E., a simple Judaean shepherd named Amos, made his appearance at a feast at the shrine of Beth-el, in the Kingdom of Samaria, then at the height of its power. His denunciation of the assembled

people—their greed, their dishonesty, their exploitation of the poor—was unsparing. He disturbed the self-satisfaction of those who heard him by the unprecedented theory that the Divine choice, on which they prided themselves, indicated a greater responsibility, not freedom from it. He warned them that their superficial religiosity could not save them on the day of punishment which was impending. The essential quality of true religion was clean living, justice, and righteousness, not the mechanical observance of an external piety. The whole tirade has been described as one of the marvels of literature for its comprehensiveness, variety, compactness, methodical argument, eloquence, and force of expression.

Slightly posterior to Amos was Hosea. Like his precursor, he was preoccupied with the imminence of an Assyrian invasion. The ultimate triumph of the rising northern power appeared to him inevitable. Though God had dearly cherished his people in the past, they had proved unfaithful to him, like a pampered woman, careless of her marriage vows. In consequence, their downfall was a foregone conclusion. If their God nurtured a special regard for them, He would express it, not by undue favor, but by the sharpness of the punishment which He would mete out. Almost contemporaneously, Micah, essentially a man of the people, foretold disaster upon the whole community, Judah as well as Israel, in consequence of the manifold sins of the inhabitants, particularly their systematic exploitation of the poor. To this fundamental point social justice, the Hebrew prophet never fails to recur.

The northern kingdom was tottering to its fall; and the

pivot of Hebraic life, with the center of interest, had been
transferred to Judah. Isaiah, a statesman and an aristocrat
(according to tradition, he was a member of the royal
house), was a commanding figure in the court of Hezekiah
and his immediate predecessors. In periods of unrivalled
eloquence he denounced the luxury and the frivolity, which
pervaded the whole land and for which retribution could
not be delayed. Assyria was, in his view, the instrument
through which the iniquities of the people were to be
purged.

Yet his prophecies had their more comforting side. The
triumph of the foreign power was not to be final, nor was
the Hebrew state to be utterly overthrown. At the moment,
the country was profaning itself by its secular interests, and
it was about to receive its lesson. Nevertheless, the people
might look forward to their ultimate destiny with optimism, so long as they clung to the religious ideals of their
fathers, reverted to a purer and simpler manner of life, and
did not entangle themselves in foreign alliances. Isaiah, in
his denunciation of moral shortcomings, coupled with
shrewd political insight and his confidence in a brighter
future, represents the Hebrew prophet at his highest and
most characteristic. If Judah weathered the storm which
was about to break over her, it was due largely to his statesmanlike advice; and the Golden Age, to which mankind
has intermittently been striving from that day to this, has
always been colored, if not inspired, by the graphic picture
which he drew.

Lesser figures now begin to appear on the scene in comparative profusion. The Scythian invasion, which menaced

the existence of the whole country about 626 B.C.E., evoked
the stirring addresses of Zephaniah, who saw in these ruthless invaders, too, an instrument in the Lord's hand to punish the crass injustice of the ruling order. The fall of Nineveh, and of the Assyrian power with it, was greeted in exultant rhapsodies by Nahum. Habakkuk grappled with the
moral problem raised by God's use of the idolatrous
Babylonian Empire, newly arisen to reeminence, and its
apparent triumph over all the neighboring nations. Without a doubt there were many others (such as Huldah, the
prophetess, of whom we obtain a fleeting glimpse during
the reign of Josiah), equally polished and equally forceful,
all record of whose allocutions has perished.

Throughout the alternations of hope and despair which
preceded the final debacle, the background is filled by the
somber utterances of Jeremiah, a priest from Anathoth,
near Jerusalem. His writings reevoke the man; a powerful, fearless orator, refusing to admit that loyalty to his
country could justify him in doing violence to his conscience, foretelling disaster because disaster was merited,
and suffering continual persecution because he refused to
be silent when silence was acceptable at court. Like Isaiah,
he stood for neutrality in external politics. He was opposed
to any intrigues with Egypt or with any other power. He
anticipated the inevitable triumph of the all-powerful
Babylonian, and lived to know his anticipations realized.
But he saw no reason why defeat or even exile should put
an end to the national existence, or to the distinctive
national conceptions. It was in this that his supreme
historical importance resides.

3.   In the eighteenth year of the reign of Josiah (621 B.C.E.), there had taken place in Jerusalem an episode which stands in close connection with the prophetic utterances. During the restoration works in the Temple, there was found a copy of the long-forgotten "Law of Moses." According to the modern critical view, what was actually in question was a revised code of the earlier laws, corresponding in the main to what we now call the Book of Deuteronomy. This had been compiled by the priests, and was now presented under the guise of an ancient composition of immemorial antiquity. The traditional view, on the other hand, envisages the Pentateuch as we now have it, which, in that case, must have fallen into entire oblivion during past generations.

The publication and diffusion of this codex, whatever its nature, its origin, and its authorship, was of cardinal importance in the spiritual history of the Hebrew people. We have already seen (see p. 43) something of the immediate spiritual revival which resulted. The repercussions did not, however, end with this. From now on, the "Law of Moses" no longer signified a half-forgotten body of regulations, known only through oral tradition, but an ascertainable written corpus, accessible to every man who could read. It was a code which, however much it may breathe the spirit of the age in which it was composed, is immeasurably superior to anything else of its day. The differences between the two are even more significant than their similarities. In many respects, the Mosaic code provides an ideal which even our modern age has failed to realize. It breathes throughout, besides its stern monotheism, that ideal of "righteousness," of charity towards one's neighbor, and of justice to the poor, which was at the basis of the teaching of the Prophets. In subsequent years, when the latter referred (as they so often did) to the neglect of the "Law of Moses," it was this code that they had in mind. And it was this which constituted the nucleus of the body of literature which the exiles took with them into Babylonia, to preserve their distinctive consciousness and conceptions, when all else in the traditional scheme of life had toppled in ruins about their heads.

BOOK TWO

THE JEW
(circa 586-425 B.C.E.)

VI. THE RETURN FROM EXILE

1.   In the course of the year 538 B.C.E. a succession of convoys wound their way along the ancient caravan routes which cross the vast expanse of desert to the west of Mesopotamia. It was no ordinary movement of wayfarers or of merchants; it was a people returning to meet its destiny.

The population deported from Palestine by the Babylonians in successive campaigns from 597 B.C.E. to 586 B.C.E., contrary to all historical precedent and actual expectation, had not lost their distinctiveness. Long before the catastrophe, men of foresight had predicted their vicissitudes, which thus appeared in retrospect in the light of a punishment rather than a disaster. Their devotion to the one God whom their forefathers had discovered became strengthened, and not extinguished through the apparent triumph of an alien deity. In their exile, too, eloquent teachers (like Ezekiel, one of the group settled at Tel-Aviv*), had arisen among them to perpetuate the prophetic tradition, exhorting them in passionate orations, to preserve their confidence and their faith. The unwilling emigrants had accordingly retained their racial, their linguistic, and their religious identity.

The Babylonian Empire had fallen with the same striking suddenness with which it first appeared. Under Nabonidus, a petty Elamite chieftain named Cyrus rose in

*The Mound of Spring, a name revived in modern Palestine (p. 373).

57

rebellion and, advancing from success to success, established a new Persian Empire. Marching south, he overwhelmed the Babylonian forces under Belshazzar, the heir-apparent. Then, aided by treachery within the gates, he seized the capital during the course of a state banquet (538 B.C.E.). He purported to come in the guise, not of a conqueror, but of a deliverer. It is not extraordinary, therefore, that he extended his favor to the people which Babylonian ruthlessness had uprooted from the land of Judah. In the actual year of the fall of Babylon (538 B.C.E), he issued an edict authorizing any persons who so desired to return to Jerusalem, and there rebuild a Temple for the worship of the Most High God. Thus the enthusiastic hopes which had been centered about his advance by certain sections of the exiles, whose sentiments are expressed in the lyrical outbursts of the second half of the book of Isaiah, became fulfilled.

2.   It was of these returning exiles that the convoys which crossed the desert in 538 were composed. According to contemporary records, they numbered in all something over 40,000 souls; those who preferred to remain in Mesopotamia supporting the expedition with monetary contributions. The expedition was under the leadership of a member of the late royal house, Zerubbabel, probably a son of King Jehoiachin. Another outstanding figure was Jeshua ben Jehozadak, a member of a distinguished priestly family.

As the caravans successively entered the country, one may imagine that they dispersed, each family going to re assert its claim on the plot of land which it previously owned. That autumn, however, they came together in Jerusalem in order to reinstitute Divine worship at the Temple. On the occasion of the solemnity at the beginning of the seventh month (subsequently known as the New Year), the debris was cleared away from the middle of the ruined courts, and a rough altar set up. From that date, for a period of three and a half centuries, the regular sequence of worship, morning and evening, was uninterrupted.

From this point, preparations for the complete restoration of the Temple were pressed on. Two years after the return, the foundation stones were laid. The old pomp seemed to be revived in the stately ceremonial and in the bursts of psalmody led by the Levites of the clan of B'ne Asaph. A shout of jubilation from the assembled people reechoed across the hills. But many of the older men, who could remember the splendor of the former building upon this site, wept at the recollection of the glory that had been, and of its tragic end. The sentiments, in either case, proved premature, as, owing to political intrigues on the part of the neighboring peoples in Palestine, the work was soon suspended.

Meanwhile, the returned exiles settled down in their new homes. Gradually, the streets of Jerusalem began to be cleared of ruins, and its houses to be repaired. Some sort of spiritual life slowly manifested itself; and teachers like Haggai and Zachariah ben Iddo arose to fill the place of Jeremiah and Hosea. Zerubbabel, who had led the return, apparently died very shortly after. On the death of Cyrus (529 B.C.E.) the peace of the state which he had built up was disturbed by a succession of rebellions and civil wars, the effects of which Palestine cannot have escaped. It was only in 521 B.C.E., when power fell into the capable hands of Darius I, the real creator of the Persian Empire, that order was restored. The interregnum led to a revival of nationalist feeling. The fiery Haggai, aghast at the rebuilding of private houses while the national shrine still lay in ruins, had meanwhile been pleading for the task of reconstruction to be taken in hand once more, and he foretold that the glory of this second House would be greater than that of its precursor.

Accordingly, in the second year of Darius, in the winter of 520 B.C.E., the work was recommenced after a cessation of sixteen years; the revival of activity being so marked as to make modern critics date the real beginning of the national rebirth from this point. In the spring of 515 B.C.E., after five years' further labor, notwithstanding the interference of an over-zealous Persian official, the building was completed and dedicated.

3.   The political condition of the restored community, meanwhile, was very different from that of their fathers of a century before. The territory on which they settled was restricted to a very small area around Jerusalem. It included no more than thirty rural settlements, scattered over a radius of a few square miles. During the Captivity, the surrounding tribes had pushed forward and occupied many outlying tracts which had previously belonged to Judah. Most important was the half-idolatrous residue of the Israelitish kingdom to the north, with its heterogeneous

admixture of foreign military settlers. They felt a distinct sense of kinship with the returned emigrés, and had a sincere, if not exclusive veneration for the incorporeal deity worshipped in Jerusalem. At the outset, they had shown a cordial feeling, and had desired to collaborate in restoring the national shrine. The others would not hear of it.

Their attitude was not altogether one of unreasoning intolerance. Their revival was both national and religious. From the former point of view, they did not welcome the intrusion of aliens at the nerve-center of their polity; from the latter, they were unwilling to endanger their newly-purified monotheism by association with elements whose motives and whose principles were by no means above suspicion. In revenge, the rival elements systematically obstructed, by fair means and foul, the work of reconstruction. It was due to their intrigues that the rebuilding of the Temple was suspended between 536 B.C.E. and 528 B.C.E.; and the recurrent dispute between the neighbors was to remain during the whole of the following century the keynote of Palestinian politics.

Palestine at this time formed part of the fifth of the twenty Satrapies of the Empire of the Achaemenids—that of the Western Provinces, with its administrative center at Damascus. This extended from the Orontes to the borders of Egypt, comprising also Syria, Phoenicia, and Cyprus. The colony itself was under the direct rule of a governor, who was, however, considered subordinate to his colleague at Samaria. The seat of administration was Jerusalem, where the governor resided in a fortress called the Birah, overlooking the Temple.

Those carried into exile by the Babylonians had belonged to all of the various "tribes" which comprised the former kingdom. In exile, however, they had become consolidated around that of Judah, as had indeed been the tendency for some little time before the final tragedy. After the return, they settled down promiscuously. The old territorial distinctions were thus abandoned. Gradually, therefore, the entire population became known as men of Judah (*Yehudim*), or Jews.*

4.   It is fortunate that the Jewish people was not restricted to Palestine. Many still remained in Babylon, and they were watching affairs with pathetic eagerness. Political emissaries, casual visitors, returning pilgrims, kept them in touch with local conditions: and the national feeling still alive amongst them resulted every now and again in the migration westwards of some further band of enthusiasts. One of the most memorable of these expeditions took place in the reign of Artaxerxes Longimanus. There was about his court a certain devoted Jew named Nehemiah who had attained high office, as royal cup-bearer. Greatly perturbed by the news brought from Palestine by his brother, Hanani, he obtained permission from the King in 445 B.C.E. to visit Jerusalem, "the city of his fathers' sepulchres." Like Zerub-

*Individual families (apart from those of the tribe of Levi, which for special reasons has retained its individuality to the present day) continued to trace their origin down to the beginning of the Christian Era, or even after. Some of them belonged to those tribes formerly included in the northern kingdom. We may deduce from this that the Jews were recruited during the exile by some of those deported previously to the same regions by the Assyrians, or after it by some who remained in the country.

babel before him, he was given full civil authority as Governor, an office filled during the intervening period by strangers.

Three days after his arrival, the new governor rode around the walls of the city by moonlight, followed by a few trusted retainers. The account which had reached him was accurate in all its details. In consequence of disturbances possibly more recent than the siege of a century and a half before, the fortifications were in a state of utter ruin, the walls being broken down and the gates lying in ashes. Jerusalem was, in fact, virtually an open city, exposed to any onslaught. On the following day, Nehemiah summoned together the principal citizens and informed them of the authority which he had received, and of the measures he proposed to take. His news was greeted enthusiastically; and, led by the priests and crafts guilds, the people set themselves energetically to the task of reconstruction, laborers streaming in also from the surrounding countryside and subordinate townships.

The sub-Satrap of Samaria, Sanballat, jealously watched while this was going on. Unable to prohibit it, he embarked upon a campaign of obstructionism, the devices to which he resorted ranging from accusations of treason levied against Nehemiah, to an attempt at his assassination. At one time the devoted band at Jerusalem had to go about their work armed, so as to be prepared against a surprise attack. Nevertheless, in spite of many interruptions, the work of reconstruction was completed in little more than two months, and the walls of Jerusalem were dedicated with great solemnity.

The area enclosed in the fortifications was sparsely in-
habited, the population being insufficient to defend it in
case of emergency. It was accordingly agreed that one family out of every ten from the countryside should be selected
by lot to live in the capital, though most of them probably
continued to cultivate their holdings outside the walls. The
inhabitants were organized into watches, and the gates
strictly closed each night. The Jewish settlement in Palestine, instead of being an agglomeration of rural colonies,
was now the nucleus of a state, with at least one stronghold
which might hold an invader at bay.

The security of the capital once assured, Nehemiah
threw himself, with the same zeal and organizing ability,
into the work of moral regeneration. In the long night of
the Babylonian Exile, the conception of the "Law of Moses"
had gained a stronger, more intimate hold upon the consciousness of the Jewish people; but it was not yet observed
in all its details by the masses. Ezra, a royal scribe of
priestly descent, who had led a large party from Mesopotamia thirteen years previous, in 458 B.C.E., had indeed
been authorized to make an inquiry into the general state
of the country, and to enforce such reforms as he thought
fit. In fact, he had done little beyond securing the appointment of a commission to inquire into the mixed marriages
which had been made, and to enforce the severance of all
extraneous family ties. He had subsequently remained in
Jerusalem with his enthusiasm for the "Law" still burning
within him though he was unable to give effect to his
ideals. His zeal was now reinforced by Nehemiah's
executive genius.

On the anniversary of the rededication of the altar two generations before, Ezra recited the Law before the assembled people from a pulpit of wood, while a number of Levites assisted him in expounding it. The function had an immediate effect. The Feast of Tabernacles, which was only a few days off, was observed with unprecedented zeal. On its conclusion, a special fast was ordained to express the general contrition. Immediately afterwards, the whole of the assembled people entered into a solemn League and Covenant. A formal contract was drawn up, binding all who subscribed to observe certain fundamental prescriptions. To this, the chiefs of all the clans, headed by the governor himself, affixed their seals. It was a memorable gathering, marking the beginning of the implicit reign of Law over the Jewish people; and it seems to have lived in the popular recollection as the Great Assembly, to which the last of the prophets were supposed to have handed on the torch of tradition.

As ever, religious and social problems were closely interwoven. The period was one of great economic stress. In order to discharge their obligations, many of the proletariat had been compelled to mortgage their holdings to their wealthier brethren. Some insolvent debtors were made to forfeit their liberty; while impecunious parents sold their children outright as slaves. The governor, to whom these complaints were loudly voiced, was quick to sympathize. He summoned a meeting of the notables, whom he upbraided for their rapacious conduct. In consequence, they agreed to restore the holdings on which they had foreclosed and to remit henceforth, in accordance with the prescrip-

tions of the Mosaic code, the interest charged on loans. As
a further means of ameliorating the condition of the country, Nehemiah waived his right to the tribute which former
governors had exacted. Simultaneously, he rigorously enforced the observance of the Sabbath. From the previous
sunset, he kept the gates of Jerusalem closed, putting some
of his own retainers in charge; and he took drastic steps to
prevent buying and selling from being continued outside
the walls.

Nehemiah had been unable to carry all the patrician
houses with him in his reforms. When in 433 B.C.E., he
was recalled to Susa, after twelve years of unremitting activity, a reaction set in. Close relations were reestablished
with the rival center of government at Samaria, with which
the Judaean notables were in close and constant communication. Intermarriage had begun again on such a scale
that, to patriotic eyes, the existence of the Hebrew language
seemed endangered. The High Priest, Eliashib, had permitted one of his grandsons, a certain Menasseh, to marry
a daughter of Sanballat, the Governor of Samaria; while
the latter's secretary, Tobiah, was actually permitted to
occupy a chamber in the Temple on the occasion of his
visits to Jerusalem. Reports regarding this state of affairs
brought Nehemiah back to Palestine, after a lengthy absence. He must have been advanced in years by now, but
he had lost none of his vigor. Tobiah's property was thrown
out of the Temple, and the chamber which he had occupied, restored to its former use. Menasseh, the arch-
offender, was expelled from the community outright. The
errant priest, followed by others who shared his views,

sought refuge with his wife's kinsfolk in Samaria. Here, under his auspices, the usages of the Temple of Jerusalem were imitated in a rival sanctuary which was now erected on Mount Gerizim. The breach between Jews and Samaritans thus became complete.

5.   Jewish tradition has tended to subordinate the name of Nehemiah to that of Ezra, notwithstanding the fact that the latter appears in the original sources as a personality less active, less authoritative, and less distinct. Later literature speaks of Ezra, the Scribe, almost as a second Moses; and numerous religious institutions of hoary antiquity are traced back to his initiative. There is in this something more than pure fancy. For the essential part of the work of resettlement in Palestine lay not so much in the political, as in the literary and spiritual sphere.

The modern critical school ascribes to Ezra, not merely the enforcement, but the redaction and even the authorship of a substantial portion of what subsequently became known as the *Torah*—the Law of Moses. Whether or not this is the case, it remains an indisputable fact that, with Ezra, the reign of the Torah over the Jewish people began. It is significant that the institution of the public reading and interpretation of the Scriptures are associated traditionally with this period. Houses of prayer were now set up, perhaps for the first time, in localities distant from the Temple; a practice encouraged by the exigencies of the Babylonian exile. In them, the Torah was not only read, but also expounded. The diffusion of this fundamental literature was aided by the new "Assyrian" alphabet which had become familiar during the Exile, an advance over the angular Phoenician forms, hitherto universally employed.

The Torah was far from being a dry code. It served as the basis of human life and conduct in every branch; and it was constantly scrutinized and rescrutinized for fuller implications. The system, with all its extensions and rigors, came to be adopted with an ungrudging zeal. The Jews had returned from the Exile a half-educated band. Their religious ideals were concentrated in Temple worship; and they were ignorant of what were subsequently considered the fundamental practices of their faith. The succeeding period is obscure in the extreme. But, when the curtain rises again to its full height, four centuries after the Return, the scene is very different. We find a people devotedly monotheistic, with a faith and a standard of life which mark them off from all other peoples. Each action of their daily existence is governed by their Torah, whose every letter and every implication they endeavor to carry into effect. They are distinguished from other men by the rigorous observance of certain religious practices, such as the Sabbath, which are to remain henceforth quintessentially characteristic of them. They came back into Palestine, as it were, still Israelites, at one in essence with their ancestors of the period of the Exodus or of the Monarchy. The work of Ezra and his followers converted them into Jews, almost undistinguishable from their descendants of the Middle Ages.

In the traditional view, the memoirs of Nehemiah constituted the last of the canonical books of the Hebrew Bible. The succeeding period was, from the literary standpoint, an utter blank. The modern critical school has endeavored to correct this impression. What was hitherto considered a period of intellectual quiescence now appears as one of unparalleled literary activity. It is regarded as the period of the final redaction of the Pentateuch; of the composition of literary masterpieces such as the books of Job or Joel, of idylls like Ruth, of poems like the Song of Songs, of narratives such as the book of Jonah, of many of the immortal poems contained in the Psalms, of philosophical meditations like Ecclesiastes, and of maxims like those contained in the book of Proverbs. The question cannot be said, even now, to be finally settled. It is corrected periodically in points of detail; and serious arguments may be advanced against the thesis as a whole. Nevertheless, the problem must be approached from the standpoint of scientific inquiry, and not of prejudice. The modern view, indeed, robs many parts of the Old Testament of something of their immemorial antiquity. It compensates, however, by establishing, in the course of the Dark Age which succeeded the return from Babylon, a period of literary activity which makes it comparable in the annals of human culture with the Golden Age of Athens, or the Renaissance in Italy.

VII.

THE STRUGGLE AGAINST HELLENISM

1.   From the close of the period of Nehemiah's activity, an almost complete darkness falls upon Palestinian affairs. Within the country, it was a period of consolidation. In political affairs, we read of the succession of High Priests. We are informed of a persecution throughout the Persian Empire, which was foiled through the influence of a Jewish woman, named Esther, at Court. Finally, in 334 B.C.E., Alexander of Macedon descended like a whirlwind on Asia, and the Persian Empire collapsed before his onslaught.

An old legend, which tells how the conqueror was appeased by a visit from the High Priest while preparing to march on Jerusalem, is indicative of the pacific acceptance of the new regime by the Jews of Palestine. On the death of the great conqueror, his Empire fell to pieces. His principal generals quarrelled fiercely among themselves for control either of the whole or of some fragment of his Empire. The Ptolemies, who seized Egypt, showed themselves kindly and tolerant rulers, content to allow Judaea almost complete autonomy, subject only to the payment of a moderate annual tribute. It was, according to an ancient legend, under the auspices of the second of the dynasty, Ptolemy Philadelphus (285-247 B.C.E.), that the Bible was translated into Greek by seventy elders sent from Jerusalem, the so-called "Septuagint" version.* The absence of

*See p. 91.

any other authority in the political sphere crystallized national sentiment more and more around the person of the High Priest. We read at this period of one Simon, called the Just, who represented to later ages the ideal leader and teacher, and was considered the prototype of the Rabbis of subsequent generations. After his death, the sacerdotal office became more and more secularized in character.

Meanwhile, war had been carried on intermittently between the Ptolemies and the house of Seleucus, which had established itself in Syria. For brief periods (295, 219-217, 202 B.C.E.) the latter managed to occupy Palestine. The Ptolemies always succeeded in resuming control until 198 B.C.E., when Antiochus the Great secured an overwhelming victory over the Egyptian forces at Paneas, near the sources of the Jordan: and the country passed definitely under Seleucid rule.

2. Not long after, in 175 B.C.E., Antiochus IV, ascended the throne of Seleucus. He had been born in Athens, and was intensely proud of the fact that he had once been elected chief magistrate of that city. This strengthened to an inordinate degree his naturally keen admiration of Greek culture, which represented to his mind the acme of human progress and perfection. It became the object of his life to "civilize" his dominions, as he considered it, by the introduction of Greek standards of life. The shallow, unbalanced nature, which caused him to assume the name of Epiphanes (the illustrious), converted this ambition into something little less than a mania.

Under the royal direction, the process of Hellenization

penetrated into every corner of the state, and made feverish progress. Judaea (where a sycophantic section of the population supported the royal policy) did not remain immune. Nothing was left undone to convert Jerusalem into a Greek city. Buildings were constructed in the Hellenic style. A gymnasium was established in the shadow of the citadel, in which—an abomination in Jewish eyes—young men exercised naked. Priests neglected their duties in the Temple to join in the fashionable craze. Greek names became common, or the old Hebraic ones were transmuted. Yet the infiltration did not go rapidly or deeply enough for the King, who resented the fact that religious separatism still continued.

A sordid intrigue for the High Priesthood gave him the opportunity to intervene more directly. When he was forced by the Romans to withdraw from Egypt in 168 B.C.E., he took the final step. If Egypt was to be maintained in perpetuity as a rival power, it became all the more important that the southern outpost of the Syrian Empire should be thoroughly organized as a Seleucid province. As he marched northward, Antiochus detached his general, Apollonius, to occupy Jerusalem. He was admitted without difficulty. On the following Sabbath, however, when (as he had heard) the Jews would not put up any resistance, he turned his forces loose on the population. Large numbers of inoffensive persons were butchered, while others were sold into slavery. The city walls were razed to the ground. On the site of the citadel of David, a new fortress, known as the *Acra,* was constructed, to hold the city in check.

After these preliminaries a systematic attempt was begun to Hellenize the country by force. No form of separatism was henceforth permitted. A proclamation was issued which ordered the fusion of all the nationalities of the Empire, without exception, into one people, and the general acceptance of the Greek religion. An elderly Athenian philosopher was dispatched to Jerusalem to supervise the enforcement of the new order. It pleased his fancy to identify the God of the Jews with the Olympian Jove. A bearded image of this deity was set up upon the altar, and the Jews were informed that this was the God of Heaven whom they were henceforth to revere. Amongst themselves, however, they referred to it with a shudder of horror as the Abomination of Desolation.

The courts of the Temple were thronged with Greek soldiers and their paramours, performing the licentious heathen rites. To increase the horror of pious Jews, swine were sacrificed on the altar. In the various provincial center, shrines to lesser deities were set up. On the other hand, the observance of any of the practices of the Jewish religion was a penal offense. The sacred scrolls in which the Law of Moses was written were destroyed or defiled whenever they were found. Special watch was kept for such as observed the Sabbath and festivals, or practiced the rite of circumcision. All this was enforced with the utmost harshness.

The Jews were, as yet, an obscure people, insignificant as far as numbers were concerned. Antiochus, however, had attacked the one thing they held sacred. His attempt to Hellenize the country, successful up to a certain point,

broke against this obstacle. The first blow was struck by
an old priest of the house of Hasmon, named Mattathias,
whose family possessions lay at Modin, between Jerusalem
and the seacoast. The occasion was the setting up at this
place of a pagan altar, at which the assembled populace
was expected to make sacrifices. As one of the local notables
went up to set the example, Mattathias cut him down.
Then, with his five sons, he turned against the royal commissioner, who shared the same fate. After destroying the
altar, they escaped into the hills, followed by the more
intransigent element in the population, and raised the
standard of revolt.

3.   Around the old priest, in the mountain fastnesses
of Judaea, there gradually gathered a considerable band of
malcontents. *Hassidim,* they called themselves: the "pious,"
who refused to contaminate themselves by worship of
idols. At intervals, sweeping down by night into the valleys, they made raids on the country towns and villages,
where they killed the royal officers and the Hellenized
Jews who supported them.

The Hasmonaean revolt followed the lines of so many
other successful movements of the sort in the world's history. The rebels would probably have been incapable of
making a stand in the field had their oppressors put forward their full strength. At the beginning, however, the
government refused to take the menace seriously. Hence
the patriots were able to score some notable successes
against minor detachments which were marching light-
heartedly against them. Once or twice they even managed

to ambush more important bodies, the defeat of which supplied them not only with training and confidence, but also with munitions. When the government at last realized the importance of the movement and put an adequate army into the field, the country was reoccupied without great difficulty. But it was impossible to follow the insurgents into their native hill-country, where they knew every inch of the ground and could count upon the sympathy of the whole population, and every successive attempt to do so met with disaster. And so the Syrians were driven to adopt the policy which so many other governments have done under similar circumstances. A truce was concluded which conceded a great part of the demands of the rebels, and this finally satisfied the more moderate elements.

From now on, the patriotic leaders consolidated their position: sometimes by force of arms, and sometimes by shrewd bargaining, in which they took advantage of every temporary weakness or embarrassment of their former tyrants. Belated attempts to suppress them would meet with much the same result as at the outset, until the Syrians were at last forced to concede complete independence. A gradual process such as this may lack some of the spectacular dash of popular appeal, but it requires not only heroism, but also patience, self-denial, and statesmanship, in an unusual degree.

The movement was peculiarly fortunate in its leaders. It is not often that history can show in one family such examples of perfect devotion and self-sacrifice as that of the Hasmonaean brothers, who followed Mattathias as leaders of the revolt. Three in succession were at the head of the

Jewish state. Two fell in the field, under circumstances of exceptional gallantry; another was ambushed at a dark period in his people's fortunes; another was put to death in cold blood by the national enemy, jealous of his success; the survivor was murdered for dynastic reasons. Of the five, not one died a natural death.

Mattathias had died not long after he raised the standard of revolt. On his death-bed, he advised his followers to choose as their military leader his third son, Judah, known as the Maccabee.* The insurgents were never overwhelmed, and on more than one occasion, cut to pieces in a surprise attack the forces sent against them. Such an engagement, brilliant, though not decisive, took place in the pass of Emmaus in 165 B.C.E., when an army led by Gorgias was almost annihilated while endeavoring to penetrate to Jerusalem. Similarly, while Antiochus was engaged in his last campaign in Parthia in 164 B.C.E., Lysias, who had been left behind as regent of the kingdom, suffered a severe check in an attempt to reach the capital from the south. He accordingly attempted to pacify the country by adopting a more moderate policy. An edict was issued restoring the liberty of worship. Judah was permitted to reoccupy Jerusalem. The Temple was cleansed, the pagan altars were destroyed, and on Kislev 25th, the same day of the year on which pagan worship had been instituted three years before, the sacred edifice was rededicated to its original usage. It was the date of the winter solstice, and, with the

* The generally accepted derivation of this word is from *Makkabah*, a hammer; the name being thus a close parallel to that of Charles Martel (The Hammer) in European history.

annual feast of dedication, or *Hanukkah*, there has ever since been associated the kindling of lights characteristic of the ancient celebration of this day.

4.   Victory upon the main issue had been won. The practice of Judaism in its traditional form was once more legalized. However, the revolt had altered and extended in scope. The persecution had brought about a revival of the national spirit, and for the first time since the Exile, a movement for complete independence developed. Emboldened by success, Judah embarked upon wider activities. A prolonged campaign ensued. After Antiochus' death in 163 B.C.E., and the seizure of the Syrian throne by Demetrius Soter, Judah scored a signal success over Nicanor, commander of the elephant corps near Beth Horon. This victory was long commemorated by a public holiday.

A month later, the Syrian general Bacchides returned with an overwhelming force. Judah, followed by a handful of only eight hundred men, threw himself in the path of the invaders at Elasa, north of Beth Horon, but unsuccessfully. His little band was defeated, and he himself died fighting. The surviving Hasmonaean brothers withdrew to the wilds beyond the Jordan, with their few remaining followers. The eldest, John, was waylaid by some unfriendly tribesmen and put to death while attempting to convey the baggage to the Nabataean Arabs. There remained only Simon, the second brother, and Jonathan, the youngest, who took over the military command.

After a futile attempt to follow Bacchides arrived at the conclusion that the best course was to conclude a pacific arrangement with them. A truce was therefore arranged, the rebel leaders being permitted to return to Judaea unmolested on condition that they disbanded their forces, and did not approach the capital. Jonathan therefore established himself at Michmash, where his headquarters became once more the center of patriotic sentiment. In the absence of any superior authority, he developed from a proscribed rebel into an independent ruler, dominating all Judaea outside the capital.

5.   It was a dynastic dispute which gave the opportunity for the final step. As the reign of Demetrius Soter had progressed, his difficulties increased. A youth named Alexander Balas, who bore a remarkable physical resemblance to the dead Antiochus Epiphanes, gave himself out to be that monarch's son. With powerful foreign support, he made a bid for the throne, and civil disturbances continued to rack the country over a long period. Both factions now endeavored to obtain the assistance of the Judaean military chieftain and his veterans. Gifts, titles, honors, privileges, and bribes were showered upon Jonathan by both sides. Almost at the outset he was authorized by Demetrius to enter Jerusalem, and invested with the vacant office of High Priest, with all of the religious and political authority which it implied. He was thus officially recognized as head of the Jewish state, and on the Feast of Tabernacles, in 152 B.C.E., he officiated in the Temple for the first time.

In the end, this triumphant progress aroused the jealousy of Tryphon, an unscrupulous military leader, who, for the moment, dominated Syrian affairs. The latter lured Jonathan to meet him for a friendly conference at Ptolemais, where he had him seized, ultimately putting him to death. But, owing to the unique devotion and ability of the Hasmonaean brothers, this act of treachery proved fruitless. Simon, the last survivor of Mattathias' five sons, automatically took over command. When Tryphon declared himself sovereign in 142 B.C.E., Simon had ample grounds for withdrawing the titular allegiance which had hitherto been maintained towards successive Syrian rulers. Even the *Acra* at Jerusalem was at last evacuated by the Syrian troops, and it was entered by the national forces, amid delirious scenes of rejoicing, in the summer of 141 B.C.E. In the autumn of the following year, Simon's title was approved by a national assembly, which confirmed him in the offices of High Priest, Prince, and military commander, henceforth to be hereditary in his house. Not long after they began to strike their own coins, the first ever issued by the Jewish state, a token of the newly won independence. To this period belongs, too, the consolidation of the alliance with Rome, first entered into perhaps by Judah the Maccabee.

The Syrians did not abandon all hope of regaining their lost influence. In 138 B.C.E., Antiochus VII, the last strong representative of the house of Seleucus, endeavored to reimpose the tribute, and to obtain the evacuation of the recent territorial acquisitions. His forces were heavily defeated by John Hyrcanus, the old High Priest's son. Two years later, Simon was assassinated and the reins of government were assumed by his warlike son. Antiochus, con-

sidering the moment ripe for another attempt, again
marched upon Jerusalem, and reduced it, after a lengthy
siege. Thanks, however, to the intervention of the Romans,
the advancing power with which successive members of
the Hasmonaean house had been careful to maintain
friendly relations, he did not push his victory to an extreme.
Though he insisted on the reassertion of his suzerain rights
and the payment of an indemnity, he allowed John
Hyrcanus to continue in office as a feudatory prince, and
even permitted the retention of recent conquests. It seemed
indeed as though the interlude of independence of the past
ten years had been no more than a passing phase. But, not
long after, in 129 B.C.E., Antiochus was killed in battle. The
Seleucid Empire fell to pieces in a final maze of civil war,
and John Hyrcanus was able to resume the independent
status which his father had won and enjoyed. It was the
beginning of a brief golden age of political freedom which
was to last for less than three-quarters of a century.

VIII. THE HASMONAEAN STATE

1.   With the long hegemony of John Hyrcanus (133-104 B.C.E.), a period of national expansion of unique importance in the growth of the Jewish people reached its climax. Following the example set by Jonathan and Simon, he pushed forward the frontiers of the state on every side. East of the Jordan, he occupied Medeba and the adjacent territory. A sharp campaign subjected the Samaritans, whose sanctuary on Mount Gerizim was destroyed. The age-long enmity between the Jews and Idumaeans, or Edomites, which had found its expression in the raids of Judah the Maccabee, culminated in the final conquest of the country, the inhabitants of which were compelled to accept the Jewish religion.

The death of John Hyrcanus, in 104 B.C.E., was followed by a dynastic struggle between his children. His eldest son, Judah or Aristobulus, succeeded him, assuming the title of king. In his short reign, of only one year, he extended the boundaries of the state even further to the north, conquering the rest of Galilee and part of the territory about Mount Lebanon, which he forcibly Judaized. He was followed on the throne by his able but unscrupulous brother, Alexander Jannaeus, or Jannai (103-76 B.C.E.). His campaigns were not uniformly successful. Nevertheless, he was able to extend his frontiers along the Philistine coast towards Egypt, and above all on the other side of the Jordan.

The Jewish state now rivalled or exceeded in size what had hitherto been its greatest extension in the glorious days of David and of Solomon. It comprised the whole of Palestine proper and the adjacent territories, from the Lake of Huleh down to the borders of Egypt. On the East, it embraced wide areas in Transjordania, known as Perea; on the west, it included almost the whole of the coastal plain. Ships sculptured on the family tomb of the Hasmonaeans near Modin, and depicted on the coins minted by successive rulers, indicated the maritime ambitions of the dynasty. The kingdom was not by any means homogeneous. Here and there were Greek cities, with only a small Jewish element amongst their population. The Samaritans, in spite of their overthrow, continued to resist assimilation. But other parts of the country became completely Judaized, their inhabitants being counted henceforth an integral part of the Jewish people. The Edomites, hereditary enemies for untold generations, came to exercise an important, and at times preponderant, influence upon internal affairs. Fertile Galilee was reckoned from this time one of the principal centers of Judaism, whether from the point of view of numbers, of sentiment, or of devotion. Within a century of the Hasmonaean revolt, the area of the Jewish state had been increased perhaps tenfold, and its population in proportion.

2.   In the course of this period, there had been an increasing rift between the ruling house and certain elements of their subjects. The Hasmonaean brothers had risen to power as the leaders of a popular revolt. The as-

sumption of the title of king, in addition to that of High
Priest, by Judah Aristobulus and his successors introduced
a completely fresh element into the constitution. A powerful section of the people objected to the overwhelming concentration of authority in the hands of one person.

The Hasmonaean dynasty could, of course, count upon
the support of the priestly element, powerful, wealthy, and
cultured. But in recent years, the opposition to the priesthood had been growing. In the period of the First Temple,
and even after the return from exile, they had been regarded as the official depositories of learning and of tradition. But, since the days of Ezra, the Torah had been the
property of the whole people. It had been publicly read and
expounded, at frequent intervals, in every town and village, and the deference previously centered about the Priests
had come to be given to any person who showed himself a
skillful exponent of Holy Writ (*Rabbi,* or "My Master,"
such a person would be called by his disciples in later generations). Tradition had gradually broadened, from precedent to precedent, the decisions or practices of one Rabbi
served as guidance for successive generations; a considerable body of oral tradition grew up to reinforce or supplement or clarify the biblical text; fresh ideas were assimilated and given a Jewish tinge. Thus, there had come into
existence a teaching more modern, more pliable, more living, than that which the Temple priesthood could provide.
Comfort for the vicissitudes of this world was found in
the doctrine of the immortality of the soul and the resur-
rection of the dead, which the Priests, not finding any specific biblical authority for it, strenuously denied.

Two parties had thus developed, one of them looking to
the Temple as the center of instruction, as well as of sacrificial worship, while the other sought enlightenment where-
ever it might be found. The one was essentially conservative, and the other eclectic, in point of doctrine and practice. The one was recruited especially from the priesthood,
backed up by the aristocracy and landowners, and the other
amongst the lower and middle classes. The former supported the absolute monarchy, vested in the hereditary
High Priests; whereas, the latter tended to be democratic.
Gradually the one party came to be known after the
priestly house of Zadok, ancestors of the Hasmonaeans, as
Zadokim, or Sadducees, while the others were given the
name of *Perushim* (Pharisees), or Seceders.*

While the Hasmonaean dynasty retained its primitive
simplicity, and the danger from without remained threatening, national unity continued to be maintained. Towards
the close of the reign of John Hyrcanus, the character of
the ruling house began to deteriorate. Rabbinical tradition
speaks wistfully of the change in this ruler, who "served in
the High Priesthood for seventy years, but in the end became a Sadducee." His successor, Aristobulus, assumed the
title of king, aped Greek customs, and plunged into an
unnatural palace-feud which resulted in the imprisonment
of his mother and the murder of his brother. Alexander
Jannai himself acted in the manner of an oriental despot,
unscrupulous, bloodthirsty, and passionate; and he main-

*These are the most probable, though by no means the only, suggested
derivations of the two terms. The mysterious, semi-monastic sect of this
period, the Essenes, played no part in political affairs, and too little is
known about them to justify a detailed account here (*see* p. 92).

tained his authority by the swords of foreign mercenaries. It was in his reign that the final rift occurred.

At a banquet given on the return of the King from a triumphant military expedition, a Pharisee leader openly bade him dissociate the civil and religious functions which he enjoyed, giving up either the one or the other. On a succeeding Feast of Tabernacles, while he was officiating in the Temple, the King-Priest retaliated by publicly expressing his contempt of Pharisaic teaching, pouring out the libation of water at his feet instead of on the altar; a trivial point, but one which indicated his attitude towards new ceremonial not prescribed in the Pentateuch. The people, enraged, pelted him with the citrons which they were carrying in honor of the feast; and order was restored only at the expense of much bloodshed.*

Civil war raged furiously for many years. Towards the close of the reign, opposition was crushed. Realizing, however, that it would not be easy for a ruler less vigorous than himself to maintain his position without the support of all elements, Jannai laid down on his death-bed as a cardinal point of policy that a reconciliation should be effected.

He was succeeded on the throne by his wife, Salome Alexandra (76-67 B.C.E.). Her brother, Simeon ben Shetah, was one of the leaders of the Pharisee party, and she was accordingly all the more inclined to follow her husband's advice. The fact of her accession illustrates the high status of woman in Jewish life of the period; for neither of her two sons was so young as to justify a Regency. The elder,

*Another account places this episode in the reign of John Hyrcanus, Jannai's father.

Hyrcanus, who was of an inactive and accommodating temperament, was invested with the office of High Priest; the younger, Aristobulus, received the military command. Salome's seven years of rule were peaceful by comparison with the constant warfare of the previous reigns. The elderly queen (she was nearly seventy years of age at the time of her accession) managed to maintain the equilibrium between the two warring elements in the state.

The sympathies of the monarchical party become centered in the dashing Aristobulus, who appeared to have inherited the charm and the warlike instincts of his house. While his mother was on her death-bed, he made a bid for the throne with Sadducean support; and, almost as soon as the breath was out of her body, he turned his arms against his brother, who had been recognized the legitimate heir. During the course of the civil war which ensued, an intervention took place which was to change permanently the face of Palestinian affairs, and to put an end for good to these futile dynastic disputes.

3.   Rome, blindly following her Imperial destinies, had been blundering on, in these last few years, from conquest to conquest. Her influence had long been felt in Asia, where she was now advancing by rapid strides. When, shortly after Salome's death, Pompey arrived in Damascus, deputations from the rival claimants to the throne waited upon him and solicited his support. The Roman was so long pondering over his decision that Aristobulus anticipated the worst, and fled to Jerusalem. Only when he found himself pursued, he realized that resistance was useless and,

making his way to the enemy camp, offered to surrender the city. His followers within the walls refused to obey his instructions, and established themselves on the almost impregnable Temple mount. Here they held out for three months, until one Sabbath (or, according to another account, on the Day of Atonement), in the year 63 B.C.E., their fortifications were stormed, and the defenders massacred.

The capture of Jerusalem by Pompey marked the end of the exceptional period of complete independence which the Hasmonaean kingdom had enjoyed since the days of John Hyrcanus. The remarkable recent expansion of the national boundaries was partially cancelled. However, the work of Judaization in the north of the country had been so thorough and so successful that it was out of the question to sever it anew. Henceforth, therefore, the center of Jewish life resided in two distinct areas, Judaea and Galilee, cut off from the coast by the Greek cities, and from one another by the Samaritan belt. Judaea retained also both Idumaea to the south, and the area of recent conquest, known as Perea, on the eastern side of the Jordan. These territories were left under the rule of the High Priest, Hyrcanus, who lost the title of king and governed the country as a Roman tributary. A few years later, 57 B.C.E., in consequence of a local revolt, he was deprived of all political authority, the country being divided into five districts immediately subject to the Proconsul of Syria. Thereafter, so long as the Roman Empire retained its might, and for long years after the political connection of the Jews with the country was ended, Palestine remained in fact (if not always in name) a Roman province.

4.   The recent reawakening had been accompanied, as is almost invariably the case in history, by a cultural revival. It found an outlet in an outburst of building, in the monumental tomb constructed for the Hasmonaeans near Modin, in the earliest Jewish coinage. But, above all, it expressed itself in literature. While the "abomination of desolation" still stood in the Temple, perhaps before the Hasmonaeans raised the standard of revolt, a zealous believer is thought to have composed the book of Daniel, the last to enter into the canon of the Scriptures. In this, in words ascribed to a figure purported to have flourished in Babylon nearly four centuries before, an attempt was made to show that the present was the final effort to suppress the Jewish people and their holy city. The Babylonians, Medes, and Persians, had done their worst. Now it was the turn of the Greek, the "little horn," as the author contemptuously qualified Antiochus. But this, too, would end in failure, and it would be followed by the final triumph of the Saints of the Most High.

This mystical composition served to strengthen the conviction of the *Hassidim*, as they strove for victory. And, when they achieved it, they expressed their exultation in a burst of song. The so-called Hallel or "Praise" Psalms (cxiii-cxviii), which the Jewish people has ever since associated with any occasion of public thanksgiving, are believed to have been composed to celebrate the Hasmonaean triumph; allusions to contemporary events have been traced in several others; and in any case there can be little doubt that the collection was edited and received its final form at this time.

The national vicissitudes and triumph are reflected, too, in various additions to the books of Esther and of Daniel. Joshua, son of Sirach, a contemporary of Mattathias, the Hasmonaean, composed Ecclesiasticus, a wisdom book containing counsels for daily life. A fictional account of a hypothetical deliverance of the Jewish people from the Assyrians through the devotion of a woman named Judith was presumably written to encourage the national morale during the struggle; while the beginning of the reign of Alexander Jannai witnessed the composition of the First Book of Maccabees, a semi-official history of the recent war. The original Hebrew text of all these works is lost.* They are extant only in ancient Greek renderings included in the supplement to the Bible, known as the Apocrypha; and for a long time were almost entirely unknown in Jewish circles. They remain, however, notwithstanding the shackles of a foreign tongue, a striking testimony of the literary activity which was fostered by the Hasmonaean triumphs.

5.   The Jewish people, during the course of this period, was not confined wholly to Palestine and the immediately adjacent territories; its expansion outside the country was fully as noteworthy as its consolidation within it. Already in the first century B.C.E. the geographer Strabo spoke of the Jews as having penetrated into all states, so that it was difficult to find a single place which had not

*Most of the book of Ecclesiasticus was, however, brought to light in the lumber-room (*Genizah*) of a Cairo synagogue, one of the most amazing literary discoveries of recent times.

received them. This serves to indicate the vast and growing importance of the Diaspora* (as it was called) during this period. The Jews were a small people; but Judaism was already a world religion.

Nowhere was the Jewish settlement more important than in Egypt. Individuals had migrated thither probably even in the days of the First Temple; a considerable body had transferred themselves *en masse* after the national debacle. Subsequently, a miniature sanctuary was established by the Aramaic-speaking military colony settled at Elephantine, which continued to exist till the fourth century. The Aramaic records relating to the colony, discovered there not long ago, throw a striking side-light upon the age, and were, until the more recent discoveries at Lachish, the oldest original, written documents extant bearing on Jewish history.

After the Greek conquest, the migration was accentuated. Jews followed the expedition of Alexander the Great, and were included amongst those settled by him in his new city of Alexandria. For many years after, Palestine was an appanage of Egypt, and the greater country exercised a powerful attraction, as always, on the inhabitants of the smaller. Its Jewish population increased apace. In the whole of the country, they are said to have numbered as many as one million. There was an important offshoot from an early date in Cyrene. In Alexandria there were some hundred thousand, occupying two out of the five sections into which the city was divided. They were permitted to live according to their traditional law, under their own Eth-

---

*The word is from the Greek meaning "scattering." The Hebrew equivalent is *Golah* (Exile).

narch,* with his council of seventy elders; while they were represented in the municipality by their communal leaders. At Leontopolis, a Temple, founded during the persecutions in Palestine by Onias, son of the dispossessed High Priest Onias III, on the model of that of Jerusalem, continued to exist for nearly two and a half centuries. The Egyptian Jews entered into every branch of life. They were merchants, artisans, farmers, laborers. Many were settled in military allotments in various parts of the country, some rising to high rank in the administraton. In every respect, excepting religiously, they were thoroughly assimilated to their environment.

Egypt was, at this time, the greatest center of Hellenic culture. The Jews could not fail to be influenced by this fact. They speedily relinquished the language of their fathers in favor of Greek; they universally adopted Hellenic names (a process which had made great progress even in Palestine); and they produced a whole literature in the vernacular to satisfy their cultural requirements. As early as the third century B.C.E. there had been begun, under royal patronage, that Greek translation of the Hebrew Scriptures which goes by the name of the Septuagint, and which enjoyed unquestioned authority in Alexandrian Jewry. Imitations of, and supplements to the Bible (mostly comprised in the Apocrypha or the looser collection known as the Pseudepigrapha) were composed in Greek in Alexandria, heavily tinged with the local philosophical conceptions. As was natural, many writers abandoned the traditional models, with the result that there grew up an en-

*i. e. Ruler of a People (Greek).

tirely independent literature, intended to familiarize Hellenized Jews with their own national culture, and to demonstrate to Gentile critics and observers the superiority, or at least rationality, of Judaism. There were historians, who wrote accounts of the kings of Judah; archaeologists, who studied Hebrew antiquities; poets, who composed dramas or epics on biblical subjects; apologists, who defended their people against the anti-Semites of the day; and philosophers who examined the Mosaic laws and proved that they did not conflict with, or perhaps even anticipated, the fashionable Greek culture.

This tendency, already present in the third century B.C.E., and active in the second, continued even after the Roman occupation of Egypt, in the middle of the first. It culminated in the noble figure of Philo of Alexandria (20 B.C.E.- 45 C.E.), through whose work Hellenic Jewish culture is best known to the modern world. The Egyptian scene was vivid, crowded, and conspicuously modern in tone. It was, however, in Palestine that the heart of the Jewish nation, and the main tradition of Jewish culture were still to be found.

NOTE TO CHAPTER VIII

Since these pages were first written, an entire literature relating to this period has been discovered among the so-called Dead Sea Scrolls. These writings were found in caves in the neighborhood of what appears to have been a monastic establishment, at Qumran, not far from Jericho. The scrolls demonstrate the intense religious vitality and literary productivity of the Jewish people at the beginning of the Christian era. Many scholars believe that they are part of the literature and disciplinary code of the hitherto mysterious Essenes (*see footnote,* p. 84); others are of the opinion that they emanate from a hyper-patriotic faction, the Zealots, who emerged somewhat later (*see* pp. 100-109). Together with this vast and varied original literature there have been found many Hebrew biblical manuscripts written something like a thousand years earlier than any previously known.

IX. THE HEGEMONY OF ROME

1.   Ever since the beginning of the petty dynastic dispute which had lost Judaea her independence, the blundering Hyrcanus had been under the influence of a certain Antipater. The latter was an Idumaean, a member of the race whose forcible conversion to Judaism had been one of the outstanding episodes of recent history. It had been on his advice, and at his instigation, that Hyrcanus had consistently acted during the prolonged struggle for the throne. After the Roman occupation, Antipater was recognized the principal personality in Jerusalem, and probably became farmer of taxes for the whole country.

Roman rapacity was responsible, meanwhile, for a whole succession of rebellions, but, notwithstanding all temptations, the High Priest was induced by his wily advisor to remain faithful. With consummate skill, Antipater managed to retain the favor of whatever faction was uppermost in Rome during the civil wars which had now begun. The conflict which broke out in 49 B.C.E. between Julius Caesar and Pompey called for all his finesse, but in the end he was found ranged on the side of the victor. Caesar showed his gratitude by restoring Hyrcanus some of his political power, with the title of "Ethnarch," and reuniting with Palestine part of the territory taken away by Pompey. His assassination on the Ides of March 44 B.C.E., was mourned by the Jews as a national loss.

93

The High Priest's authority remained purely nominal.
The Romans were the overlords of the country; Antipater
was the force behind the throne; and the latter's two sons,
Phezahel and Herod, were appointed governors of Jerusalem and Galilee respectively. The latter, though younger in
years, was the abler and the more strenuous, and gradually
began to occupy the front of the stage. When, in 43 B.C.E.,
Antipater was poisoned by a rival, it was to this son that
he transmitted his authority in the state.

When the triumph of Philippi made Mark Anthony
master of Asia, Herod's honeyed words and lavish promises outweighed the impression caused by the Jewish deputations who appeared before the victor to complain at the
harshness of the regime. The result was a further promo-
tion. Hyrcanus was deprived of the shreds of political authority which he had nominally enjoyed during the past
few years. This was now divided between Herod and his
brother, who were given the title of *tetrarch*.*

Not long after, a revolt, with Parthian support, resulted
in a temporary restoration of the Hasmonaeans in the person of Antigonus, son of Aristobulus (40-37 B.C.E.), and
deprived Phezahel of his life. Herod, however, realized
that the fate of Palestine had to be decided, not in the east,
but in Rome. Thither he made his way, and his personal
suppleness and lavish gifts secured the support both of
Anthony and of Octavian, the two rulers of the Roman
Empire. His new patrons had no difficulty in securing his
nomination by the Senate as tributary King of Judaea.

*Literally, "ruler of a fourth part," but loosely applied to any subor-
dinate prince.

With the aid of a couple of legions and his wild Idumaean
kinsmen, the country was reconquered. Jerusalem was captured after a five months' siege, and the last Hasmonaean
sovereign put to death. During the course of the campaign, Herod married Miriam (Mariamne), a grand-
daughter of Hyrcanus II. Thus the usurper was able to
attract some of the popular sympathy which still lingered
about the name of the Maccabees, and to begin his long
reign with a semblance of legitimate right.

2.   "I had sooner be Herod's swine than his son,"
was the commentary of the Emperor Augustus, Herod's
friend, upon his creature's family record. This is the aspect
of the reign which has captured the popular recollection.
The new ruler was supremely able and energetic. He lacked
entirely, however, the qualities which appeal to the imagination. He was cold, calculating, and cruel. He was aware
that his rule was profoundly distasteful to his people, and
that their sympathies inclined to the remnants of the old
royal house, which had delivered them from foreign oppression and ushered in a brief period of glorious freedom.
But, in consequence of his marriage, he himself was closely
allied with the Hasmonaeans. His own children, descended
from them on their mother's side, were therefore his most
dangerous rivals. As his reign continued, and other possible claimants disappeared from the scene, his mind became more and more suspicious even of his nearest kin,
until his life closed under the shadow of the darkest tragedy of all.

Almost the first act of his reign was the arrest and execution of forty-five members of the leading aristocratic families of the realm. He was persuaded against his will to appoint his wife's handsome young brother, another Aristobulus, to the High Priesthood (an office to which he could not aspire himself), but the popularity which the latter achieved aroused his enmity, and he had him drowned. The aged and mutilated Hyrcanus, his wife's grandfather, formerly King and High Priest, was murdered for fear that he might again become a dangerous competitor for the throne. The climax came in 26 B.C.E. when his own wife, Mariamne, was put to death on a suspicion of conspiracy and infidelity, an outrage which the perpetrator himself soon repented, and from the effects of which he never recovered. A less blood-stained period followed, if only for lack of victims. Herod's children by Mariamne, Alexander and Aristobulus, were, however, growing to manhood; and the King could see that by virtue of their descent on their mother's side, they appealed to the popular sentiment as he had never been able to do. Gradually, his mind became filled with gnawing suspicion even against them. In the end, the two young princes were formally arraigned on a charge of treachery, and after the travesty of trial, were strangled in prison (7 B.C.E.).

It is entirely wrong to regard this succession of palace tragedies as constituting the essential feature of the reign. Cold and cruel as Herod was, he counted nevertheless amongst the most competent rulers of his day, and his reign was memorable, for more reasons than one, in the annals of the Jewish people. The ultimate Roman overlordship was at all times plain. The tribute paid was heavy.

Roman legionaries were never absent from Jerusalem and Roman institutions prevailed in the country in an increasing degree. Yet, within these limitations, there was a considerable element of success, and even glory, in the reign. In spite of all turns of the wheel of political fortune, the Jewish king managed to maintain his position. So long as he did nothing which conflicted with the wishes of his suzerains, his power was absolute. The old constitution of the country was overruled. The *Sanhedrin* or Council, previously the most important deliberative authority, was deprived of all executive or advisory power, so that it became in an increasing degree an academic and religious council. Everything was done to prevent national sentiment from crystallizing again around the High Priesthood, as had been the case in former days. The occupant of the dignity was changed with indecorous frequency, and the sacred robes which constituted the insignia of office were kept in the royal custody.

In compensation, there was a long period of peace, broken only by local revolts or border raids. In consequence of successive grants, the boundaries of the kingdom were enlarged almost to the extent of the old Hasmonaean state. A period of intensive development followed. The wealth and population of the country rapidly increased. Taxation was heavy, but the proceeds were largely devoted to public works. The seaports along the Mediterranean coast were developed, and communications opened up through them with the western world. Samaria was rebuilt and called Sebaste,* in honor of the Emperor. Straton's

* *Sebastos* is the Greek equivalent of the Roman *Augustus*.

Tower, an unimportant coast town, was developed into the city of Caesarea, modern even to its drainage, which ultimately became one of the most important seaports of the Levant. Magnificent royal palaces were built in Jerusalem and elsewhere. On the other hand, the King attempted to conciliate his subjects, adorn his capital, and perpetuate his name at the same time, by reconstructing the Temple, which had stood without substantial alteration since the return from the Exile. The work occupied many years, and the building, when finished, was one of the wonders of the Mediterranean world.

Nothing earned Herod so much domestic unpopularity as his devotion which he showed to the fashionable Hellenic culture, to the complete neglect of everything Jewish. In all his building operations (excepting possibly the Temple) the classical style of architecture was employed. The urban centers throughout Palestine, and especially the new cities which he developed, came entirely under Greek and Roman influence. In Jerusalem, itself, he constructed a Hippodrome, where the games which had so scandalized a former generation were carried on. The Hellenization against which the Hasmonaeans had fought thus became deeply implanted in a period of profound peace. When the King died, in a welter of blood, in 4 B.C.E., vast strides had already been made, under his inspiration, in the process which was to end with the extrusion of Judaism from the country.

3.   Herod's death was succeeded by a general flare-up of insurrection, which was put down with needless ruth-

lessness by the Roman legionaries. Meanwhile the future of the kingdom was decided in Italy. By other wives than the unfortunate Mariamne, Herod had left several children. In accordance with the terms of his will, Palestine was divided up between them. One, Archelaus, was invested with the rule of the central part of the country, including Judaea and Samaria; his brother, Antipas, was nominated *tetrarch* of Galilee and Perea; Philip was given the northeastern province. In only one important respect were the terms of Herod's final dispositions neglected. Archelaus was deprived of the title of king, which his father had enjoyed, and had to content himself with that of Ethnarch, which accentuated his subordination to Rome. Ten years later (6 c.e.), the Emperor Augustus took advantage of the complaints voiced by his subjects to depose him and annex his territories.

The kernel of the Jewish homeland was henceforth a Roman possession, nakedly and without disguise. Its constitution and administration were much the same as that of any other province of the Empire. It was ruled over by a Procurator, who was himself subordinate to the Legate of Syria. Jerusalem, notoriously recalcitrant and troublesome, was deprived even of the titular dignity of capital, the seat of administration being removed to Caesarea. Ample garrisons were stationed throughout the country. The taxation, heavier than ever before, was farmed out to private contractors, or publicans. The High Priesthood was kept rigorously subordinated and prevented from attaining independent authority. Within these limits, there was a certain degree of local autonomy, but the ever-present

Roman legionaries, and the activities of the publicans, served as constant reminders of the overlordship of an alien power.

The country was in a continuous state of discontent, which flared up from time to time into actual rebellion. The upper classes were opposed to violence, believing that deliverance would come from heaven in God's own time. The ordinary people, however, were not always amenable to their influence. Groaning under the weight of the foreign oppression, they looked forward to salvation with increasing eagerness. Assuredly, God would have mercy upon their affliction and deliver them, as he had done their fathers in days of similar distress. The Hasmonaeans had failed them. Then it would be a descendant of the royal house of David who would be sent to deliver them and prove to be the Lord's Anointed, the Messiah. Large numbers were determined to chase out the oppressor by force of arms, just as Judah the Maccabee had done two hundred years before, and to avenge themselves on those who favored alien rule.

In the mountains of Galilee (still nominally under the *tetrarch* Antipas, though, in fact, a Roman province) a state of revolt became endemic. A certain Judah, whose father Hezekiah had been executed by Herod, and who had himself risen in arms at the time of the tyrant's death, put himself at the head of the insurgents. He was defeated and put to death. Nevertheless, his spirit continued to inspire his sympathizers, who for long years after looked up to his sons as their leaders. They became known as the *Kannaim* or Zealots; and, in the remoter parts of the country, they cut down without scruple any person who appeared too friendly towards the Roman oppressor. At the Pilgrim Festivals, Jerusalem continued a hot-bed of excitement; and, on one occasion, in the year 33 C.E., a popular religious revivalist from Galilee named Joshua (Jesus), who laid claim to Davidic descent, was crucified on Passover eve, after a summary trial, by the nervous administration.* Further acts of violence were perpetuated in subsequent years under the same Procurator, Pontius Pilate, who was ultimately dismissed as a result of the complaints levelled at him from all quarters.

In the following period, the state of affairs became even more delicate. Peace had been maintained in Palestine only by treating the religious susceptibilites of the Jews with the utmost regard. The current interpretation of the second commandment precluded any "graven image" whatsoever. Accordingly, taught by bitter experience, the Roman legions went so far as to discard their Eagles, and even effigies of the Emperor, before entering Jerusalem; the tactless Pilate had been forced to remove the shields bearing the Imperial insignia which he had placed in the governor's palace; and the Legate of Syria, passing through Judaea immediately afterwards, refrained from marching his army to Jerusalem with their standards. The half-mad Emperor, Caius Caligula, failed to appreciate all this. It had become customary throughout the Roman dominions for the Emperor to be adored as Divine, and for his effigy to be set up in all the Temples. That the Jews did not

---

*For a fuller account of Jesus and the rise of Christianity, see p. 140 ff.

follow this example appeared to him a deliberate affront. Shortly after his accession to the throne in 37 C.E., he made an attempt to enforce the erection of his statue in the synagogues of Alexandria (if not elsewhere), and even in the central shrine at Jerusalem. The governor of Syria, who was entrusted with the execution of this mission, was wise enough to temporize and the Emperor was assassinated before his resolution could be enforced. A repetition of a general revolt like that against Antiochus Epiphanes was, almost providentially, averted.

4.   There followed a brief glimmer of brighter things, the last that Jewish Palestine was destined to know. Aristobulus, the murdered son of Herod and Mariamne, had left behind him one child, a boy, named Agrippa after the Emperor's son. He had been brought up at the Roman court with Caius Caligula, with whom he was on most intimate terms. One of Caligula's first actions was to order his friend's release, and to nominate him successor to the Tetrarch Philip, who had just died. In addition, he was given the title of king. In subsequent years, further gifts were showered upon him by the Emperor and his successor, Claudius (41-54 C.E.), until his dominions were almost co-extensive with those of his grandfather, embracing the whole of Palestine.

Agrippa united in his veins the blood of Herod and of the Hasmonaeans. His vigor and his adroitness testified to the first, his personal charm, his popularity, and his intense Jewish feeling, to the second. Long years after his death, men continued to speak of his piety and of his

scrupulous observance of the Mosaic code. But, in spite
of the royal state which he enjoyed and the show of independence, the shadow of Rome remained only too apparent,
and, when, after a brief reign (41-44 C.E.), the popular
Jewish monarch died suddenly, at Caesarea, it was thought
safest to bring the dynasty to an end. His young son,
Agrippa II, retained a sentimental hold on the popular
imagination. He was, after all, the Jewish King, if not
King of the Jews, and he was not slow in speaking whether
in Rome or elsewhere, at any time when the interests of
his people were involved. His actual political authority
was, however, confined to an unimportant area, with a
mixed population, in the far north. The rest of the country was once more annexed to the province of Syria, being
governed by a succession of tyrannical Procurators as it
had been before the recent interlude.

5.   The period which followed was one of misgovern-
ment, accentuated by an utter absence of appreciation of
Jewish standards of life and religious ideals. One Procurator after another trampled on the susceptibilities of the
people. Their exploitation at the hands of the Roman tax-
gatherers drove the populace to sullen hatred of the existing state of affairs. Everywhere the Zealots became increasingly active, and an extremist party, who became
known as Assassins, sprang up amongst them. At intervals,
the latter would come down from their mountain fastnesses
and raid the villages and townships, looting the houses of
Roman sympathizers, and killing their occupants without
remorse. Intermarriage with a Gentile was sometimes

sufficient to cost a man his life. An attempt of the Procurator Felix (52-60 C.E.) to suppress the rebels ended in
failure. Their leader, Eleazer, was treacherously seized
and sent to Rome, where he perished, but his fate stimulated his followers to greater efforts.

From Galilee, their activities extended into Judaea.
Roman partisans were unsafe even in Jerusalem, where
they ran the risk of falling under the dagger of some
enthusiast who mingled with the crowd and escaped
before his crime was discovered. One day the High Priest,
himself, who was adjudged to have shown himself too
accommodating, was assassinated by members of the patriotic party. In Caesarea, a state of semi-overt warfare
existed between the Jewish and the Gentile population.

After an interregnum which allowed the forces of disorder to gain a stronger hold, a new Procurator named
Florus arrived in 64 C.E., to find Judaea seething with discontent. Nevertheless, he followed the rapacious example
of his precursors. His maladministration became more and
more glaring, culminating in the seizure of seventeen tal-
ents of gold from the Temple Treasury. A riot ensued,
and a basket was passed round by some witty citizen into
which the charitably inclined might drop coins for the
relief of the indigent Procurator. Furious at this insult,
the latter turned his troops loose on the city, part of which
was sacked, and the disorder was put down in blood. Two
cohorts were summoned from Caesarea to reinforce the
garrison. After much trouble, the High Priest persuaded
the citizens to give them a friendly reception. Their over-
tures were treated with contempt, and the anti-Roman

demonstration flared up again. There was fighting up and down the steep streets, where a hail of missiles from the housetops greeted every Roman helmet. The insurgents seized the Temple mount, and all efforts to dislodge them proved of no avail. The city was now untenable, and the legionaries withdrew to the citadel and the royal palace. Ultimately, they agreed to lay down their arms, but, as they left their stronghold, they were attacked and butchered to a man.

Judaea and Galilee were now in full revolt. The events at Jerusalem exacerbated feelings in Caesarea, always a hot-bed of religious animosity; and here, on the day of the slaughter of the garrison at Jerusalem, the Jews were set upon by their Gentile neighbors and massacred. Racial riots swept through the whole of Syria. Every place where Jews were in the majority they rose in revolt. Marauding parties raided the neighboring Gentile townships, some of which were reduced to ashes. Elsewhere, reprisals were carried out against the Jews. At length, Gallus, the Imperial Legate in Syria, determined to strike, and led a strong force to suppress the revolt. He met with no opposition on his way to Jerusalem, where he camped outside the walls and defeated a sortie with ease. The insurgents remained unintimidated by this display of force, and the troops at Gallus' disposal were inadequate to carry out a formal siege. There was no alternative but to withdraw. As it passed through the historic gorge of Beth-Horon, the Roman force was surrounded and attacked. The retreat developed into a rout. The invaders were able to extricate themselves only after the loss of six thousand men and the whole of their baggage (autumn of 66 c. e.). It was one of the most signal defeats inflicted upon the Roman armies since the establishment of the Empire. Henceforth, all possibility of conciliation was at an end.

6.   Meanwhile, the revolutionary government had continued in control at Jerusalem, authority being exercised by a general assembly of citizens in the courts of the Temple. Steps were immediately taken to prepare for the inevitable Roman onslaught, and commissioners were sent to the various provinces to take over the administration and to make ready the defense. For a very brief period, from the autumn of 66 c.e., Jewish Palestine enjoyed a last glimpse of independence. The country was filled with warlike preparations. Coins were again struck, in token of the restored independence. Yet, even in this grave hour, there was no unity. The Assassins continued active. The extremists intrigued continually against the more moderate elements; and energy, which should have been turned against the common enemy, was wasted in operations against internal opponents.

Preparatory measures on the other side were meanwhile being pressed on. Vespasian, one of the ablest living Roman generals, who had achieved a high reputation as the conqueror of Britain, was despatched to Syria to direct operations. During the winter of 66-67 c.e., he was at Antioch, recruiting his forces. Early in the following year, he advanced to Ptolemais, on the edge of the area that had revolted. Here he was joined by his son Titus, who had brought up a legion from Egypt. Galilee was in no condition to put up a defense. The governor who had been appointed to the command of this province in the patriotic interest on the outbreak of the revolt, was a certain Joseph ben Mattathias, the priest, better known to posterity as Josephus. His principal recommendation was a recent visit to Rome, where, it was presumed, he had learned something of Roman methods. But his sincerity was suspected. The more earnest patriots, grouped about the fervent John of Gish-halab, or Gischala, opposed Josephus tooth and nail.

The past year had thus been wasted in internal squabbles and intrigues, sometimes accompanied by bloodshed. In spite of a few spectacular measures carried out by Josephus, no serious steps had been taken to put the country in a state of defense. Accordingly, the Jewish resistance crumbled before the Roman advance (spring—67 c.e.). The raw Jewish levies could not face the legions in the field, and dispersed without striking a blow. Josephus retired to Jotapata, occupying an almost impregnable position in the mountains. After a defense of two months, the city was captured and Josephus, saving his life by a stratagem, went over brazenly to the Romans, an act of treachery to which the Jewish people is indebted for its one-sided though minute knowledge of this period. The full force of the Roman armies was brought to bear upon the remaining strongholds, one by one, and, before the autumn rains had brought the campaign to a halt, the whole of Galilee and northern Palestine was once more in Roman hands.

The effect in Jerusalem was the reverse of what might have been expected. The patriots who managed to escape from the disaster, made their way to the capital, where they reinforced the extremists. The revolution thus entered upon a second more violent stage. It was a Jacobin sequel to the orderly change of government which had taken place in the first instance. When the moderates, headed by the ex-High Priest Hannan (Annanus) took up arms and drove the Zealots from the city (though they were unable to dislodge them from the Temple), a rumor was circulated that they had the intention of surrendering outright to the Romans. The Zealot leaders countered this menace by sending for reinforcements to their friends in Idumaea, recent converts to Judaism, but nonetheless devoted to the Jewish cause. On the latter's arrival in the city, during a heavy downpour, they effected a juncture with their allies, and a combined attack was delivered against the common enemy. A veritable reign of terror set in. The leaders of the moderate party were butchered. A revolutionary tribunal was set up, which condemned its opponents to death without compunction. The original leaders of the revolt were thus swept out of the way. The administration was now in the hands of the extremists, headed by John of Gischala, Josephus' former opponent, who had managed to escape from his native city after holding out bravely for some months.

Vespasian had determined to isolate the capital before striking his final blow. During the winter of 67-68 c.e., he reduced the majority of the territories beyond the Jordan to obedience. In the spring, he marched southwards. The towns in the Judaean lowlands were captured one by one. A strong force was left in Idumaea to overawe the coun-

try. Then, wheeling northward, he occupied Jericho. With
the exception of a small strip around Jerusalem, the whole
of the country was now in Roman hands. The commander-
in-chief returned to Caesarea to make final preparations for
besieging the capital. While he was here, news arrived of
the death of the Emperor Nero. The political outlook became so uncertain (all the more so when Nero's successor,
Galba, was assassinated the following January) that for the
moment, it seemed inadvisable to recommence the campaign. In Jerusalem, meanwhile, John of Gischala was supreme. He showed in his administration many of the qualities of a real statesman. Yet satisfaction with his rule was
by no means universal. Civil warfare broke out once more,
and the streets again flowed with blood. It proved impossible, however, to dislodge the Zealots from the Temple
mount, even though they were hopelessly disunited.

Internal dissensions were put an end to by the advance
of the Romans. While Vespasian was at Caesarea making
preparations for further operations, news came through of
the elevation of Vitellius to the throne of the Caesars by
the army of the Rhine. His own legionaries, indignant,
proclaimed their own general Emperor. The latter abandoned the campaign and hastened Romeward to assert his
claim. At Alexandria the news reached him that Vitellius
had been assassinated, and that his own title was now
virtually unopposed. Before embarking, therefore, he sent
his son Titus back to complete the conquest of Judaea. In
the spring of the year 70 c.e., the new commander arrived
at Jerusalem. The ranks of the besieged closed in face of
danger. But, for the past three years, they had been fritter-

ing away their energies in internal discord, and they were now in no condition to withstand a siege. The lower city was stormed without much difficulty, after a breach had been made in the walls, but the upper city and the Temple mount continued to hold out. The defenders fought with unbelievable valor. God, himself, they thought, was on their side, and, when all seemed blackest, He would assuredly miraculously intervene to deliver them, as He had so often done in the days of their fathers. By midsummer, conditions had become so extreme that the regular sequence of morning and evening sacrifice had to be discontinued at the altar, for the first time since the triumph of Judas the Maccabee. On the ninth day of Ab, almost the exact anniversary of the destruction of Jerusalem by Nebuchadnezzar, the Temple was stormed, and (whether by accident or by design) committed to the flames.

The upper city held out for a month longer; but before the Jewish New Year had come around, all was in Roman hands. The few fastnesses which still resisted were reduced without much difficulty, with the exception of Masada, an impregnable port on the Dead Sea, which continued to hold out under the Zealot leader, Eleazar. In the spring of 73 C.E., this too fell, and the last vestige of Jewish independence was crushed. The Imperial City witnessed yet another triumph, graced by the presence and the slaughter of the surviving heroes of the struggle; and the classical world gave a sigh of relief at the thought that a city which they considered a bulwark of obscurantism, and which they conceived had withstood the tide of progress for so many centuries, had at last been swept away.

X. THE PATRIARCHATE

1.   Contrary to what is generally imagined, the fall
of Jerusalem was only an episode in the history of the Jewish people, rather than the close of an epoch. It is true that
Jerusalem and the Temple lay in ruins, and were forbidden
to be rebuilt. In consequence of disorders which the fugitives from Palestine stirred up in subsequent years in
Egypt and Cyrene, even the imitative sanctuary at
Leontopolis, founded by the High Priest Onias nearly two
and a half centuries before, was closed. It is true that the
voluntary annual tax of half a shekel, which had hitherto
been collected throughout the Diaspora on behalf of the
Temple of Jerusalem, was made compulsory, and assigned
to the Imperial Treasury at Rome, under the title *Fiscus
Judaicus*. It is true that the people as a whole sat in mourning for those who had fallen in the war, and for the glory
that was gone from Israel. Yet, in spite of all this, the state
of Palestine, when order was restored, did not materially
differ from its previous condition. The population of
Judaea and Galilee, at least, remained preponderantly Jewish. The country continued to be administered by a Roman
Governor resident at Caesarea. The Jewish state had fallen
a century and a half earlier, when Pompey captured Jerusalem. The constitutional position of the Jewish people,
after the great revolt was suppressed, remained substantially
the same as before it began.

One important new development, and one only, took place. The spokesmen of the Jewish people had hitherto been the rulers of the house of Herod, but the last male representative of that house, Agrippa II, was estranged from his people, and had not much longer to live. The High Priest had been hardly less prominent, but, with the destruction of the Temple, the High Priesthood itself had come to an end. Even before the fall of Jerusalem, there had been a category which enjoyed almost equal, if not superior, consideration. The Rabbis, scholars who expounded the Holy Writ, had always been looked up to by the people with reverence. Now, there was no one else to revere. It happened that, before Jerusalem fell, one of the outstanding scholars of his generation, Johanan ben Zakkai, had managed to escape from the city—according to legend in a coffin borne by his disciples. Titus had permitted him to settle in the seaport of Jabneh (Jamnia), near Jaffa, and to open a school for the study and exposition of the traditional lore. The most eminent of contemporary scholars gathered round him there. The Sanhedrin, formerly the highest Council of State, became reconstituted from members chosen for their erudition rather than for political influence or wealth. As its head was elected Gamaliel, a descendant of the great Hillel, one of the most beloved figures of the Herodian era, whose teachings and whose personality were still cherished more than those of any other scholar of his generation.

This body ultimately acquired semi-official status. Its President or Nasi ("Patriarch," as he was called in the outside world), became recognized as the representative of the Jewish people in its relations with the Roman authorities. Over a period of three and a half centuries, the dignity was transmitted in this family from father to son.

With the fall of the Temple, the Sadducees, whose whole existence had been bound up with its worship, lost their separate individuality. The Pharisee scholars were left masters of the field. The internecine academic strife which had so long prevailed among them, between the disciples of Hillel and those of his more stringent rival, Shammai, was amicably settled. Under these auspices, life in Palestine was reorganized. There was a double system of government, that of the Romans with their subordinate officials and tax-gatherers, centering upon the Procurator at Caesarea, and that of the scholars, revolving about the Sanhedrin and the Patriarch in Jabneh. The people voluntarily set aside tithes for the priest, and gave offerings to the charity-collector sent around by the schools, with a better grace than they paid their taxes to the Roman publican. Courts, for deciding legal cases in accordance with Jewish law, continued to be maintained in every town, with the Sanhedrin as coordinating authority over them. The Synagogue and the house of study became more than ever before the centers of local life. The scholastic system was developed, until it attained a perfection unrealized in Europe until the nineteenth century was far advanced, and the population continued to lead a full, and on the whole, a tranquil Jewish existence.

2. The work of reconstruction was interrupted by an outstanding triumph, followed by a terrible catastrophe. A

people confident of Divine succor could not accept defeat as a final solution. For nearly a generation, Palestine was kept in cowed subjection. But, forty-five years after the fall of Jerusalem, the eastern frontier of the Roman Empire was again in a blaze, and the Jews of the Levant and Africa, inspired with a vague Messianic hope, rose simultaneously, with a spontaneity and cohesion which make one suspect a master-mind behind the movement. As far afield as Mesopotamia, Egypt, Cyrene, and Cyprus, the revolt assumed menacing proportions. It was put down, with an excess of cruelty, only after much blood had been shed on either side (115 c.e.)

For the moment, thanks to a formidable display of severity, peace was maintained in Palestine. However, shortly after the accession of the Emperor Hadrian, an insurrection on an imposing scale took place here as well (132 c.e.). At its head was a leader of gigantic strength and rare fascination of character named Simon bar Kozeba, or, as his admirers called him, Bar Kocheba (the Son of a Star). Amongst those who rallied around him was the outstanding scholar of his generation, Akiba ben Joseph, whose whole-hearted adherence gave the movement exceptional significance. It spread with lightning rapidity. No Josephus was present to write an account of the revolt; but it seems to have met at the outset with very considerable success. The Roman garrisons were driven out of the southern part of the country at least. Jerusalem was captured. An attempt seems to have been made to restore the Temple. Coinage was struck of a perfection hitherto unparalleled, and bearing an inscription in the old Hebrew characters, commemorating the liberation of the Holy City from the Romans.

For three years, the insurgents held out. At last, Julius Severus was recalled from Britain to take charge of operations. The Roman military machine, once its full weight was exerted, was invincible. The country was methodically reduced, and Jerusalem recaptured. The last place to offer a resistance was the mountain-fastness of Beth-Ther, between Jerusalem and the sea coast. In 135 c.e., after a long and stubborn defense, it fell—on the ninth of Ab, the anniversary of the double national disaster. The rebels were systematically hunted down. Those leaders of the revolt who had not fallen in battle, like Bar Kocheba himself, were cruelly put to death, as was Rabbi Akiba ben Joseph. A harrow was drawn over the site of Jerusalem, and a new city erected, under the name *Aelia Capitolina,* into which no Jew was allowed to set foot. The rest of Judaea lay in ruins, its population almost annihilated by the war and wholesale enslavement which followed. No longer was the stretch of territory about the ancient capital to remain the heart of the Jewish people. The center of national life was removed to the north of the country, to Galilee. From this time the Jews were in a minority in the land of their fathers; and, even there, the most populous settlements were in that area least closely associated with the bygone national glories.

3.   The suppression of the revolt was followed by an interlude of religious persecution. Like Antiochus Epiphanes before him, Hadrian seems to have hoped to sup-

press the existence of the Jews as a race by forbidding the
exercise of their religion. Until his reign was at an end,
the fundamental practices of Judaism remained proscribed. Even the teaching of the law was forbidden, and
tradition recalled ten outstanding scholars who suffered
martyrdom rather than comply. Ultimately, Hadrian's
successor, Antoninus Pius, came to the conclusion that the
new policy was unwise, and freedom of conscience was
restored (138 c.e.). The intolerant laws were rescinded,
with the significant reservation that circumcision might be
practiced henceforth only on persons of the Jewish race.
Conversionism, as it had hitherto been carried out widely
throughout the Empire, thus became a capital offense.
From this enactment may be dated the close of the missionary activities of Judaism on a large scale.

The survivors of the school of Jabneh managed to reestablish themselves at Usha, in Galilee. Here the Sanhedrin was set up anew; and it decided upon a series of
measures for the reorganization of national life, shattered
by the recent disaster. Simon, son of the late Patriarch
Gamaliel, was elected *Nasi*. He was a man of no great
scholarship, a fact which demonstrates the commanding
position which the family had by now established in the
affections of the nation. He was succeeded in his office by
his son Judah (170-217 c.e.), under whom the Patriarchate
reached its fullest development. The state which he maintained was little less than royal. His personality dominated
the Sanhedrin. He made a point of seeing that Hebrew
was spoken in his household, considering it to be, with
Greek, the only tongue fitted for cultured intercourse.

When the state of his health forced him to take up his residence in the mountain air of Sepphoris, that place became one of the centers of national sentiment. It was under his auspices that there took place the great codification of the traditional jurisprudence known as the Mishnah (*see* p. 127), which was to form the basis of the national culture and literature in succeeding generations.

Judah, who died in 217 c.e., was the last commanding figure in the Patriarchate. He was followed by a monotonous succession of Gamaliels, Judahs, and Hillels. Scholarship was by now a superfluous qualification for the office, which had definitely become hereditary. Politically, however, its lustre was undiminished. The authority of the Patriarch (now established permanently at Tiberias), was recognized to the utmost ends of the Diaspora, from which a voluntary tribute flowed in for the upkeep of his state, as had previously been the case for the maintenance of the Temple. Under his rule, the Jews of Palestine continued a compact group, nursing their traditional culture, and maintaining at least juridical autonomy. But they were a dwindling community. Christianity was slowly extruding Judaism from the country of its birth. Economically, the country was in decline. The devastation effected by the Romans in suppressing the two great revolts of 68-70 c.e. and 132-135 c.e. left a permanent mark, from which it never recovered. There is evidence of a progressive dessication, of a diminution of rainfall which was robbing the whole of the Arabian Peninsula and the adjacent lands of their fertility. Taxation became crushingly heavy. Every civil and military disturbance tended to affect the Jews more than any other section of the population, excepting, perhaps, their unhappy kinsmen, the Samaritans, who were no less unruly, and whose history was even more chequered.

There was one last ray of hope before the darkness finally gathered. The Emperor Julian (known as "the Apostate," *see* p. 143), in his reaction against Christianity, showed distinct favor to Judaism, and, in a letter to his "brother, the venerable Patriarch Hillel II" (320-365 C.E.) he announced his intention to rebuild the Temple at Jerusalem, on his return from his projected campaign against the Persians. But he never returned, and exultant Christian writers regarded the disappointment of the Jewish hopes as a final proof that the Divine favor had departed.

The end was now near. When in the course of the fourth century the ramshackle Roman Empire became divided into two separate states, Palestine naturally fell to the lot of the Eastern or Byzantine division. In 399 C.E., Honorius, Emperor of the West, jealous at the transmission of bullion from his dominions to those of his rival, prohibited the collection in Italy of the voluntary tax which every Jew had hitherto sent each year for the maintainence of the Patriarchate. It was a severe blow, which must have been keenly felt in the miniature court in Tiberias. In the following year, the Patriarch Judah IV (385-400 C.E.) was succeeded by his son, Gamaliel VI. Twenty-five years later, the latter died, without leaving male issue; and Theodosius II, seized the opportunity to abolish the office entirely (425 C.E.).

Thus, the last vestige of Jewish independence, the last

shadow of the glories of the past age, was swept away. It
was true that Jews were still to be found in Palestine in
some numbers. Synagogues of considerable magnificence,
like that recently excavated at Beth Alpha, continued to
be constructed. Schools and scholars managed to maintain
themselves at Tiberias and elsewhere. The biblical text was
scanned by the so-called Massorites, and a certain amount
of legalistic literature (long lost, but in part recovered in
the course of the past few years) was compiled. At the time
of the great struggle between the Persians and Byzantines
for the mastery of Palestine in the reign of Heraclius, the
Jews of the country, led by a certain Benjamin of Tiberias,
took the part of the Persians, and had to pay a terrible
price when their previous masters returned (628 c.e.). It
was not until the time of the Crusades that the dwindling
Jewish settlement in Palestine finally decayed, and, even
down to our own days, it is said that there remain a couple
of village communities in remote corners of Galilee who
were never uprooted throughout the millennia from their
ancestral soil. With the abolition of the Patriarchate, however, it may be said that the last vestige of Jewish
autonomy, which had existed since the return from exile
nearly one thousand years before, passed away, and the last
feeble succession to the political authority of the house of
David, of the High Priests, and of the Hasmonaeans,
henceforth belonged to the past. The Jew was now in the
fullest sense of the word, divorced from his land. It is now
that the most characteristic, and most amazing chapter in
his history was to begin.

XI. THE MESOPOTAMIAN CENTER

1.   The period of the decline of the Patriarchate in Palestine coincided with the heyday of a new center of Jewish life in Mesopotamia. Not all of the Jewish exiles deported by the Babylonians had seized the opportunity to return to Palestine with Sheshbazzar and Ezra. Throughout the six centuries when the Second Temple had stood in Jerusalem, a second important center of population had remained, under Persian and then under Parthian rule, in the land of the Twin Rivers. They called themselves, and were known in the Jewish world as "The Captivity" (*Golah*). They appear to have been engaged for the most part in agriculture, but there were important settlements in the towns of Nehardea and Nisibis on the Euphrates. In the first century c.e., the entire royal house of the vassal-principality of Adiabene on the Tigris embraced Judaism. The Rabbis told fantastic stories regarding the punctiliousness of the observance of Queen Helena and her household. She herself, with some of her family, was buried outside the walls of Jerusalem; and at the time of the great war against Rome in 68-70 c.e., the King of Adiabene and his brother fought gallantly on the Jewish side.

The recognized head of Babylonian Jewry, in its dealings with the state, was the Prince or Head of the Captivity (*Resh Galutha,* generally known as "Exilarch"), legendarily, a descendant of David. The state which he

upheld was almost royal. He maintained lavish hospitality at his table, and it was through his medium that
the government exacted the taxation, usually of crushing
weight, imposed on the Jewish community. The vernacular of Mesopotamian Jewry was Aramaic, a language
closely akin to Hebrew, which by now had lost its currency even in Palestine. Juridically at least, the community
was completely autonomous. Internal disputes were settled
according to Jewish law, and if only for that reason it was
natural that the traditional learning continued to be
eagerly cultivated. Throughout the period of the Patriarchate, therefore, relations with Palestine remained close
and constant. Babylonian scholars went to perfect themselves at the feet of the great masters of Tiberias or
Sepphoris. On the other hand, with the deterioration of
conditions in Syria, many families migrated eastward in
order to enjoy the more congenial surroundings of their
Mesopotamian co-religionists.

2.   Excepting as regards spiritual and intellectual life,
about which we are peculiarly well informed, our knowledge of affairs in Mesopotamia remains scanty in the subsequent period (from 226 c.e.) when the province was under the rule of the Persian sovereigns of the Sassanid line.
Notwithstanding the intense literary activity which was the
distinguishing feature of the period, conditions do not appear to have been ideal. The influence of the Magi, as the
priests of the Zoroastrian religion were called, sometimes
resulted in a persecution of other creeds. On the other
hand, some rulers, like King Sapor I (241-272 c.e.), were

remembered lovingly for the favor which they showed to their Jewish subjects.

3.   In the middle of the fifth century, the conditions of the "Exile" in Mesopotamia took a definite turn for the worse. The ever-present religious prejudice found its outlet in a long succession of persecutions. This came to a head in the sixth century when the Persian ruler, Kobad, adopted a new faith, Zendicism, which, according to its enemies at least, inculcated not only the community of property, but also of wives. At length the Exilarch, Mar Zutra II, rose in armed revolt. For seven years he managed to maintain his independence, in the region about Mahoza, with the support of some of the non-Jewish, as well as Jewish population. Ultimately, he was borne down by weight of numbers, and after his defeat he was crucified upon the bridge of his native place (520 C.E.). His little son, Mar Zutra III, born on the day of his death, was carried off to Palestine, where an attempt was made to revive the dignity of Patriarch in his favor.

The Jews of Mesopotamia never wholly recovered the prosperity and influence which they had enjoyed previous to these tragic events, though, under the last Persian rulers, conditions improved to some extent. The precise details of these vicissitudes, however, matter little. The fleeting glimpses which we have are sufficient to illustrate the background of the thriving, well-organized life of the Jews in Babylonia in the first few centuries of the Christian Era. The total population was to be reckoned by hundreds of thousands, perhaps by millions. Numerically, by the time of the decay of the Patriarchate, it had equalled, or perhaps even outstripped that of Palestine. Above all, it had become the seat of a unique intellectual life which was to have a permanent influence upon the being and the mentality of the Jewish people at large.

XII.

THE DEVELOPMENT *of the* TALMUD

1.　　　The distinctive feature of Hebrew history in the period of the First Temple had been the Prophet, and its distinctive product had been the Bible. In the period of the Second Temple, with its sequel down to the divorce of the Jews from the lands with which they had hitherto been exclusively associated, the distinctive feature was the Rabbi, and its literary monument, the Talmud.

The one was a logical and natural outcome of the other. Once the Jew was provided with a written text, containing the history of his people, the moral teachings which ideally should govern its life, and the national code of jurisprudence and of religious practice, the next step was the rise of a class of teachers. On the one hand, these expounded the sacred text; on the other, they decided on legal cases which were brought to them for solution. Long before the destruction of Jerusalem (as we have seen), the teachers of the Law, or Rabbis, had begun to occupy a prominent position in national life. The legendary chain of tradition associates them with the last of the Prophets, and regards Simon the Just, the High Priest of the time of Alexander the Great, as the first of the new line. Even in the age of Herod, the Rabbi, as the New Testament amply reminds us, was important, if not all-important; and towering figures such as Hillel and Shammai had come to the fore.

The fall of Jerusalem swept away aristocracy and priest-hood. Nothing was left but the scholar; and, thanks to the policy of Rabbi Johanan ben Zakkai, the scholar became the dominating influence in the affairs of the Jew-ish nation for many centuries to come. The national ideal was henceforth not the priest, the warrior, or the land-owner, but the student; and aristocracy was reckoned in terms of the learning, rather than the wealth of a man's family.

The tragedy of the Bar Kocheba rising and its relentless suppression proved all but fatal to the intellectual life of Palestine. So important had been the part played in it by outstanding scholars, like Rabbi Akiba himself, that an at-tempt was made by the Roman authorities to suppress the schools entirely. Judah ben Baba secured the chain of tra-dition, at the cost of his life, by secretly ordaining some of Akiba's leading disciples after their master's martyrdom. Slowly the old life reestablished itself in Galilee, under the leadership of outstanding scholars such as the kindly Rabbi Meir, who earned his living as a scribe, or Simon ben Jochai, later to be regarded as the founder of Jewish mysticism.

Hitherto, the teachings of the Rabbis had centered upon no written text other than the Bible. But there had already grown up about this a vast amount of oral lore. No written code can cover all possible emergencies. From the very be-ginning there had been questions and difficulties con-cerning one point or another on which there was no direct guidance in the Torah. Legal disputes on business or matrimonial matters, upon which the Scriptures were silent, were brought before the Courts daily for settlement. Moreover, it was logical to extend the scope of the biblical precepts in certain cases a little further: to "make a fence round the law," as it was expressed, so as to prevent a person from infringing upon it unawares. The general issue was not what a man must do and what a man must not. It was, rather, what a man should do and should not, if he desired to carry out the Torah in its every detail; it was a code of life, rather than one of law. Gradually, there came into being various hermeneutic rules, or canons of interpretation, according to which the Scriptures should be understood; the most important system being one formulated by Rabbi Ishmael, a contemporary of Akiba.

In this way there had grown up, in addition to the written code, a vast amount of "case law," which was handed down in the schools from generation to generation by word of mouth. Much of it, indeed, was of such antiquity that it was regarded as tradition received by Moses himself at Sinai. It was Rabbi Akiba ben Joseph who began to reduce this heterogeneous mass to order. In the first place, he enlarged the tendency and method of finding justification in the biblical text for every item of the traditional extension. Thus an unusual spelling, or the duplication of some word, served to correlate a recent development of legal practice with the ancient written code. Secondly, he was the first scholar to arrange the accumulated traditions according to subject matter. His pupil, Rabbi Meir, revised and elaborated the body of teaching which his master had assembled. It is probable, though not certain, that these scholars continued to rely

on oral instruction, without committing anything to writing. The phenomenal Oriental memory might have made
it possible for this method of transmission to continue in-
definitely, granted tranquil conditions. But conditions in
Palestine were far from tranquil; and by the end of the
second century, the living tradition appeared to be
dwindling with startling rapidity.

Under these circumstances, a final redaction was undertaken under the auspices of the Patriarch Judah I, with
whose name the enterprise is associated. Traditions handed
down in the names of some one hundred and fifty scholars
were collected and scrutinized. The material gathered by
Akiba and Meir was revised, supplemented, and, where
necessary, rearranged. Traditions of doubtful validity were
excluded. The division according to subjects was perfected.
In cases of dispute, the majority ruling and the accepted
view were indicated. The whole was arranged in six "Orders," each divided into Tractates, Chapters, and Clauses.
The language employed was pure, vigorous Hebrew, for
which the Patriarch had a predilection. This new code
was called the *Mishnah,* or Teaching; those Rabbis who
had collaborated in its production, from Hillel and his
predecessors down to the Editor himself, being subsequently known (after an Aramaic word derived from the
same root) as *Tannaim.*

2.   No sooner was the work completed than fresh
discussions began to center round it. It was no more possible for it than for the Pentateuch to be so comprehensive
as to meet all conceivable cases. Fresh problems of a re-

ligious or legal nature were always arising, and were
brought to the schools for decision. They would be examined carefully from all sides, in the light of the *Mishnah*
or of less authoritative independent compilations, such as
the *Tosephta* (supplement) or *Baraita* (outside statements)
which stood in the same relation to the former as the
Apocrypha does to the Bible. Moreover, there was a vast
amount of traditional lore—history, legend, ethical teaching—which had not found its way into the severely practical code drawn up by the Patriarch. All this formed the
subject-matter of the lectures and discussions in the schools.

In the generation succeeding the compilation of the
Mishnah, notwithstanding the political and economic de-
cadence of the country, there were scholars qualified to
take their place by the side of the most illustrious of the
former age—men like the tolerant Johanan bar Nappaha
(d. 279 c.e.), the son of a blacksmith, or his brother-in-law,
Simon ben Lakish, who had been a gladiator before the
other's influence turned him into a student.

The overwhelming passion for study was not confined
to Palestine. For many generations previous, young students
had come in considerable numbers from Mesopotamia to
frequent its schools. One of the most brilliant students who
sat at the feet of Judah I was Abba the Tall (d. 247 c.e.);
"Rab," or Master *par excellence,* as he was subsequently
called. This scholar, a Babylonian by birth, founded a
school of his own at Sura, on his return to his native land.
A rival institution was situated at Nehardea, the principal
Jewish settlement. This was brought to a high pitch of
excellence by a certain Samuel (d. 254 c.e.), Abba the Tall's

contemporary, and the exponent of a rival system of jurisprudence, who was at the same time a physician, anatomist,
and astronomer. On the sack of Nehardea by the Palmyran
forces (c. 261 c.e.), this academy was transferred, after
many vicissitudes, to Mahoza on the Tigris, near the site
of Bagdad. In the meantime, a more important center of
study had come into existence at Pumbeditha, a few miles
from Sura. For the next eight centuries, with slight interruptions, the schools of Sura and Pumbeditha continued
to dominate Jewish learning.

The organization of intellectual life in Mesopotamia, as
in Palestine, differed radically from the European conception. There was no professional class who studied in order
to qualify for some appointment. To absorb himself in the
law of God was regarded as the privilege and the duty of
every man, from the highest to the lowest. The Exilarch
himself was sometimes a capable scholar. An agriculturist
or artisan would attend the school each day after the
morning and evening services, working in his fields or
shop in the interval. During the day, eager students would
be unflagging in their attendance on some famous Rabbi,
listening to his verdict on cases which were brought him
for decision, and mentally noting not only his arguments
and precedents, but also his small-talk, his conduct, and his
most trivial habits. In the spring and autumn, when agricultural work was suspended, students would flock to the
academies from every part of the country, and for a whole
month instruction was continuous. This (the *Kallah,* as it
was termed) corresponded in its way to the modern university extension system, though carried on with an inten-

sity and generality unparalleled in our more sophisticated
age.

3.   As the years passed, the mass of the material
which was treated of in the schools of Palestine and of
Mesopotamia became immense. The groundwork was the
Mishnah itself, with the case-law, hypothetical or actual,
which had accumulated since its redaction. This was
known as the *Halakha* (way of walking, manner of life).
But, in addition, there was the *Haggada* or "Telling" comprising everything that was not *Halakha*: the Humanities
of the rabbinical teaching, as it were. Everything was in
it: history, folk-lore, medicine, biology, biography, ethical
teaching, astronomy, science, logic, personal reminiscences
of the great teachers of the past, and above all, a vast
amount of downright legend, sometimes very beautiful,
sometimes a little puerile. All this heterogeneous mass,
Halakha and *Haggada* together, was currently known as
the Teaching, or *Talmud,* the Rabbis of the generation
taking their name after the *Amoraim,* or Interpreters, who
acted as the mouthpiece of prominent scholars when they
lectured.

The Talmud was repeated, by word of mouth, in the
course of discussions in the schools, or of public discourses
in the synagogues. By slow degrees these discussions, too,
though they always remained subject to additions and modifications, became stereotyped and crystallized. In Palestine, the foundations at least of the definite form were laid
by Rabbi Johanan bar Nappaha, before his death in 279 C.E.
However, the disturbed state of the country and the

dwindling of the schools prevented this, the so-called Palestinian (or, less accurately, Jerusalem) Talmud from becoming fully developed. The parallel body of lore which came
into existence in Mesopotamia is considerably greater both
in bulk and in importance. Its redaction was due to Ashi
(375-427 c.e.), principal of the school of Sura. Subsequent
generations continued to make additions and alterations.
However, by the close of the fifth century, the Zoroastrian
persecutions made it appear likely that the Mesopotamian
schools would soon go the same way as those of Palestine;
and Rabina II, a successor of Ashi's, took what was regarded as the momentous step of committing the whole
vast agglomeration to writing. Its final redaction was effected by the "Saboraim" (or Reasoners) who lived after
Rabina II. Thus the so-called Babylonian Talmud came
into being.

The importance in Jewish life of the Talmud (with
which we may associate the contemporary Palestinian compilation, the *Midrash,* containing the homiletic and legendary embellishment of the biblical story), is by no means
purely academic. It comprises the accumulated wisdom of
the Jewish people over many centuries. No aspect of Hebrew thought, and no subject of human interest, is unrepresented in it. The period of the redaction coincided
with the growth of independent centers of life in far-
distant regions, cut off politically and linguistically from
the former nuclei. The Jewish people was about to enter
on an entirely different phase of its existence, in countries
of which their fathers had never heard, in callings with
which they had previously been unfamiliar, in the face of

difficulties hitherto unimaginable. They possessed, to bring with them into their new life, a code, not merely of religion or of law, but of civilization.

The way of life which the Talmud so minutely illustrated and prescribed made the whole people of Israel one, wheresoever they might be found, into however many political factions they might be divided. It gave them the characteristic imprint which distinguished them from all other peoples, as well as their phenomenal power of resistance and cohesion. Its dialectic sharpened their wits, and conferred upon them a preternatural mental acuteness. But there was more in it even than this. For the Talmud gave the persecuted Jew of the Middle Ages another world into which he could escape, when the vicissitudes of that in which he lived had become too great to bear. It gave him a fatherland, which he could carry about with him, when his own land was lost. And, if the Jew were able to maintain his identity in the course of the long centuries to come, under conditions such as no other people has ever been known to surmount, it is to the Talmud, above all, that the credit is due.

BOOK THREE

DIASPORA
(425-1492)

XIII. THE DIASPORA IN EUROPE

1. As early as the period of the Assyrian and Babylonian campaigns in Palestine, the forefathers of the Jewish people first came into touch with Europe and the European races. Even before the close of the Biblical Age, Hebrews were perhaps settled within the periphery of the Hellenic world. The conquest of the Babylonian Empire by Persia brought the mass of Jewry under the rule of a power which had continual association with Europe. The constant succession of wars, the international traffic in slaves, and the inevitable process of commerce, all tended to bring isolated settlers to Greece and her colonies. After the Battle of Issus (333 B.C.E.), when the Persian Empire was overthrown by Alexander, the Near East became Hellenized, and the Jews of Palestine and the neighboring centers came definitely into the European orbit.

The revolt of the Maccabees, essentially a reaction against Hellenism, actually resulted in bringing the Jews into touch, for the first time, with their ultimate enemy, Rome. After Pompey's capture of Jerusalem (63 B.C.E.), Palestine was virtually a Roman province, and belonged to that vast nexus of subject territories which looked to Rome as their capital.

In celebration of his success, Pompey had sent to grace his triumph the Golden Vine from the Temple, together with many of the prisoners. According to the practice of

135

the times, the latter were sold as slaves. Similarly, from 190
B.C.E. onwards, in all the Roman campaigns in Asia Minor
(already, from its propinquity to Mesopotamia, a center
of Jewish settlement), Jews had been captured and enslaved. The same was the case in the many Judaean revolts,
culminating in the insurrection of 66-70 C.E. and in the
Bar Kocheba war of 132-135 C.E., in which the number of
captives was reckoned by hundreds of thousands. The
greater proportion, probably found their way to Italy; but
others were distributed throughout the Empire, from Spain
and Gaul on the one side to Phrygia on the other.

But the Jew was a bad servant. This was due in part
to his independent temperament. A more important factor,
perhaps, was his stubborn adherence to the practices of his
ancestral faith, which would not permit him to work on
the Sabbath, or to eat the food provided by his master.
Hence it was natural that in the end the purchaser tried
to rid himself of what appeared to be an unprofitable bar-
gain. Moreover, the intense racial solidarity which the
Jews felt more than any other people prompted them to
help one another to freedom whenever the opportunity
presented itself.

It must not be imagined, however, that the origin of the
Jewish settlement in Europe was due entirely to the slave
element. Commerce is a factor more potent, though not
always more prominent, than warfare. Palestinian merchants as a matter of course established connections with
the capital of the Empire and of the world. As we have
already seen, there was, from early times, a very considerable Jewish settlement in Alexandria, the greatest com-

mercial center of the Mediterranean. It is not to be doubted that the earliest arrivals in Rome comprised also a large number of traders who came thence, probably in connection with the grain trade in which Egypt played so important a part: and there were other colonies all along the line of communication between the two cities.

2.   The Diaspora, or Scattering, of the Jewish people dates back therefore, even as far as Europe is concerned, to a very early period. Abundant testimony exists to show how numerous Jews were in Greece and the adjacent islands, even before the fall of Jerusalem. If this was the case even when the Jewish state maintained some vestige of independence, it can be imagined to what an extent the process of dispersion was accentuated after the final tragedy, when Palestine was a mere province of the Empire, and when successive revolts had glutted the market with slaves. It is almost certain that by the third century, the process of penetration had reached even the most distant provinces. We have positive evidence of the existence of Jews in over forty places in Italy, as well as in Scythia, Dalmatia, France, the Crimea, and elsewhere. In Spain, and even in Germany, their numbers at the beginning of the fourth century were already so considerable as to justify special mention in the legislation of the period. But places with regard to which certain proof survives must necessarily be in the minority. Just as today a Jewish community exists in every city of the United States of America which has a population of 50,000 souls, a railway station, and a public theatre, so one was to be found in all probability in

every *municipium* of the Roman Empire, sufficiently important to have its forum and its hippodrome.

By the time of the decline of the Roman Empire, the Jew was thus thoroughly acclimatized in Europe and identified with that European civilization which, whether for better or for worse, was to mould the destinies of the world.

3.   The condition of the Jews under the Romans was, on the whole, indistinguishable from that of any other of the many peoples of the Empire. Even the notorious unruliness of their co-religionists in Palestine did not prejudice their position to any extent. From certain points of view, they were actually privileged. To the Roman, religion was not of paramount importance in life. To sacrifice to the gods was the duty of every decent citizen. The Emperor himself was worshipped as a deity. It was nothing more than patriotic to adore his effigy; to refrain from doing so was regarded as a token of disloyalty. An exception was made only in favor of that strange people whose religion was different from all other religions: who admitted no image into their places of worship; and who had been prepared to rise in revolt rather than set up Caligula's statue in the Temple. From that time onward, no attempt had been made to repeat the experiment.

It was not that the Jews were popular. Contemporary poets jeered at their manner of life, singling out for ridicule in particular their strange habit of resting every seventh day. In spite of this, the practices of Judaism were studied sympathetically in all classes. It was not easy for the ordinary woman, and especially for the ordinary man, to assume the heavy yoke of the *Torah*. Yet large numbers became semi-proselytes, refraining from idol-worship, and following Jewish tradition in such matters as the Sabbath and abstention from forbidden food. At one period, this modified Judaism seems to have become positively fashionable, especially among women; and we read of adherents in the highest ranks of society, sometimes in the sphere of the Imperial Court itself.

Even after the Jewish War, Judaism continued to be regarded as a tolerated cult—the only cult, indeed, legally recognized in addition to the official one. There was as yet no thought of restricting the activities of its adherents in any way. In their ordinary life, they enjoyed the most complete freedom. We find them in all activities, from artists to fortune-tellers, and from actors to mendicants. Finally in consequence of the famous Edict of Caracalla of 212 c.e., all free inhabitants of the Empire, without distinction, were created Roman citizens. This, in point of fact, was dictated by financial considerations, being intended to make all alike liable to taxation. But as a matter of course, they shared the advantages of citizenship as well as its burdens. The Jews of the Empire were henceforth Roman citizens in every respect, distinguished from the rest perhaps by one or two privileges, but not by any disability (other than the obligation to pay the *Fiscus Judaicus*).* It was a condition of affairs which was not to prevail again in Europe until the nineteenth century.

See p. 111.

XIV. THE TRIUMPH OF CHRISTIANITY

1.   This was the state of the Jews of the civilized world at the period of the triumph of Christianity. Cursory reference has already been made (page 101) to Joshua or Jesus of Nazareth, a Galilean enthusiast who was executed in Jerusalem during the procuratorship of Pontius Pilate. He was one of many who had been put to death in a similar fashion at that period for daring to champion the cause of their people. In Jesus of Nazareth, however, there was a double strain. On the one hand, he claimed (so, at least, many of his followers believed) to be the promised Messiah who was to deliver his people from foreign bondage. On the other, he followed the tradition of the moral and social reformers who had always been so characteristic a feature in Hebrew history. In his wanderings through the country he urged the people to amend their manner of life. His utterances were not entirely original. He quoted and elaborated the teachings of contemporary Rabbis as he had heard them repeated in the synagogue of his native place. It was in the spirit of the ancient prophets of Israel that he censured the exploitation of the poor by the rich and the stranglehold which formalism could establish upon religion.

Under such circumstances, no man could have failed to concentrate upon himself an overwhelming degree of opposition—from the Romans whose rule was threatened by his political aspirations, from the fashionable religious leaders whose example he condemned, from the priesthood for his attempt to reform the Temple worship by violence, and from the moneyed classes whom he reviled with a poor man's virulence. When he died on the cross, it was to be imagined that his influence would have died with him, as was the case with so many of his contemporaries. However, his personal magnetism must have been amazingly great. The group of disciples who had followed him continued to cherish his memory and to look forward to a second coming which would achieve all that had been left undone at the time of his death. Gradually new adherents gathered round them. Their opponents in Greek-speaking Antioch referred to them contemptuously as "Christians," after the *Christos* or "Anointed one" (Messiah), whose teachings they followed. The name, like so many others first applied in contempt, became generally adopted, and under it the Hebraic ideals which the new faith embodied were to become part of the common heritage of the Western world.

The turning point came when a Jewish tentmaker named Saul of Tarsus, known to the outside world as Paul, as he was nearing Damascus on his way from Jerusalem, suddenly became convinced of the Messianic claims of the dead leader, whose followers he had strenuously opposed before this. Henceforth, he was one of the most prominent, and indubitably the most fiery of all members of the circle.

With his burning faith, his unquenchable courage, his strange personal fascination, he was an incomparable prop-

agandist. Few Jews have ever influenced the world to the
same extent. It was due to him more than to any other
person that Christianity assumed the form in which we
now know it, and that it ultimately swept the world. He
undertook a succession of missionary journeys to win over
disciples for the new cause. In every community in which
he arrived, he found a synagogue which served as the
scene and subsequently as the center of his activities. But
he gradually became convinced that it was impossible for
Christianity to make headway while it was weighed down
with the yoke of the Jewish law, its adherents having to
submit to circumcision and to conform to the elaborate
dietary restrictions. Not without difficulty, he managed to
achieve an almost complete break with the past. The ceremonial regulations of the Old Testament were utterly
abrogated. The fundamental Hebraic doctrines of Christianity became merged with the philosophical conceptions
of the Greek world, and with mystical currents which
were abroad at this time throughout the Roman Empire.

This facile synthesis had a general appeal and met with
instantaneous success. Despite occasional persecutions, its
adherents soon numbered hundreds of thousands.
Eventually the rising doctrine was adopted by the Emperor Constantine (307-337 c.e.) and before long became
the official faith of the Roman Empire.

2.   The famous Edict of Toleration, issued by Constantine the Great at Milan in 313 c. e., indicated the beginning of the ascendancy of Christianity. In the provisions
of the new law, Judaism was included with other faiths.

Its position was thus maintained juridically. In fact, however, it soon began to deteriorate. Christianity, though dominant, was not yet sufficiently sure of itself to show real tolerance. The line of demarcation between the two faiths was still, in some respects, a little indistinct. The fathers of the Church were engaged in a perpetual struggle to make it clearer and more sharply defined, in order to prevent Christians from following Jewish rites, perhaps unwittingly, and so falling under Jewish influence. Moreover, Christianity still regarded Judaism as a dangerous rival—to be repressed, if it could not be suppressed. This attitude found its expression in the Edicts of a succession of Church Councils, to culminate in that held at Nicaea in 325 c.e. at which even the calendar and the religious week were manipulated in order to prevent future confusion with Judaism.

This clerical attitude was henceforth to be adopted, almost in its entirety, by the State. In the Imperial Edicts, the fact soon became apparent. From "a distinguished religion, certainly permissible" as it had been referred to previously, Judaism now became "a sacrilegious gathering" or "nefarious sect." In 329, Jews were forbidden to have Christian slaves in their possession, or to convert those who were pagans. Proselytes, and those who had won them over, were menaced by the penalty of death. Intermarriage between Jews and Christians was forbidden under the pain of capital punishment. Apostasy was not only protected, but even encouraged. There was a brief intermission under Julian the Apostate, 361-363 c.e., due not so much to his friendly sentiments toward Judaism as to his antipathy towards Christianity. On his death, however, the reaction was resumed to the full, coming to its height under the Emperor Theodosius II (408-450 c.e.)—"the first Christian Inquisitor." The latter's famous code, which formed the basis of European jurisprudence, embodied all the prevailing anti-Jewish conceptions and regulations. These restrictive measures thus became part and parcel of the legal background of the mediaeval world which was about to come into being.

4.   The Roman Empire in the West staggered to its fall in a welter of foreign invasion, and Rome was sacked by the hordes of Alaric in 410 c.e. Our knowledge of Jewish as of general history, is vague in the mist of the Dark Ages which succeeded. Jewish communities continued to exist, however, in Spain, in Northern Africa, in France, and in Italy. They must have suffered with the rest of the population during the long succession of warfare. A period of greater tranquility, and less obscurity, came only when the barbarians settled down and adopted the Christian religion. The effect of this upon the Jew was far from favorable. Hitherto he had been reckoned, with the conquered Romans, as a natural enemy of the new regime, standing completely outside the ordinary body politic. But the conquered Roman was now a fellow-Christian and a brother, and the position of inferiority was left to the Jew alone.

There was one compensation. In many cases, the barbarians had felt attracted to the Arian form of Christianity, with its purer monotheism, in sharp contrast to the Trinitarian doctrines of the so-called "Catholics." Accordingly they tended to treat the Jews with favor, if only to enlist their support against their own rivals. Arianism, however, was not destined to prevail. The triumph of Catholicism was a question only of years; and, in the sixth century, it definitely gained the upper hand.

5.   Orthodox Christianity, whether in its eastern form in the Byzantine Empire, or in its western under the aegis of the Popes at Rome, showed itself less tolerant than the schismatics had been. Gregory the Great, Pope from 590 to 604 c.e., set the example which was to be followed by later generations, and which was to remain the norm in Christian Europe until the Middle Ages were at an end. Positive persecution was indeed discouraged and forced baptism deprecated. The Jews might enjoy liberty of worship and maintain their synagogues, though they were allowed neither to erect new ones nor to embellish the old. On the other hand, they were not to be encouraged to fresh "insolence." Proselytism on their part was to be sternly repressed. The imitation of Jewish rites by Christians was prohibited. Their ownership of Christian slaves was not to be tolerated under any condition. Even the employment of Jewish physicians, who might obtain physical and, ultimately, moral control over their patients was not to be allowed, and secular rulers were sternly warned against appointing any Jewish officials, in however unimportant a capacity.

In a long series of letters written to places as far afield as France to the north, and Sicily to the south, the Pope

enforced this policy. However, its niceties could hardly
be appreciated by subordinate ecclesiastics, and even less
by ignorant civil potentates. In France, where Jews had
settled in considerable numbers even in Roman times,
there was a succession of attacks headed by the local
bishops, and leading in some cases (not withstanding the
Papal disapproval) to mass baptism. Meanwhile, in the
Byzantine Empire (which embraced Greece, southern Italy
and northern Africa, in addition to the old Roman provinces in Asia), under the threat of attacks by the Arab
tribesmen, the reaction assumed yet darker colors. The
Emperor Heraclius (610-641 c.e.) went so far as to prohibit completely the public exercise of Judaism; and it
seems that he attempted to secure the imitation of his
example throughout Europe. In any case, at this period,
there was a simultaneous persecution in all the countries
of the West in which Catholicism had recently established
itself. In Gaul, in 626 c.e., King Dagobert ordered a general
expulsion of all the Jews excepting those who consented to
adopt the dominant religion. A like policy was adopted by
his neighbors in Burgundy and in the Kingdom of
Lombardy. But it was in Spain that the reaction reached its
greatest height.

Here the Jews had been settled from time immemorial;
legendarily, from the period of the First Temple, and certainly before the destruction of Jerusalem by Titus. Their
numbers at the beginning of the fourth century were
already so great that a Church Council held at Elvira
found it necessary to pass special regulations in order to
check the excessive familiarity which was held to prevail

between them and their Christian neighbors. Under the Visigothic regime which established itself upon the ruins of the Roman colony, the Arian form of Christianity was adopted. The Jews now had small ground for complaint and seem, indeed, to have been especially favored. But after their conversion to Catholicism, their new rulers showed the persecutory zeal so characteristic of the neophyte. In 589 c.e., when King Recared adopted orthodox Catholicism, the current clerical legislation was put into effect also in Spain. Slave-owning, conversionism, and inter-marriage on the part of Jews were all prohibited under the severest penalties; and they were excluded from all positions of authority or trust under the State. Later rulers were a trifle more tolerant. But from 616 c.e., when King Sisebut mounted the throne, the darkness became complete. For a period of nearly a century the open practice of Judaism was absolutely proscribed. Successive Church Councils, held at Toledo under the presidency of the King, formulated minute regulations by which former Jews and their descendants might be weaned away from their ancestral faith. Their children were seized and taken away to be brought up in orthodox Catholic households; and a somewhat pathetic letter is extant from the former Jews of the capital intimating their sheer physical inability, notwithstanding their own desires, to demonstrate their orthodoxy by eating of the pig's flesh.

Naturally, in the majority of cases, the conversions were feigned, and in the privacy of the home, Jewish rites and customs continued to be observed as far as possible. Yet officially, save for occasional brief intermissions, the practice of Judaism in Spain was forbidden down to the last days of Visigothic rule, and those who persisted in its observance were driven into exile. A universal upheaval was required to restore freedom to the Spanish Jews and to initiate what was to be their age of greatest glory.

XV. THE HEGEMONY OF ISLAM

1.   In the spring of the year 622 c.e., a moody Arab camel-driver fled in fear of his life from his native city of Mecca, and the history of Mohammedanism began. To Mohammed himself, the Jews were no strangers. Long before his time, they had been familiar in Arabia. In the fifth century, the ruler of Yemen had been converted to Judaism, and his kingdom remained half-Jewish until it fell in 525 c.e. before a combined attack of the Abyssinians and Byzantines. In the northwest of the peninsula, Jews continued even after this date to be powerful and numerous. Like their neighbors, they were divided into tribes, frequently at war amongst themselves. They were said to have introduced the culture of the date-palm into the region; and, in the towns, they were famous as goldsmiths and artisans. Several oases and cities were entirely in their hands. Their poets and their poetesses were famous, and are still remembered in the annals of Arabic literature. Their relations with their neighbors were generally cordial. Many of the latter were attracted by the principles of Judaism; and their folk-lore had become an integral part of the background of the whole country.

When Mohammed launched his new religion, he looked upon the Jews as the section of the community in which it might most easily be propagated. It was similar to Judaism in its insistence upon strict monotheism, in essential rites such as that of circumcision, in its dietary laws, in its reverence for the Holy City of Jerusalem. The prophet's own utterances, later to be included in the Koran, embodied vast amounts of the Jewish history and legend with which he, like so many of his contemporaries, had been familiar from his youth upward. Yet, to his supreme disappointment, the Jews held themselves aloof. At the beginning, he was forced to tolerate them. But when he gained his outstanding victory over the inhabitants of Mecca at Badr, in 624 C.E., his attitude changed. The Jews of Medina were suddenly attacked, and driven into exile. Subsequently, one after another of the independent Jewish tribes were assaulted and in most cases either expelled, exterminated, or forced to embrace Islam. Those who remained were permitted to do so only on the condition of paying their conqueror a tribute of one-half of all their produce. Thus the new faith began to live up to its slogan: *There is one God, and Mohammed is his Prophet.*

This policy continued to be followed by the Prophet up to the time of his death, in 632 C.E. His immediate successors, the first Caliphs, followed his policy to its logical extreme, expelling all Jews and Christians from the territories subject to them. Under the rule of Omar, however, the Arab tribes burst forth from the Peninsula and initiated that phenomenal career of conquest which was to subject half the known world. Within the next few years, Egypt, Palestine, Syria, Mesopotamia, Persia—all the traditional seats of Jewish settlement and culture in the Near East—were overrun. It was impossible for the Caliph to treat the vast mass of non-Moslems who had now sub-

mitted to his rule in the same heartless, though supremely
logical, fashion which had been the lot of those of Arabia.
If his new dominions were not to be depopulated, it was
necessary to be more tolerant. Accordingly, the official
policy of Islam towards other faiths underwent a complete change. They were indeed to be punished severely
if found reviling the Prophet or luring his followers away
from their faith. They were to be subjected to a number
of vexatious restrictions. They were to wear a distinctive
dress. They were to pay a heavy poll-tax. They were not
to be allowed to bear arms, or to ride on horse-back. But
they were henceforth to be allowed to exist, and permitted
the exercise of their religion. In the course of time, the
various restrictions came to be disregarded; but the essential tolerance of Islam, in practice if not in theory, was to
remain one of the most important factors in Jewish history
for many centuries to come.

2. For the moment, the most important center of
Jewish population was still Mesopotamia, where the ancient schools still flourished and the memory of the Talmudic era was still fresh. It was natural for the new Arab
rulers to make use of existing institutions in their relations
with subject peoples. As far as the Jews were concerned,
the obvious medium was the Exilarch, or *Resh Galutha,*
looked up to by his co-religionists by virtue not only of his
political position, but also of his legendary descent from
David. From the new rulers, the dignity received official
recognition, its incumbent being confirmed in the right
of internal jurisdiction, as well as endowed with privileges

of the spectacular sort that appealed to the Oriental mind.

Almost on an equal footing with the Exilarchs in the popular imagination, and superior to them in the eyes of posterity, were the heads of the two great Academies of Sura and Pumpeditha, at which the scholarly traditions of the previous age were still cherished. These worthies were now known as *Geonim,* or Excellencies (singular *Gaon*); and it is as the "Age of the Geonim" that the period is generally remembered. In their respective academies they still continued to foster and to develop the traditions of the *Tannaim,* the *Amoraim,* and the *Saboraim* (the expounders of the Oral Law who had immediately preceded them*). The seat of Judaism was no longer confined to Mesopotamia and the neighboring lands. Jews had wandered far and wide, and were no longer in personal touch with the great centers of Jewish population in the East. But, wherever they were, they still required guidance on matters connected with the Jewish Law and religion; and it was natural for them to direct their inquiries (accompanied frequently by contributions for the upkeep of the Colleges) to the sages of the Mesopotamian seats of learning. An increasing proportion of the energies of the Geonim was thus occupied by their correspondence, addressed to almost every corner of the known world, from Spain and Germany on the one side to Northern Africa and Egypt on the other. These Gaonic *Responsa,* as they are generally called, touched on every conceivable subject in which Judaism itself was interested: Biblical exegesis, elucidations of the Talmud, religious questions, marital regulations,

*See p. 131.

business law. The earliest known Jewish liturgies, and the first of all Jewish literary histories, were composed by various Geonim in response to inquiries addressed to them by eager students in what was then regarded as the Far West.

The most pressing problem with which the Geonim were faced was the rise of the Karaite schism. There had always been two tendencies in the Jewish people; the one of them regarding Judaism as a living, organic tradition, continually growing, continually changing, yet in essence always the same, and represented in every age by its Rabbis and teachers; the other thinking of it as fixed and immutable, with its final expression in a specific code of laws.

It was the latter conception which the Karaites championed. According to a tradition emanating from the opponents of the new body, therefore not to be taken over-literally, the occasion for the schism was a disputed succession to the dignity of Exilarch in the year 767 c.e. The disappointed candidate, Anan ben David, seeing himself passed over in favor of a younger brother, found consolation by organizing a rival body over which to rule. He rejected entirely the authority of the Rabbis, whose opposition had ousted him from the coveted dignity. He branded the Talmud as an imposture, and those who followed it as dupes. He refused to admit the weight of tradition in interpreting Jewish law and practice. He recognized the authority only of the Bible (*Mikra*) after which his followers became known as the *B'ne Mikra,* or *Karaim* (Scripturalists); their opponents receiving the title of Rabbanites. Under Anan's guidance, the new faith, with its apotheosis of the literal interpretation of the Scriptures, was arid and uninspiring to a degree. The eating of almost any sort of meat was forbidden; no lights or fires could be kindled on the Sabbath Day; recourse to physicians in times of sickness was considered an impiety; and a hundred other impossible restrictions were introduced, for all of which Scriptural authority was discovered. Teachers of a latter generation, however, in particular Benjamin of Nehawend (c. 830 c.e.) and Daniel al-Kumisi (c. 900 c.e.) showed greater humanity and insight in their treatment of the Scriptures, borrowing some of their methodology and ideas even from the hated Rabbanites. The new reading of Judaism made immediate headway. It was looked upon with favor in the outside world; and it gained tens of thousands of adherents amongst the less learned Jews, who had found the arguments of the Rabbis above their heads, but always had the Bible at hand to consult. The movement spread from Mesopotamia to the surrounding territories. It had a foothold in Palestine itself; it established a powerful colony in Egypt; it had adherents as far afield even as Spain. At one time, it appeared that the new interpretation was likely to gain the upper hand, and that rabbinic Judaism would be reduced to the position of an unimportant sect. That this did not take place was due largely to the efforts of one man.

3.   Saadiah ben Joseph (882-942 c.e.), the greatest of the Geonim, was a native of Egypt, who was summoned to Mesopotamia in 928 c.e. as head of the decaying Academy of Sura. He realized that the Karaites must be combatted with their own weapons. The Academies had contented

themselves hitherto with the exposition of the Talmud
and Jewish law, paying little attention to the new tendencies of the outside world. The Karaites had appealed to
reason; they must be followed, and defeated, upon their
own ground. They had appealed to the Bible against the
Talmud; the Rabbis must turn their attention again to the
Bible, and show that Jewish tradition was implicit in it.

In one composition after the other he dealt with the
specific questions at issue. A translation of the Scriptures
into the vernacular, still classical in some Arabic-speaking
countries, carried the war into the enemy's territory. No
longer was it possible to say that the Jews who followed
the Talmud were ignorant of the Bible; and the commentary which accompanied certain of the books, together
with the lexicon of words which occur once only in the
Scriptures, inculcated some further idea of traditional
hermeneutics. A treatise on "Beliefs and Opinions"
(*Emunoth VeDeoth*) provided a metaphysical basis for traditional Judaism, and laid the foundations of Jewish
philosophy.

There were still to be occasional outbursts of rancour,
sudden spurts of activity, and sporadic interchanges of
polemics. But Karaism was henceforth a lost cause—mori-
bund through its essential aridity. Its adherents are still to
be found in Egypt, in Poland, and above all in the Crimea.
But, by the time that Saadiah was borne to his grave, the
great battle to which he had devoted his life was all but
won.

From the period of Saadiah, the Jewish settlement in
Mesopotamia underwent a rapid decline. The Arabian

Peninsula, and the countries bordering upon it, were slowly becoming less fertile and less able to support their population. In consequence, the inhabitants were gradually driven to seek their livelihood elsewhere. It was this, to a large extent, which had stimulated the Arabs to burst out of their former home and to overrun half the known world. The same factors were operative also with the Jews. Family after family was leaving the region in which their ancestors had been settled from time immemorial, and following on the heels of the Arab invaders, to seek its fortune in fresh fields of opportunity further west. Exilarch indeed still succeeded Exilarch; Gaon followed upon Gaon. Scholars, like Sherira (968-998 C.E.) or Hai (968-1038 C.E.) continued to uphold worthily the academic traditions of the old Academies. However, the volume of their responsa, directed to the furthest limits of the Diaspora, shows that they were now more concerned with satisfying the requirements of the new Jewish settlements than with continuing to develop the living tradition of the schools over which they presided. Hai was accordingly the last of the great Geonim; for a long time, indeed, it was thought that he was actually the last of the whole series. For two or three hundred years more, until the close of the thirteenth century, or even later, a succession of pretenders or imitators in Mesopotamia, Syria, Palestine, or Egypt continued to keep alive the memories of past glories, under various names, and with a deplorable display of petty jealousy among themselves. Their importance was however negligible, and their influence strongly localized. The first half of the eleventh century witnessed the final stage in the intellectual and political supremacy of Mesopotamian Jewry, and the interruption of the chain of tradition which dated back to the period of the First Exile. But, before the torch of learning fell from their weary hands, the Geonim had succeeded in passing it to a new, vigorous colony in the west, which was to preserve the sacred flame of the Torah for later ages.

4.   It had taken the Arabs somewhat less than a century from the date of the Hejira to sweep the Mediterranean world from end to end. In 711 c.e., an expedition under Tarik crossed the Straits of Gibraltar; and the final conquest of Spain was a matter of only four years. This change of government ushered in a fresh age for Spanish Jewry.

The Jews, impelled by the same natural urge or by the same economic necessities, streamed after the Arabs, as colonists, as traders, as agricultural settlers. The ancient communities which had continued a somewhat degraded existence, under the Byzantine rule, in Egypt and the adjacent countries of north Africa, were rejuvenated. Kairouan, the military camp founded in the neighbourhood of the ancient city of Carthage (subsequently to be the center of government for the whole province), suddenly became known as a center of learning, its scholars exchanging learned correspondence with the Babylonian Geonim even before the days of Saadiah. Spain made headway a little more slowly, but with even more dazzling results. In consequence, the most important section of Jewry, numerically, geographically, and culturally, became

Arabised. They flaunted Arab names, spoke Arabic only among themselves, adopted Moslem intellectual fashions and standards, used the vernacular for their literature and even, to some extent, for their liturgy, and considered Europe, north of the Pyrenees, as an outpost of barbarism.

From the time of Abd-ur-Rahman I (756-788 c.e.), Spain was the seat of an independent state and free from all dependence upon Bagdad. The special conditions of the country, with its large proportion of Christian or Visigothic elements, made tolerance a cardinal point of policy, the Jews enjoying it in the same way as other sections of the population. Indeed, it was only wise to favor them and thus foster their sympathies; for they constituted an important minority in a population, a large part of which was perennially disaffected. They thus entered into every walk of life. There were peasants, farmers, physicians, merchants, and artisans. For the purposes of diplomatic intercourse with the Christian states, both in the Peninsula and outside it, the Jew, with his knowledge of languages, was the ideal intermediary; and, in consequence of this, many individuals attained great influence in affairs of state. Physicians, astronomers, and astrologers (the latter two arts were at the time all but identical), similarly obtained an entrée to Court, and in some instances wielded vast power.

The outstanding figure of the period was Hasdai ibn Shaprut (c. 915-970 c.e.), with whom Jewish life in Spain suddenly emerged from the comparative obscurity which had enveloped it for the past few centuries. He owed his political importance to two factors: first, to his knowledge of medicine, which had originally brought him in touch with the Caliph Abd-ur-Rahman III, who appointed him Court Physician; and secondly, to his acquaintance with the Latin tongue, at that time the international language of letters and diplomatic intercourse. From being simply his physician, Hasdai became in consequence of this the Caliph's confidant and advisor. Without bearing the title of vizier, he was in reality Minister of Foreign Affairs. Negotiations of the highest delicacy, both in the country and beyond its borders, were entrusted to him. In addition, he was made Inspector-General of the Customs for the port of Cordova, the income of which he presumably enjoyed as a reward for his services. On the death of Abd-ur-Rahman (961 c.e.), his son Hakam II, retained Hasdai in his service, and he appears to have continued to enjoy the royal favor until his death.

In his prosperity, Hasdai did not forget his own people. Every Embassy which was sent to Cordova from foreign powers was interrogated by him as to the conditions of the Jews in its native land. It was this which led to the famous interchange of correspondence with the kingdom of the Khazars, the independent State to the north of the Black Sea, the ruling classes of which had accepted Judaism in the eighth century. (*See* p. 264.) Hasdai used his influence to ameliorate the condition of the Jews in the south of France, and made representations at the Byzantine Court to avert a persecution which seemed imminent. Unlike the majority of his imitators in a later age, Hasdai ibn Shaprut was also a magnificent patron of learning, and it was under his aegis, as we shall see, that Spanish Jewish scholarship burst upon the world.

5.   A turning point came in the history of Moslem Spain some forty years after Hasdai's death, when a horde of Berber mercenaries from North Africa captured Cordova, and the Caliphate was broken up. The Jewish community of the capital had hitherto been by far the most numerous and the most influential of the whole country. Now its members, its scholars, its statesmen, its men of business were scattered throughout the Peninsula. Hebrew life and culture, hitherto unduly concentrated, became diffused. On the ruins of the Caliphate, there grew up a number of independent kingdoms governed by the local aristocracy or successful military leaders. The new rulers turned for help in the involved and difficult labor of administration to those whose acumen best qualified them for the task. Hence it came about that, in one after another of these petty courts, Jews rose to high rank; in some cases not merely as advisors, as in former days, but with the formal rank of *vizier*.

The earliest and most famous of all was Samuel ibn Nagdela (993-1055 c.e.), poet, scholar, and statesman. He personified, in his own many-sided activity, all the finest characteristics of his age. A man of good education, though of humble social status, Nagdela had fled after the sack of Cordova to Malaga. Here he got into touch accidentally with the vizier of King Habbus of Granada, whom he served for some time in the capacity of Secretary. His acumen soon became notorious at Court; his counsel was asked on all important State matters; and on his death-bed in 1020 c.e., the vizier advised Habbus to appoint the learned Jew as his successor. Thus, for a period of a quarter of a century, Nagdela was almost omnipotent, being allowed to manage all the affairs of State so long as a sufficient supply of money was forthcoming for his royal master to dissipate.

Many stories were recounted of his wisdom and tact. He not only patronized letters, Arabic as well as Hebrew, but was himself one of the outstanding litterateurs of his age. Though hardly a literary genius of the first rank, his interests extended to every field of Jewish scholarship; and he is the most representative, if not the most gifted, figure in contemporary literary life. As a poet he was prolific and capable, though he lacked fire. He wrote lengthy works in imitation of the biblical books of Ecclesiastes, Proverbs, and Psalms. He was the author of a comprehensive dictionary of biblical Hebrew. As a Talmudist, he ranked as one of the most distinguished scholars of the period. He presided at Granada over an Academy of his own, and was the author of more than one work which was regarded with admiration by contemporaries, and may still be studied with profit. He excelled as a patron of learning. Scholars and poets flourished under his patronage, and commemorated him gratefully in their verses. Contemporaries, with one accord, hailed him as their prince; and it is as Samuel ha-nagid, or Samuel the Prince, that he is still remembered today.

Ibn Nagdela died, universally mourned, about the year 1055 C.E. He was succeeded, as a matter of course, by his son, Joseph, who continued in office until a wave of jealousy brought about his fall, accompanied by a general attack upon the Jews of the state, in 1066 C.E.

The events in Granada did not affect the position in the other Arab states in more than one of which individual Jews rose to similar positions of eminence. This blaze of glory was not destined to be of long duration. The crescent was no longer supreme south of the Pyrenees. In the mountainous region of Asturias, the hunted Visigoths had managed to put up a successful resistance, and to stem the Moslem advance. From the eighth century this little nucleus had begun to expand; and by now there were half a dozen Christian states, controlling some of the fairest provinces in the Peninsula. After the capture of Toledo in 1085 c.e., the Andalusian rulers saw no prospect of being able to check without aid the triumphant advance of the Christian powers. There was only one quarter from which this aid could be forthcoming. The whole of northwestern Africa was now comprised in the Empire of the fanatical Berber tribes known as al-Moravides (whose name is still preserved in the English *marabout*). An embassy asking for assistance was sent to them by the Moslem powers of Spain. Without waiting for a formal agreement, they poured into the Peninsula. The Moslem and Christian armies encountered at Zalaca, near Badajoz. The battle resulted in a decisive victory for the Crescent. Though Toledo continued in Christian hands, the unity of Moslem Spain was restored before long under Almoravidan supremacy. The new rulers brought with them a tendency to the primitive sternness, simplicity, and fanaticism of Islam. Gone was the favored position which Jewish statesmen had enjoyed at the various local courts; and in 1107 c.e. an attempt was made to secure, by force, the conversion of the

Jews of Lucena, the principal and the wealthiest community in Spain.

But it was not long before the conquerors, like others similarly circumstanced, began to lose their original zeal. Their desert fanaticism became undermined by the softer Andalusian atmosphere. The enlightened traditions of the Caliphate were revived in their Courts; and, once more, Jewish physicians or astronomers came to exercise considerable influence in affairs of State. Meanwhile, however, another wave of reforming zeal had sprung up among the Moslems of northern Africa. The Berber tribes of the Atlas region had rallied round the banner of religious Puritanism, and set up a powerful state. Their insistence upon the dogma of the Divine Unity led to their assuming the name of al-Mohades, or Unitarians (the root is akin to that of the Hebrew *ehad*). As was the case sixty years previous, they received an appeal for help from their co-religionists in Spain, hard-pressed once more by the Christian advance. In 1146 c.e., the al-Mohades crossed the Straits.

From the first days of their expansion, the new sect had revived the stern policy of early Islam in relation to other religions. There could be no question of non-conformity. All who were not Moslems must be forced to don the turban; the only alternatives were extermination or expulsion. Once more, as in the days of the Visigothic kings, the cities of southern Spain were filled with insincere converts from Judaism to the dominant faith; while the high roads leading from the Moslem territories were crowded with fugitives, seeking refuge in a more tolerant land.

By 1172 C.E. the al-Mohades had restored unity once more to Moslem Spain, the last of the independent rulers having submitted to them. Not a single professing Jew was now left in the south of the country. The glory of the Andalusian communities was at an end. It was fortunate that the Christian Kingdoms had by now begun to make headway in the north, providing a haven of refuge in which Jewish life could take root and flourish again.

XVI. THE NORTHERN CENTERS

1.   Peace and order had been brought to Western Europe, for the first time since the Barbarian invasions, by the conquests and organizing genius of Charles the Great, or Charlemagne, who was crowned Emperor at Rome on Christmas Day, 800. He was not only a strong ruler, able to override the theological prejudices of the time, but also a far-seeing one, who could realize the important contribution which the Jews could make to the economic life of his Empire.

Accordingly, he and his house, as a consistent policy, set about patronizing them, and encouraging their immigration. Charter after charter is extant in which the royal house extends protection and privileges to some Jewish merchant. When in 797, an embassy was sent to Haroun-al-Raschid at Bagdad, a Jew named Isaac was attached to it as interpreter. His principals died on the way, and it was Isaac alone who returned, bringing with him in triumph the elephant sent by the Caliph in token of his esteem. Jewish tradition has chosen to preserve the name of Charlemagne, the prototype of his house, in more than one ancient legend, in connection with favors bestowed upon their fathers.

During the succeeding period, we find numerous Jewish communities established throughout the Carolingian dominions. Traders starting from the Mediterranean ports scoured half the known world, as far as India and China, for their wares. They pressed north and east, along all the trade routes, into Germany and beyond. From the land of the Slavs (Canaan, as they called it) they brought back the most profitable merchandise of all—slaves, to recruit the harem or the bodyguard of the Caliph of Cordova. The ecclesiastical authorities, indeed, looked askance at this. It was not, by any means, for reasons of humanity—civilization had not progressed so far. But they strenuously objected to the sale of a true believer into slavery to an infidel, and frequently intervened to prevent it. Successive Church Councils reenacted, with monotonous regularity, the old canonical restrictions, which the State was urged to put into effect. Yet they were generally neglected, with the completest connivance of the Court. In the first half of the ninth century, Agobard and Amulo, successive Archbishops of Lyons, wrote, labored, and intrigued incessantly, to have the petty code in all its details enforced in their diocese by the civil power, but apparently without result.

Even after the fall of the Carolingian dynasty, the House of Capet continued their policy of protection. Though there were occasional darker chapters, conditions continued such as to encourage immigration. The area of settlement, originally most marked in the south of the country, gradually spread. Before long, the northeastern corner of France, too, was filled with thriving communities, to be found in every township, almost in every village, and, for the next three centuries, this section of France constituted one of the most important centers of Jewish life and culture.

2.   The German communities seem to have been in the main an off-shoot of these, the earliest being situated in the commercial emporia with which the Franco-Jewish merchants carried on their trade. In Roman times, there had been a colony at Cologne, and no doubt in some neighboring *municipia* as well. This region remained the center of settlement down to the period of the Crusades. In addition to the immigrants who came eastward from Champagne, there were others who pressed northward, from one commercial center to the other, up the valleys of the Danube and of the Elbe. In the ninth century already, mention is found of Jews at Augsburg and at Metz. In the tenth, they were settled in Worms, Mayence, Prague, Magdeburg, Merseburg, Ratisbon, and other places. By the close of the eleventh, Jews were as numerous all along the Rhineland as they were in the adjacent areas of France.

The last of the great countries of Western Europe to receive a Jewish settlement was England. No conclusive evidence exists for the presence here of Jews in Roman or Saxon times, though it is not out of the question that some isolated merchants may have found their way thus far. But, with the Norman conquest in 1066, England entered, for the first time since the downfall of the Roman Empire, into the European orbit. The country was opened to foreign enterprise, and the Jews were not slow to take advantage of the opportunities which offered themselves. At Rouen, the capital of Normandy, a community had existed in all probability since the beginning of the eleventh century, and it was natural for its members to cross the channel and settle in the new realm which their Duke had conquered. By the close of the reign, a community had established itself in London, and there were others in the principal provincial cities, especially York, Oxford, Norwich, and Bristol.

3.   The settlement of the Jew in England was the culminating point in the movement which brought the masses of Jewry from East to West. It had been in the East, in Palestine, that the Jewish people had been formed, and in the East, in Palestine and then in Mesopotamia, that it had developed its characteristic forms of life. But (as we have seen) these ancient centers were dwindling. On the other hand, those of the Occident were increasing in importance. As early as the ninth century, an important role had been filled by the Jews of Spain. From the middle of the eleventh, France, Germany, and the adjacent countries were to share with the Iberian peninsula the hegemony—spiritual, intellectual, numerical, economic—of Jewish life. Communities continued to exist, in numbers which were far from negligible, in the East—in the Byzantine Empire, in Mesopotamia, in Arabia, in Egypt, in Persia, and even further east, in India and China. Their importance in Jewish life, and in the civilization of the world, was not, however, destined to be crucial. That section of the Jewish people which was to count for something in the history of humanity, and for most in the history of Hebraic culture, was henceforth to be associated permanently with Europe—with European culture, with the European outlook, and for many generations at least, with European soil.

XVII. THE NEW LEARNING

1.   That a large body of people was able to transfer itself from one end of the Mediterranean world to the other, at the period of the great national displacements which succeeded the classical age, was not an unexampled, nor even a remarkable, feat. What rendered the Jewish migration memorable, and perhaps unique, was the fact that they managed to transfer with them not only their religion, but also their civilization.

That the transference was feasible is to be ascribed in part to the circumstances of the Saracen conquest. The revival of Arabic literature found its echo throughout the Mediterranean world, from Bagdad to Cordova. The Jewish communities could not hold themselves aloof from this intellectual stir. For the moment, indeed, Jewish scholarship was almost arabized. The Arabic language was widely used even for semi-sacred purposes; Arab methods were closely studied; and Arab models were sedulously copied. The immediate consequence was a revival of belles-lettres. Hebrew poetry was written on secular models; lexicons were composed in the literary tradition of the age; and just as, centuries earlier, Philo and the Hellenists of Alexandria had considered that Plato had said the final word in human thought, students now believed the Aristotelian philosophy, which the Arabs had taken over from the Greeks, the acme of intellectual achievement.

Wandering scholars brought the new fashions to Andalusia, where the intellectual revival in the tenth century
under the Ommayad Caliphs could not fail to have repercussions in Jewish circles. The importance of Moslem Spain
in Jewish life is not therefore a question merely of numerical weight or of political influence. It constitutes a
chapter of unexampled brilliance in the history of Jewish
literature and thought.

2.   Hasdai ibn Shaprut was the Maecenas under
whose aegis the renascence was initiated and European
Jewish intellectual life began. He patronized scholars of
the new school like Menahem ben Saruk of Tortosa, author of the first complete Dictionary of Biblical Hebrew,
or the latter's caustic rival, Dunash ibn Labrat. Both were
prolific versifiers, and Dunash was one of the first to write
Hebrew verses in regular meter, in imitation—ingenious
rather than discriminating—of Arabic prosody. Subsequently, Hebrew poetry above all took root in Spain,
flourishing there as it has done nowhere else outside Palestine. Samuel ibn Nagdela was himself a poet, as we
have seen already, if not an inspired one. He made himself memorable, moreover, for his patronage of Solomon
ibn Gabirol of Malaga (? 1021-1056), "the nightingale of
piety," whose hymns immeasurably enriched the synagogal
liturgy, and whose philosophical composition, preserved
in Latin under the name *Fons Vitae,* became a classic
among mediaeval Catholic schoolmen, who did not dream
that its author was a Jew.

In the following generation, Moses ibn Ezra (died about

1139) of Granada equalled Ibn Gabirol in poetic fire, and excelled him perhaps in depth of human feeling. The latter's kinsman, Abraham ibn Ezra (1092-1167) might have rivalled him but for his amazing versatility. A native of Toledo, he could never find rest in any one place, and wandered about throughout the known world, from Spain to Italy, from Italy to France, from France to England, and perhaps back again to Spain. He stands in the front rank of Hebrew poets and hymnologists, wrote grammatical, philosophical, and astronomical works, and was the author of a classical commentary upon the Bible, in which he shows a glimmering of the principles of what is now known as Higher Criticism.

The humanistic tradition of Spanish Jewry reached its climax with Judah ha-Levi (1086-1141). Although by profession a physician, he was by vocation a poet. Never perhaps has any other person acquired such extraordinary mastery over a language no longer spoken. Nothing Jewish and nothing human, was strange to his muse, neither the pleasure of friendship, nor the ecstasies of passion, nor the grandeurs of nature, nor the mysteries of religion. Above all, he developed a transcendental passion for the Holy Land; and his hymns to Zion compare in their heartrending appeal to any of the greatest love-lyrics in world literature. Following the footsteps of Saadiah, the poet also composed a philosophical work, *The Khuzari,* in the form of a dialogue between a Jewish savant and the King of the Khazars (won over to Judaism not long before, *see* p. 264), in which he vindicated the rational basis of Judaism. Judah ha-Levi's life was as harmonious as his literary

productions. It is told how, in the end, he succumbed to
the mystical charms of the mistress whom he had so often
celebrated in song, and set out for the Holy Land. As he
arrived in sight of Jerusalem, he flung himself in ecstasy
on the ground. A passing Arab horseman spurred his steed
over the recumbent body of Judah ha-Levi; and the poet
sobbed out his last breath with the immortal cadences of
his greatest ode to Zion.

3.   Less dazzling, but perhaps more vital, than the
humanistic revival with which we have been dealing
hitherto, was the transplantation of that unique literary
monument, which embodied and, over long centuries, was
to mould the Jewish conception of life. The origins of Talmudic scholarship in Europe will always be associated with
a romantic story told by an ancient chronicler. It is recounted how four Rabbis, collecting contributions for the
upkeep of the ancient academies of Babylonia, set sail in
972 from the seaport of Bari, in south Italy, already a seat
of learning. The ship was captured by an Andalusian cor-
sair, and the four captives were sold in four different ports,
in which they implanted the lore of their native land. One
of them, Moses ben Enoch, was taken to Cordova, where
he was ransomed by the Jewish community. One day he
found his way to the house of study. Notwithstanding his
rags, his genius was immediately recognized, and he was
installed with universal approval at the head of a school
which served henceforth as a center for the whole of the
Peninsula. He was succeeded by his son Enoch, who had
been captured with him, and the two between them man-

aged to transfer to Andalusia the method of Talmudic study which had hitherto been characteristic of the Mesopotamian schools, and which could not be communicated excepting by means of oral instruction.

When, in the middle of the eleventh century, Isaac al-Fasi (i.e. of Fez: 1013-1103) emigrated from North Africa to Spain, where he became principal of a famous school established at Lucena, the supremacy of the latter country in rabbinic scholarship was assured. Al-Fasi was recognized to be one of the greatest luminaries of his age, and his classical compendium of the Talmud, with its elimination of irrelevancies and its clear-cut decisions, had already acquired for him considerable reputation.

Italy, too, had by now begun to produce great scholars in this field. Their greatest literary monument was the dictionary (*Arukh*) of Nathan of Rome (c. 1050-1100), al-Fasi's contemporary. This, which is indispensable to philologists and students of folk-lore even today, provided yet another instrument by which the learning of Palestine and Mesopotamia could become accessible to western Europe.

4.   It was, however, to the north of the Alps and of the Pyrenees that Talmudic scholarship was especially cherished. Here it came to its prime with startling suddenness. We know almost nothing about literary life in the Franco-German communities previous to about the year 1000. This was the heyday of a certain Gershom ben Judah, a native of Metz, who passed the majority of his life at Mayence, on the Rhine. Such were this scholar's attainments that he is still remembered as "the Light of the

Exile." Very little of his work has survived, other than a
hymn commemorating a persecution on the Rhineland in
1012, some responsa, and a few glosses on the Talmud. He
is, however, famous as the author of a series of regulations,
Takkanoth, intended to adapt Jewish life to the altered
conditions which it had come to face in Europe; in particular, one which prohibited, in northern Jewry, the polygamy
long since abandoned in practice.

The school which Gershom of Mayence founded continued to flourish for many years. The most eminent of its
pupils was Solomon ben Isaac of Troyes, in Champagne,
universally known by the initials of his name (*R*abbi
*Sh*elomo ben *I*saac) as Rashi (1040-1105). He had studied
at Worms with scholars who had themselves sat at the
feet of Gershom. At the age of twenty-five he returned to
his native land, where he remained apparently for the
rest of his life. He earned his livelihood by winemaking,
having perhaps a vineyard of his own; but he must have
spent the best part of his waking hours poring over his
Talmudic folios. His fame spread to neighboring centers.
Enquiries for elucidation upon one point or another began
to reach him; and promising young students were sent to
study at his feet. Not content with verbal exposition, Rabbi
Solomon noted down his observations on each tractate,
submitting them to constant revision. This was the origin
of his famous Commentary upon the Babylonian Talmud,
which provided a chart for that formidable sea and rapidly attained semi-classical status. A popular commentary
on almost the entire Bible, naive and learned, though
hardly profound, supplemented the greater work, and for

many centuries served as the textbook through which the Jewish child received his first introduction to rabbinic literature.

In the generations succeeding the great teacher's death, his works became the standard of further literary activity. The Talmud was studied in the light of his commentaries; points left obscure in them were elucidated; apparent contradictions were painstakingly brought to light and reconciled with one another. This material was embodied in a series of Additions (*Tosaphoth*) to the existing matter, and the scholars responsible for them are generally known as *Tosaphists*. They were to be found throughout eastern France and the adjacent territories, especially Lorraine and the Rhineland, where every township seems to have had its little circle of eager students, clustered about some eminent Rabbi.

5.   Mediaeval Jewish intellectual life reached its climax in the commanding figure who combined the humanism of Spain with the practical interests of the northern countries, and who left no branch of Jewish learning untouched and unadorned. Moses ben Maimon (1135-1204) (or, to use the incongruous Greek form which has become usual, Moses Maimonides) was born in Cordova, of a family long distinguished for its learning. He was only thirteen years of age when his native city was captured by the al-Mohadan fanatics, and its community driven into exile. After a brief period of wandering, the family found a permanent home in Cairo. Here, Moses ben Maimon became physician to the family of Saladin.

His was an encyclopaedic mind: phenomenally well-stored, reverent yet rational, intensely logical and intolerant of confusion. It may be said that he took the whole corpus of traditional Judaism, theoretical and practical, and reduced it to order. Even before his arrival in Egypt, he had begun his masterly Arabic commentary on the Mishnah, distinguished by its clarity of thought and its lucid presentation of practical issues together with their theoretical basis. Knowledge of the Talmud appeared to him to be on the wane, and the ordinary Jew needed a new handbook of practice; his *Mishneh Torah* (Repetition of the Law) presented the whole mass of traditional teaching, written in the purest Hebrew and in a methodical and logical order. There was a widespread impression that Judaism, as a system, was antiquated; in his *Guide to the Perplexed,* Moses ben Maimon put forward a philosophy of Judaism, giving it a completely rational basis, reconciling it to the fashionable philosophy of the era, and putting some apparent crudities of the Bible into what he considered their correct perspective. It is his greatest work, and one that has formed the groundwork of Jewish philosophy from that time onward. It does not perhaps still retain its appeal in all details; but its line of approach, and the spirit in which it confronts difficulties, must always remain a model.

The admiration which the great Egyptian scholar received, though unbounded, was not universal. It was feared that his *Mishneh Torah,* professedly written for the sake of the ignorant, might in the end prove a fatal bait to the learned, and wean them away from the Talmud. Moreover, there were in it certain omissions, some intentional, some inadvertent, which attracted the attention of scholars; while part of its speculative teaching seemed to be of doubtful orthodoxy. Above all, the *Guide to the Perplexed* attracted pungent criticism, for its spirited rejection of the literal interpretation of Scriptural anthropomorphisms, its intellectualization of the faculty of prophecy, its rational explanation of every biblical precept, its dismissal of the sacrificial cult as a concession to idolatrous propensities. Even before the author's death, the storm had begun to gather. Immediately afterwards it burst; and it continued to rage intermittently for some generations. An unprecedented acrimony made itself felt in the dispute. Famous Rabbis hurled excommunications and counter-excommunications at one another. The aid of the civil power was invoked; and the climax was reached when the writings of Moses ben Maimon were denounced to the newly-established Dominican Order as prejudicial to faith, and were condemned by them to the flames (1234). Discord continued even after this; but Jewish opinion as a whole was so shocked by the episode that a reaction set in, and the reputation of the second Moses was henceforth safe.

6.   The center of these disputes had been Provence, the region lying north of the Pyrenees along the Mediterranean coast: geographically, spiritually, and linguistically a bridge between France and Spain. It stood, indeed, outside the sphere of the cultural activities of northern France and Germany, and approximated more to its southern neighbors in general humanistic and literary interests. But

the characteristic function of Provence in Jewish literary history was different from either. A very large proportion of the literature of the period had been written, not in Hebrew, but in Arabic, the international language of Mediterranean culture of the time. It could hence become accessible to the mass of Jewry only through the medium of translations. The most important of these were carried out in Provence, notably by members of the family of Ibn Tibbon, who had sought refuge there from the persecutions in Spain. They frequently had to invent their own vocabulary; their style was sometimes harsh; yet the service which they rendered to Jewish learning was immense. In addition, they translated from the Arabic into Hebrew, for the benefit of their co-religionists, numerous philosophical classics by Gentile authors ancient and modern; both original works, like those of Averroes, and translations, like those deriving from Aristotle. Another famous Provencal family of translators and scholars was that of *Kimhi*. Its most important member was David (d. 1235), who played an important part on the liberal side in the controversy about the writings of Maimonides. He compiled the grammar through which successive generations of Christian scholars acquired their knowledge of Hebrew, as well as a biblical commentary second only in renown to that of Rashi in Jewish circles, and more influential still among their neighbors in the subsequent age of reform.

At a later period, especially under the patronage of Frederick III, Holy Roman Emperor, Robert of Anjou, ruler of Naples and Provence, and Alfonso the Wise, King of Castile, a systematic series of renderings was carried out by various Jewish scholars at the courts of these monarchs. It was thus that the philosophical and scientific treasures of ancient Greece began again to penetrate the European world, bringing about that quickening of interest and that revival of learning which was to culminate with the Renaissance.

XVIII. THE $\mathcal{S}$HADOW OF THE CROSS

1.   As the eleventh century was drawing to its close, Christian Europe was stirred to its depths by the reports spread by pilgrims newly returned from Palestine, of the sacrilege perpetrated by the Moslems at the Holy Places, and the barbarous treatment of those who came to visit them. The general indignation grew; and Pope Urban II, in a sermon preached before the Council of Clermont on 26th November, 1095, summoned Christendom to take steps for the recovery of the Holy Land and its shrines from the Infidel. This was the direct occasion of the succession of Crusades which, throughout the next two centuries, attempted, with varying degrees of success, to win back Palestine for the Cross, initiating incidentally an era of martyrdom for the Jewish people which is without precedent in history.

Once religious passions are aroused, it is always difficult to restrict them to one channel. It was notorious that certain leaders had vowed that the blood of Christ should be avenged in the blood of the Jews. From the Crusader's point of view, it was supremely illogical to leave older and even more bitter opponents of the Christian faith undisturbed, perhaps even profiting from their holy venture, while they went to risk their lives and their substance in battle against the Saracens. A preliminary outbreak in Lorraine, which cost twenty-two members of the Metz community their lives, warned those of the Rhineland that danger was imminent. The forces under the command of Emico, Count of Leiningen, took the lead in an onslaught. On May 3rd, a Sabbath, the synagogue of Speyer was surrounded and attacked. Thanks to the resistance put up by the worshippers, and to the energetic measures taken by the Bishop, the outbreak was suppressed, though not before some persons had lost their lives.

On the next occasion, the Crusaders were better prepared. On Sunday, May 18th, an attack was made at Worms, with the connivance of the burghers. A few of the weakest saved themselves by submitting to baptism. The rest, with the exception of those who had found refuge in the Bishop's palace, or died at their own hands, were put to death, almost to a man. A week later, the episcopal palace itself was surrounded, and those who had sought protection in it were exterminated. Scenes of a similar nature were enacted at place after place along the Rhine valley, in some of which we know of the existence of a Jewish community so early only by reason of an exterminatory massacre at this period. On the day of the uprising at Cologne, May 30th, the community at Prague, the capital of Bohemia, where the Jew was already a familiar figure, suffered martyrdom. The climax of the campaign was reached in 1097, when the main body of the Crusaders under Godfrey de Bouillon fought their way into Jerusalem. The steep streets of the Holy City ran with blood; and all the Jews, whether Rabbanite or Karaite, were driven into one of the synagogues, which was then set on fire. This reckless slaughter marked the end of the Jewish connection with their former capital for many centuries to come.

2.   This outbreak marked the beginning of a long series which not only characterized successive Crusades, but has continued, almost without interruption, down to the present time. The whole coloring and tempo of Jewish history was henceforth different. So far did martyrdom become an occurrence of every day that the ritual codes dryly prescribed the form of benediction to be used before being put to death "for the sanctification of the Name."

From the midsummer of 1096, there was an interlude in the train of suffering. In 1146, however, the straits to which the Latin kingdom of Jerusalem had been reduced led to the organization of a new Crusade for its relief. The movement on this occasion was more compact and better organized than had been the case in 1096. Nevertheless, under the inspiration of an ignorant monk named Radulph, similar scenes of horror on a minor scale were witnessed all along the Rhine. From Germany, the infection spread to the north of France. That the excesses were kept within comparatively moderate bounds was due to the efforts of the truly saintly Bernard of Clairvaux, whose fiery oratory was the main inspiration of the Crusade, but who insisted that the Jews, though they ought not make any profit out of the Crusaders, should on no account be molested.

With the Third Crusade, the contagion invaded England, which had hitherto remained immune, and had thus offered itself as a welcome haven to refugees from the Continent. While Richard I was being crowned at West-

minster on September 3rd, 1189, a riot began, which ended
in the sack of the London Jewry and murder of many of
its inhabitants. The example was followed throughout the
country in the following spring, immediately the King
crossed the Channel. Norwich, Lynn, Dunstable, Stam-
ford, all added their names in letters of blood to the record
of Jewish martyrdom. The culminating point was reached
in York, where, after a preliminary attack, the Jews sought
refuge in the Castle and held out for some time against
a regular siege. In the end, seeing that there was no possibility of deliverance, they resolved to deprive their enemies at least of the delights of massacre. Led by their
Rabbi, all the heads of families killed their wives and
children, and then fell on one another. When, on the next
morning, the gates of the Castle were opened, barely a soul
was found alive to tell the tale of that awful night.

3.   The taste for blood once whetted, it was not
easily appeased. Popular religious passion was so far
aroused, against the Jews in particular, that before long
the pretext of a Crusade became superfluous. On Easter
Eve, 1144, the dead body of a boy named William, appren-
ticed to a skinner at Norwich, was found in a wood near
the city. Actually, it appears that he had died in a cataleptic
fit; but the story spread that he had been put to death a
day or two before by the Jews, in mockery of the Passion
of Jesus, to celebrate their Passover feast. Similar accusations of child murder for ritual purposes have been brought
up against unpopular religious minorities in all the ages;
for example, against the early Christians, at the time when

they were beginning to make headway in the **Roman** Empire, and many centuries later, against the Jesuit missionaries in China. But the accusation was levelled against the Jews, though in a peculiarly improbable form, at a propitious moment; and, in consequence, it made exceptionally rapid headway.

Soon, another element was introduced Into the story— that the object of the crime was to obtain blood for use in making the Unleavened Bread or in some other Paschal rite. The fact that consumption of animal blood in any shape or form is forbidden to the Jew by the Mosaic code, coupled with the consideration that human flesh is technically a "prohibited food," should have been sufficient to demonstrate the phenomenal absurdity of this tale, even if the fancied culprit were considered capable of habitual homicide. Princes, kings, and emperors issued edicts condemning the fable; popes anathematized it; scholars methodically disproved it; common-sense decried it. But still, the accusation continued to flourish, gaining, rather than losing, in strength. By the close of the fifteenth century, at least fifty cases may be enumerated, each with its trail of blood; yet the record is manifestly incomplete.

Sometimes, not even so specious a pretext was considered necessary. In case of a destructive conflagration, so frequent and so fatal in mediaeval towns, who should be responsible but the Jews? If there were an outbreak of plague, it was plainly they who had introduced it—provably, if they were infected first; and none the less obviously (for it clearly demonstrated their malicious forethought) if they remained immune. All heresy was assuredly fos-

tered by them; and it was they who were answerable for
all otherwise unexplained murders. They were periodically
accused of inflicting torture on the consecrated Host, notwithstanding the fact that they attached no importance
whatsoever to it. In case of an enemy invasion, especially
one by the infidel, it was taken as a matter of course that
they had invited it. During civic or dynastic disturbance,
they were plundered by each side, on the plea that they
were in sympathy with the other. Kings accused them of
complicity with rebels, and rebels asserted that they were
the instruments of the king. Sometimes, no excuse at all,
other than the imminence of the Easter season with its
reminiscences of the Passion, or even less, was necessary
for an attack to be made. And, in the ordinary vicissitudes
of war and peace—siege, capture; riot—they bore at least
their share of suffering.

4.   In the south of Europe, conditions were by no
means as bad as in England, France, and Germany. In
Italy, above all, the path of the Jews was comparatively
smooth. The popes, however much they may have desired
to prevent the contamination of Christian orthodoxy
through their means, always adhered to the principle of
formal toleration. In their dominions, alone in almost all
Europe, the Jews never knew the last extremes of massacre and expulsion. The Jews of Sicily, too, remained
numerous, if not particularly prosperous, and were generally unaffected by the storms which elsewhere had become a feature of Jewish life. On the adjacent mainland,
in the kingdom of Naples, conditions were similar until

the close of the thirteenth century, when the accession of the house of Anjou introduced northern ideals of intolerance followed by persecution and forced conversion.

Further east, in Greece and the neighboring territories, the earliest center of settlement in Europe, the old Jewish life wilted under the shadow of Byzantine fanaticism, which found its outlet from time to time in bursts of oppression and attempts to enforce conformity. Here and there, however, we obtain glimpses of flourishing communities, distinguished (as a contemporary traveler informs us) for their learning and piety.

The most important center by far of Jewish life in southern Europe was still Spain. The earliest stages of the *Reconquista* (as the Christian reconquest is generally called) had originally involved obvious danger for the Jews. As early as the tenth century, however, a change of attitude began to manifest itself. The initial religious zeal had begun to wane. If the Christian hold on the country were to be secure, it was plainly advisable to conciliate so important an element in the population as was constituted by the Jews. At the same time, by reason of their linguistic qualifications, it was sometimes found convenient to employ them on important diplomatic missions. Physicians and scientists, trained in the Arab schools, became prominent at Court; while inherent aptitude won many individuals high office in the financial administration.

Thus, the golden age of Jewish life in Spain, though without doubt largely due to the propinquity and example of the Moors, did not entirely coincide with their hegemony. Indeed, over a prolonged period, Christian tolerance

compared very favorably with al-Mohadan fanaticism. It
was under Christian rule, though to some extent under
Moslem intellectual influence, that some of the greatest
figures in the cultural life of Spanish Jewry flourished. Jewish levies fought bravely under the banner of the Cross as
well as of the Crescent, and individuals of outstanding
ability served the kings of Castile and Aragon as loyally
and with as much devotion as they had those of Granada
or of Seville.

It was in the reign of Alfonso VI of Castile (1065-1109),
that the Jews of Christian Spain reached the zenith of their
prosperity. His conquest of Toledo made him master of
one of the oldest and most flourishing Spanish communities. Notwithstanding the admonitions of the Pope, they
were left in possession of all the privileges which they had
enjoyed under the Mohammedans, and were placed in a
position of general equality with the rest of the population. Throughout this reign and those which immediately
followed, Jewish physicians, scientists, and financiers were
prominent at Court, and sometimes exercised great influence in public affairs.

For the next three quarters of a century, the condition of
the Jews in Christian Spain remained favorable. Yet the
crusading spirit had already crossed the Pyrenees and begun to disturb the friendly relations which had hitherto
existed. Papal pressure led to the enactment, if not to the
enforcement, of the anti-Jewish measures of the various
Church Councils; and at intervals a solemn protest would
be made against the appointment of Jews to positions of
trust. When, at the beginning of the thirteenth century,

a Holy War had been preached against the infidel, and large numbers of knights and adventurers streamed to Spain from all parts of Europe, they imitated the example set on the Rhineland, and began operations by attacks on the Jews of the capital and elsewhere.

The engagement of Las Navas de Tolosa, in 1212, resulted in an overwhelming victory for the Cross. The Moslem menace was finally crushed. Within a few years, the territory subject to them was reduced to insignificance. By virtue of this very fact, the position of the Jews began to deteriorate. Christianity being supreme, it was hardly necessary any more to conciliate the sympathies of a minority. Diplomatic errands to the Moslem powers ceased to have the same importance as hitherto. Even Moslem science, and hence the importance of Jewish scientists trained in the Moslem schools, began to wane. Simultaneously, the fierce religious intolerance, the exclusive nationalism, the commercial rivalries, which prevailed in the rest of Europe began to penetrate the Peninsula. Political maltreatment and popular outbreaks began to be more common. Successive rulers restricted more and more the privileges which the Jews were theoretically allowed to enjoy, even though they did not always put their legislation into practice. It took a long time, indeed, for the new spirit to permeate the country, and in some respects it never did so with the same thoroughness as elsewhere. Yet from the beginning of the thirteenth century, the tranquility of a former age began to pass, and the cloud which lowered over all Europe extended menacingly over the ancient *Juderias* of Spain.

XIX. THE SOCIAL REVOLUTION

1.   The growing insecurity of the Jews in northern
Europe was accompanied, as the Middle Ages advanced,
by a change in their economic position. In the earliest days
of their dispersal, there was little to differentiate them in
this respect from the ordinary population. The Roman
magnates who purchased Jewish slaves after successive
revolts must have destined them in the main for work
on their estates. Many, on gaining their freedom, certainly
continued to be engaged in agriculture, like their co-
religionists in Palestine, Babylonia, and Persia. Even in
northern Europe, the Jew was not entirely divorced from
the soil until the Middle Ages were well advanced. In the
south, a minority remained attached to it to the end.

One cause which tended to divorce the Jew from the
countryside is obvious. His religious practices, as they had
become evolved in the course of centuries, called for a
sympathetic social environment. Moreover, with the growth
of religious prejudice, life in isolation became increasingly
uncomfortable, if not dangerous. Constant contact with
other Jews was thus essential for security. Finally, the organization of rural society on a feudal basis afforded no
opening whatsoever for a non-believer. Semi-servile agri-
culturalists were the vassals of the Lord of the Manor and
paid him in labor or in kind; the Lord of the Manor was
the vassal of the Baron, and the Baron, in turn, of a major

Baron or of the King—the apex of this inverted pyramid—
to whom all, directly or indirectly, paid service. This organization, moreover, was based upon the idea of allegiance to a common faith, and cemented by a series of
religious oaths. As though this were not enough, the Jew
was forbidden in many places by immemorial usage, and
in most subsequently by law, from holding freehold property. In rural society, no place was thus available for him,
no gap left even into which he might insinuate himself.
Banished from the countryside, his attention was necessarily confined to the town.

A willing immigrant into a country already populated
can, as a matter of fact, hardly find any outlet for his
energies excepting in urban life. In Imperial Rome, Jews
were to be found in almost every calling, but the back-
bone of the community was the merchant class. They were
largely responsible for the importations of corn which made
possible the policy of satisfying the proletariat with "bread
and circuses." It is noteworthy that their principal center
in the capital was near the docks, and that early settlements
were situated all along the trade route which joined Rome
to Egypt, the granary of the ancient world.

The Dark Ages narrowed the broad horizons of Imperial
Rome within national limits, sweeping away the old order
of things in favor of a rude military caste. International
trade was thus thrown, as far as the northern countries of
Europe were concerned, more and more into the hands of
a class who had no country of their own, with international connections to help them, and an international
language in which to correspond. As we have seen, the

slave-trade (considered in those days no more reprehensible than the cattle-trade in ours) lay almost entirely in their hands. In legal documents of France and Germany of the ninth century, the terms "Jew" and "merchant" are used almost interchangeably. An imposing list of commodities has been drawn up beginning with oranges, going on with sugar, rice, slippers, and tambours, and ending with lilac, which probably owe their introduction in Europe in the first instance to Jewish traders.

The commercial supremacy of the Jew in Western Europe came to an end in the tenth century, with the growth of the Italian trading republics, particularly Venice and Amalfi, which rapidly gained the monopoly in Mediterranean affairs. The Crusades provided the final impetus which drove him out of mercantile life. Successive campaigns for the recovery or protection of the Holy Land brought the East and the West more closely together than they had been at any time since the Roman Empire had fallen. They developed further the power of the Italian maritime city-states. In the final result, they safeguarded pilgrims—and with them, as a matter of course, merchants —on their way to the Holy City. Thus commerce was given a powerful stimulus among the western European nations.

The Jew's personal characteristics, which had hitherto been an advantage, now told against him, for he could enjoy the privileges neither of the Christian on the one hand, nor of the Moslem on the other. The insecurity of his life made his commercial ventures more dangerous. Finally, the mediaeval organization of commerce, like the mediaeval organization of agriculture and land-tenure, left no opening for the unbeliever. In every city, buying and selling came to be confined to members of the Guild Merchant, no strangers being allowed to enter into competition with them. But the Guild Merchant was based entirely upon the conception of uniformity. It was a social body— and no burgher desired to have any social contacts with a Jew. It had its definitely religious aspects—its corporate services, its processions, perhaps its own chapel—in which a Jew could take no part. It was based on the idea of protecting the native against the competition of a foreigner, but the Jew, for however many generations his ancestors may have been resident, was always reckoned a stranger and an interloper.

In manufacture and handicrafts, the position was much the same. In the early days of his settlement in Europe, the Jew had been prominent in this sphere also. But he had little chance against a Gentile competitor, while the ecclesiastical prejudice against the subordination of a true believer to an infidel made it impossible for him to employ Gentile assistants, and so to extend the scale of his operations. Finally, the organization of the various Crafts Guilds, with their complete legal monopoly of one process of manufacture or another, left him utterly excluded. In the logical, symmetrical, all-embracing organization of urban life, as of rural life, therefore, no place was available, in northern Europe at least, for the arch-infidel.

2.   There was one indispensable economic function, however, for which mediaeval society made no provision.

The financier, or banker, or money-lender (for the terms are in fact nearly synonymous) is equally necessary in any age in which a monetary economy prevails. Nevertheless, as the Middle Ages progressed, the Catholic Church began to set its face against the lending of money at interest, under whatever conditions. The Mosaic code, indeed, envisaging a purely pastoral and agricultural life, centered about small village communities, had prohibited profit-making on any loan to one's 'brother.' The Sermon on the Mount, in its current mistranslation, enjoined the faithful to "lend expecting nothing" (the actual meaning is "never despairing"). Aristotle, second in authority only to the Bible in the Middle Ages, took up the same attitude. By slow degrees, accordingly, the Church took up an attitude of unqualified opposition to "usury," as it was called, whether the rate charged was great or small. In the Third Lateran Council, held at Rome in 1179, the attack reached its climax, Christian burial being refused to all who followed the heinous practice.

The policy was, as a matter of fact, based on a mistaken idealism, justifiable only had steps been taken by the Church to make loans available to the needy free of charge. Only the omnipresence of the Jew made it feasible for however short a time, for the prohibition was a religious one, levelled at true believers only. Thus, just at the period when the Jew was excluded from ordinary walks of life, he found an opening in this, the most unhonored and least popular of all pursuits. Rabbinical authorities disapproved of the practice; where a fellow-Jew was in question, they flatly forbade it. Nevertheless, in the end, they had to bow

to circumstances. By the thirteenth century, the majority
of Jews in those countries subject to the Catholic Church,
with the partial exception of southern Italy and Spain,
were dependent directly or indirectly, in spite of themselves, on this degraded and degrading occupation.

For a period, therefore, the Jew was in some countries
the sole capitalist. Whenever any great scheme was on
foot, his services had to be sought. For the two characteristic occupations of the Middle Ages, fighting and building, his aid was indispensable. The Crusades, fatal to him
as they were, would have been impossible in the form in
which they were undertaken had it not been for his financial assistance. Even ecclesiastical foundations had recourse
to him for any important undertaking. The transition of
Europe from a barter-economy to a money-economy, during the two and a half centuries which succeeded the First
Crusade, was certainly facilitated by his presence.

The heyday of the Jewish predominance in the world
of finance was from the middle of the twelfth century,
when on the one hand the displacement from commerce
had come to be effective, while on the other the regulations
against usury were rigidly enforced. A century later, the
Gentile usurer (legal and canonical restrictions notwithstanding) once more became a universal, though highly
unpopular figure. Legal fictions were found to get round
the impracticable regulations. Throughout Europe, Italians,
generally known under the generic name of "Lombards"
or "Cahorsins," had a bad name for their excesses in this
direction. Against the activities of these Christian competitors, with their august patronage and their vast cooperative

resources, the Jew was utterly powerless, and before long he was driven to the wall.

The Italians were mainly interested, however, in operations on the grand scale. The Jews were now forced to restrict themselves in most cases to lending money on pledge and similar petty transactions, hardly distinguishable from what we would today call pawnbroking. The rate of interest charged was always high, necessarily so, in view of the scarcity of coin and the general unruliness. Yet the Christian usurers, though they did not have to safeguard themselves to the same extent against the chances of murder and pillage, were no less exacting, and their rapacity often made the general population regret the departure of the Jewish competitors whose presence had been rendered unnecessary by the Christian usurers.

3.   An inevitable result of a special occupation, in the Middle Ages, was a special status; for any person who could not be included in the feudal scheme of things, necessarily had to find a place in the organization of society outside it. Besides, the Jews were frequently strangers in fact, and were invariably treated as such so that it was necessary for them to look for protection to the king —the Lord of all men who had no other, and the traditional protector of the merchant and foreigner. Moreover, the special taxation which they, and they alone, had been made to pay in the Roman Empire seems to have been taken in the Middle Ages as proof of the fact that they were actually the vassals of the Emperor, and hence, by imitation, of all other monarchs. The constant appeals to

the sovereign for protection during the course of the Crusades did something to spread the conception, and, in the
fourteenth century, the old Roman poll-tax was revived in
Germany under the title of *Opferpfennig* (penny offering),
as a token that the Emperor had inherited from Vespasian
and Titus the complete supremacy over the people conquered and enslaved so many hundreds of years before.

Whatever the reason, the Jews of the Middle Ages were
reckoned as royal serfs (*servi camerae regis*). This special
relationship to the crown explains much in their position
and their special tribulations. They were the king's men.
He exercised the most minute control over all their activities. He taxed them arbitrarily. For a monetary consideration or otherwise he might alienate all rights on them,
collectively or individually, to a third party. He might
confiscate their property outright. He might expel them
from the realm without giving any reason. He regulated
their internal affairs down to the least detail. Above all, he
found in them a source of income. The average revenue
derived from the Jews in northern countries has been reckoned at about one-twelfth of the total royal income. The
proportion is not vast, but it is wholly disproportionate to
their numerical importance, which was never large. Above
all, the levies were entirely arbitrary. It was possible for
the king to raise enormous sums at short notice without
any customary pretext, merely to suit his convenience.

Naturally, therefore, it was to his interest to protect the
Jews and to encourage their activities. So much of their
profits came into his coffers that he became, in a sense, the
arch-usurer of the realm. The Jews constituted a sponge,

as it were, which could be used to suck up the floating capital of the kingdom. When the treasury was empty, the sponge would be squeezed. It was only a short-sighted ruler, and there were many of them, who would display his authority by a wholesale remission of interest, or even of the whole debt, on condition that a certain proportion was paid into the Treasury. This had the automatic effect of increasing the rate of usury for the future. But, besides this, it was financially unwise, for it was obvious that the Crown stood to gain more by a few years of sleeping partnership than by the most drastic measure of confiscation. Meanwhile, the common people were filled with jealousy at the Jew's rapid accumulation of wealth. They watched the money which had once been theirs pass in an unending stream through his chests into the royal treasury. They saw the king through this means, grow, independent of constitutional checks. And so their hatred mounted up, until one day, upon a trivial pretext or none, the common people would throw themselves on the Jewish quarter, and another dark page would be added to the record of martyrdom.

4.   The Lateran Council of 1179 deeply influenced Jewish life in other directions. It marked the climax of the reaction against Albigensianism, that extraordinary heretical movement which had attained a predominant position in the south of France, and threatened the supremacy of the Catholic Church. The latter, made nervous by a movement which had at one time threatened to engulf it, suspected the Jews of complicity, and included all forms of

dissent in the counter-attack formulated at the Lateran. This accordingly witnessed the revival and reenactment of all the old anti-Jewish legislation, devised under the auspices of the early Church, but almost dormant for the past seven centuries. It absolutely prohibited Jews to have Christians in their service, or Christians to enter into the employment of Jews, even as nurses or midwives. In addition, it forbade true believers to lodge amongst the infidel, thus laying the foundation of the later Ghetto system.

The Fourth Lateran Council of 1215, under the auspices of Innocent III, the greatest Pope of the Middle Ages, went even further. Above all, the regulations instituted by certain Moslem rulers, by which all unbelievers (including of course, Christians) had to wear a distinguishing badge, were introduced for the first time into the Christian world. In practice, the badge consisted of a piece of yellow or crimson cloth—in England in the form of the two tables of stone which bore the Ten Commandments, in France, Germany, and elsewhere of a wheel or O. In some lands, where a simple badge was found inadequate, the wearing of a hat of distinctive color was ultimately prescribed. The culminative result of all this was to stigmatize the Jews in perpetuity as a race of pariahs, to single out isolated individuals for continual insult, and the whole community for attack and massacre on any outburst of popular feeling.

It must not be imagined that all the ecclesiastical regulations were immediately and consistently enforced, even in those places which were directly subject to the Church in matters temporal. Nevertheless, they remained a standard of conduct to which it was always possible to revert with increasing severity when the occasion seemed to demand it. At any time of crisis, when a fresh heresy had arisen to threaten the Church, or some peculiarly zealous Pope was elected to the throne of St. Peter, the whole of the repressive code would be renewed and put into effect, bringing disgrace and perhaps disaster into ten thousand homes.

It was not only in the political and economic spheres that the reaction affected the Jew. The counter-attack was extended to his spiritual ideals and to his literature. The Dominican Order, established as an instrument against heresy when the Albigensian peril was dying down, soon directed its activities against the Jews, and lost few opportunities of vexing them. From time to time, "disputations" would be staged under their auspices, in which some zealous but not necessarily well-informed apostate would endeavor to demonstrate the imbecility of the Talmud on the one hand, and its testimony to the truth of Christianity on the other. All possibility of fair debate was stifled by the fact that the truth of Christianity was assumed to be beyond all question. Hence the Jewish protagonists would be prevented from making a counter-attack, while any outspoken reply on their part would be characterized as blasphemous. In consequence, the results of these encounters were almost invariably adverse, and led to a general attack upon traditional literature.

These disputations often took place under the highest patronage. The first impetus was given by the apostate Nicholas Donin of La Rochelle, who in 1240 laid before Pope Gregory IX a formal denunciation of the Talmud as blasphemous and pernicious. In consequence, the Pope gave orders for the seizure of all copies of the much-decried work, and an investigation into its contents. In France, the order was immediately obeyed, all Hebrew literature being seized throughout the country on March 3rd, 1240, while the Jews were at service in their synagogues. On June 12th, a disputation upon its merits and demerits was opened at Paris, in the presence of "Saint" Louis and all his court. After the merest parody of an inquiry, Donin was adjudged to have proved his case, and the work which he had denounced was formally condemned to the flames. On Friday, June 17th, 1242, twenty-four cartloads of priceless Hebrew manuscripts were publicly burned in Paris.

This attack upon Hebrew literature was the prelude to many more: and the Talmud was persecuted with such ferocity that, notwithstanding Jewish zeal and devotion, only one ancient manuscript of the whole text is now extant. The disputation of Paris, similarly, was repeatedly imitated. Freedom of speech was granted once only in 1263, when King James of Aragon arranged a discussion between the apostate Pablo Christiani and Rabbi Moses ben Nahman (Nahmanides, 1194-1270), an exegete, legalist, and mystic, with a reputation second to none in his day. For four days the argument continued in the presence of the King and his Court. The Jewish representative easily held his own, and the King, openly recognizing this fact, dismissed him with a gift. The Churchmen, however, were furious at some of the opinions which he had expressed, and, notwithstanding the royal safeguard, it was considered advisable for Nahmanides to seek safety in exile.

At times, the attack was transferred from the Jewish literature to the Jewish liturgy, and it was alleged that certain ancient prayers, composed in an age and country where Christianity was unthought of, contained passages which could be construed as derogatory to the daughter-religion and its founder. In particular, the attack was centered upon the dignified *Alenu* prayer, composed by the *Amora* Abba the Tall (*see* p. 128f.) which referred to the vanity and insubstantiality of the objects of heathen worship. Similarly in 1278, Pope Nicholas III, imagining that the conversion of the Jews would be ensured if they were made to hear the exposition of Christian doctrine, ordered them to permit conversionist sermons to be delivered in their synagogues. Like much of the legislation of the period, this was not consistently carried out, but it was henceforth possible for any fanatical friar to march to the synagogue with a mob at his heels, to plant his crucifix in front of the Ark, and demand the hospitality of the pulpit.

5.   The description of the position of the mediaeval Jew given above is not, of course, of universal application. The nearest approach to the typical "feudal" Jewry, as it may be termed, was to be found in England, where the Jews arrived at a late date and for a specific purpose. In France and Germany there was an approximation of the same economic, and therefore constitutional status, but, by reason of the antiquity of settlement and the gradual evolution, as well as the lack of political uniformity in the two countries, it is less easy to generalize.

Even in those countries where they were utterly excluded from ordinary walks of life, the Jewish communities could not be restricted to a single occupation. The
principal householders, indeed, might be financiers or
money-lenders. Yet dependent on them, directly or indirectly, there would necessarily be numerous subordinates.
The Jewish physicians—frequently, at the same time, scholars and business men—were famous for their skill. Canon
law, indeed, forbade any true believer to make use of their
services, lest they might obtain an undue physical and even
moral control over a Christian soul. But, at any time of
emergency and often without that specious pretext, such
restrictions would be overlooked. Kings and princes frequently had a Jew as their body-physician, and a long succession were in attendance on the Popes themselves.

In a few handicrafts, the Jews long retained their predominance, especially in the south and east of Europe.
Down to a late period, they almost monopolized the dye-
ing and silk-weaving industries in Sicily and Greece, as
well as further east. Benjamin of Tudela, a Jew who tra-
versed the whole of the Mediterranean world at the close
of the twelfth century, and was the first mediaeval traveler
who generally told the truth, mentions place after place
where the community supported itself entirely by these
branches of activity. The art of goldsmith and jeweler,
facilitated by foreign intercourse, and above all desirable
for a persecuted nomad who preferred to have his possessions in the most easily transferable form, was universally represented. In Spain and southern Italy, including
Sicily, the economic degradation of the Jew made least

progress of all. The practice of handicrafts on a large scale was never abandoned. There were Jewish craft-guilds and guild-halls in the larger cities. Many individuals remained addicted to commerce, both wholesale and retail, and though money-lending and tax-farming were the callings of a minority, they were never universally followed.

6. Throughout history, from ancient Alexandria with its famous "Delta" section downward, religious and social solidarity, reinforced by Gentile aversion, brought about a tendency for the Jews to foregather in one street or quarter of each town. This received a powerful impetus when the Third Lateran Council forbade Christians to live in the immediate propinquity of the infidel, so as to avoid any possibility of being contaminated by his unbelief. The Jewish quarter everywhere had its own name. In England it was called the *Jewry*, in Germany the *Judengasse*, and so on. The homes would be grouped about the synagogue, in which the services had to be conducted in a subdued tone, lest it offend the ears of passers-by. Near this would be the school and bathhouse, together with a workroom, a hospital which served at the same time as a hostelry for strangers, and even, in larger communities, a hall for weddings and similar festivities.

Home life was exceptionally warm. The treatment of the women was more kindly than that which prevailed in ordinary society, so much so that a mediaeval Rabbi stigmatizes wife-beating as a Gentile practice. If the woman was excluded from public life, and relegated to a special section in the synagogue, it did not imply that she was an inferior. In the home she was supreme, and the home signified more in traditional Judaism than the synagogue. Housewives frequently engaged in business on a large scale, in some cases to leave their husbands more leisure for study. It is significant that the proportion of martyrs for their faith was, if anything, higher among women than among men. Child-bethrothals were common, not, as with non-Jews, for reasons of state, but (severely practical consideration) lest the parents should lose their lives before they could make arrangements for their children's happiness.

However depressed he might be by adverse circumstances and jealous neighbors, it was impossible for the Jew to discard his intellectual interests. The only calling in which he is universally found, other than finance, is medicine, and this in spite of innumerable ecclesiastical ordinances and of the difficulty which he found in studying at the universities. Many courts, especially in Spain, employed a Jewish astrologer, whose activities extended also to astronomy and cartography. A daring philosopher and exegete, Levi ben Gershon (1288-1344), perfected the quadrant, while the chronicler, Abraham Zacuto (c. 1450-c. 1515), who had lectured at Salamanca before he became Astrologer Royal at the Court of Portugal, composed the astronomical tables used by Columbus on his later expeditions, and manufactured the improved astrolabe employed by Vasco da Gama when he rounded the Cape.

At a period when the vast majority of Europeans were illiterate, the Jews insisted as a religious duty upon a system of universal education of remarkable comprehensiveness. In every land in which they penetrated, schools of rabbinic learning sprang up, in which the shrewd financiers became transmuted into acute scholars, while their clients sat drinking in their castles. The rolls of the various Exchequers bear ample witness to the wide secular activities of men whose names are immortalized in the annals of Hebrew literature. The office of Rabbi became professionalized so far as it ever was, only at a comparatively late date. To instruct the people was regarded as a privilege, and, for a long time, it was considered shameful to accept any remuneration for so obvious and so meritorious a function.

So for generation after generation, the wits of the Jew were sharpened by continuous exercise from earliest youth upon the acute Talmudic dialectic. But the Talmud meant much more to him than this. It brought him another world, vivid, calm, and peaceful, after the continuous humiliation of ordinary existence. It provided him with a second life, so different from the sordid round of everyday. After each successive outbreak was stilled, and the shouting of the mob had died down, he crept back to the ruins of his home, and put away his Jewish badge of shame, and set himself to pore again over the yellowed pages. He was transported back into the Babylonian schools of a thousand years before, and there his troubled soul found rest.

XX. EXPULSIONS AND PERSECUTIONS

1.   On November 30th, 1215, a Papal Bull put into
effect the decisions regarding the Jews reached by the
Fourth Lateran Council. Thereafter the clouds gathered
thick and fast. In country after country fanaticism gained
the upper hand. For the moment, indeed, the Jew was regarded as an indispensable pest, by reason of the fact that
recourse might be had to him for the financial assistance
which canon law forbade the true believer to provide. As
the century advanced, however, and the Cahorsins and
Lombards extended their thinly-veiled activities, he became
superfluous, and his fate was thus sealed.

Expulsion was not indeed unknown before; yet in past
centuries it had been confined to very limited areas. Now
the authority of the Crown was become a reality in the
various European states, extending over the whole country. Hence any hostile measure at the close of the thirteenth
century meant a great deal more than would have
been the case a hundred years earlier. The layman, moreover, was unable to appreciate the delicate logic of the
Papal policy, which protected and tolerated the Jews even
when it humiliated them. A secular ruler, reminded almost
daily from the pulpit or in the confessional of the multitudinous offenses of the Jewish people, sternly warned
against showing them the slightest favor, commanded to
put into execution the repressive ecclesiastical policy in its

last impossible detail, could hardly fail in the end to imagine that he would be performing a task supremely acceptable to his God if he rid his dominions of them
entirely.

2.   The first country to drive out the Jews, as the
Middle Ages were reaching their apogee, was that which
had admitted them last. The English communities never
fully recovered from the blow they had received at the time
of the accession of Richard Coeur-de-Lion to the English
throne, notwithstanding a drastic subsequent reorganization. John Lackland, indeed, conceded them in 1201 a comprehensive charter of liberties in return for a subsidy. But,
later in his reign, his attitude changed, and he began to
squeeze money out of them by a series of expedients, from
wholesale arrest down to the torture of wealthy individuals,
as typical of his shortsightedness as anything else in his
reign. During the minority of Henry III (1216-1272), under
the rule of a succession of statesmanlike regents, they were
treated with greater mildness. But, from the beginning of
his personal rule, their condition became worse and worse.
The King's own extravagance, and the rapacity of his foreign favorites, demanded a constant supply of ready
money, and it was to the Jews that he looked to supply it.
The grasping tendencies of the Crown over-reached themselves. The goose that laid the golden eggs was worn almost to death with over-production, and the results were
seen in an enormously decreased fecundity.

    Religious intolerance meanwhile came to a head. The
oppressive decrees of the Lateran Councils were put into

execution in England earlier and more consistently than in
any other country in Europe. Synagogues were periodically
confiscated on the plea that the chanting in them disturbed
the service in a neighboring Christian place of worship.
The Blood Libel and similar accusations blazed out again,
coming to a climax with the classical case of "Little St.
Hugh" of Lincoln in 1255, which cost eighteen persons
their lives. From several cities, the Jews were entirely excluded. With the outbreak of the Civil War in 1262, the
Baronial Party professed to see in the Jews the instrument
of the royal exactions and of their own impoverishment,
and there was a recrudescence of riot and massacre all over
the country.

This was the situation which confronted Edward I on
his accession to the throne in 1272. It was a state of affairs
which obviously could not be allowed to continue. The
Jews were so impoverished that their importance to the
treasury, the needs of which were increasing year by year,
had become relatively negligible. By his *Statute Concerning
the Jews* of 1275, the new King prohibited the practice of
usury, endeavoring at the same time to divert the Jews into
agriculture and other productive callings. But prejudices
on both sides were too strong, and the experiment ended
in failure. Accordingly, Edward determined to sweep
away the problem which he had failed to solve. On July
18th, 1290, a decree was issued ordering all Jews to leave
the country within a little more than three months. True
to his upright though narrow spirit, Edward extended to
the Jews in the meantime a degree of protection and security which was rare in such cases. In all, more than

16,000 persons remained steadfast to their faith, and sought
new homes overseas. The exclusion of the Jews from the
country in the subsequent period was not, indeed, absolute:
History shows that this can seldom be the case. For many
centuries to come, however, the reestablishment of a settled community was impossible. Thus the swing of the
pendulum, which had brought the center of Jewish life
from Palestine and Mesopotamia to Western Europe,
began its inexorable return toward the East.

3.   Closest akin to the Jews of England in culture,
in condition, and in history, were those of France. Here,
ever since the outbreaks which had accompanied the second
Crusade, they had lived a chequered existence. From the
close of the twelfth century, the ruling house of Capet had
developed an anti-Jewish attitude which, for sheer unrea-
sonableness and brutality of execution, was perhaps unparalleled in Europe as a dynastic policy. At the outset,
owing to the encroachments of feudalism, the royal authority was restricted to a small area in the immediate
neighborhood of Paris. Outside this district its influence
was little more than nominal. Hence the hostility of the
Crown did not affect the Jews much more than that of any
major baron would have done. The history of the Jews in
France is therefore to be understood only in relation to the
extension of the royal authority over the whole country,
which, in the end, spelled for them utter disaster.

With Louis IX (1226-1270), better remembered as
"Saint" Louis, religious zeal reinforced ancestral prejudices
in an unusual measure. The prescriptions of the Lateran

Councils were enforced with the utmost severity. A personal interest was taken in securing converts. It was under the royal auspices that the famous Disputation was held at Paris between Nicholas Donin and Rabbi Jehiel, and the Talmud was condemned to the flames. Finally, before setting out on his first Crusade in 1249, the King decreed the expulsion of the Jews from his realm, though the order, it appears, was not carried out.

The sufferings of French Jewry reached their climax under Philip the Fair (1285-1314), St. Louis' grandson. From the moment of his accession, he showed that he considered the Jews merely as a source of gold. Spoliation succeeded spoliation, wholesale imprisonment being resorted to periodically in order to prevent evasion. The climax came in 1306, when, the treasury being once more empty, the policy of Edward I of England was imitated, with significant differences. On July 22nd, all the Jews of the country were simultaneously arrested, in obedience to instructions secretly issued some time before. In prison they were informed that, for some unspecified wrongdoing, they had been condemned to exile, and must leave the realm within one month, the whole of their property being confiscated to the crown. By this time, owing to the vigorous and fortunate policy of the French crown in recent years, its authority extended over the majority of France proper, including Languedoc and Champagne, where the schools of rabbinic learning had especially flourished. The banishment spelled accordingly the end of the ancient and glorious traditions of French Jewry.

There were, indeed, a couple of brief, ignoble interludes

before the curtain finally fell. The same mercenary considerations which had prompted the expulsion of the Jews soon made it advisable to encourage their resettlement. Accordingly, in 1315, Philip the Fair's brother, Louis X, issued an edict permitting them to return to the country for a period of twelve years. The few who cared to avail themselves of this hazardous opportunity were entirely insufficient, whether in number or in intellectual calibre, to reestablish the great traditions of their fathers. Almost immediately after, they had to undergo a period of tribulation barely rivalled even in the tragic record of the Jewish Middle Ages. In 1320, a Crusading movement sprang up spontaneously amongst the shepherds of southern France, the so-called *Pastoureaux*. Few, if any, ultimately embarked for the East, but all seized the opportunity of striking a blow for the religion of Jesus nearer home. A wave of massacres of almost unprecedented horror swept through the country, community after community being annihilated. In the following year, a similar wave of feeling, diverted this time into a purely ludicrous channel, brought about a recurrence. A report was circulated widely that the Jews and lepers, brother-outcasts, had been poisoning the wells by arrangement with the infidel kings of Tunis and Granada. This ridiculous pretext was eagerly followed up. Massacres took place in many cities. An enormous indemnity was levied on the communities of the whole realm. Finally, contrary to the terms of the agreement of only seven years before, the new king, Charles IV, expelled the Jews from his dominions without notice.

A period of thirty-seven years elapsed before the experi-

ment of toleration was tried again. However, in 1359, after
the financial crisis which followed the disastrous defeat at
Poitiers, a few financiers accepted an invitation to resettle
in the country. The Crown protected them, until a charge
was brought against the Jews of Paris of having persuaded
one of their number to return to Judaism after accepting
baptism. For this heinous crime, the principal members of
the community were arrested and flogged, and it was determined to banish the whole of the wretched remnant. On
September 17th, 1394, the mad Charles VI signed the
fatal order. A few months only were granted them to sell
their property and settle their debts, a process not made
any more easy because of a subsequent order, by which
their Christian debtors were absolved from paying their
dues. Ultimately, when the time limit was expired, they
were escorted to the frontier by the royal provosts.

Some of the exiles sought refuge in the south, at Lyons,
where they were allowed by the local authorities to remain
until 1420; in the County of Provence, where they were
not finally expelled until the beginning of the sixteenth
century; or in the possessions of the Holy See about
Avignon and Carpentras, where the Papal policy of tolerance allowed them to remain permanently, in enjoyment
of toleration if of nothing else. Others crossed into Italy,
where, near Asti, they established a little group of congregations which continued until our own day to preserve
the ancient French rite of prayers. But the majority, in all
probability, made their way over the Pyrenees or across the
Rhine, where further scenes in the age-long tragedy had
meanwhile been enacted.

4.   From Germany, owing to its peculiar political conditions, there was at no time any general expulsion, as in England or in France. It figures instead in history as the classical land of Jewish martyrdom, where banishment was employed only locally and sporadically to complete the work of massacre. The famous Golden Bull of the Emperor Charles IV (1356) alienated all rights in the Jews, as in other sources of revenue, in the territories of the seven greater potentates who were members of the Electoral College. Minor rulers, bishops, and even free cities, claimed similar prerogatives, subject only to a very remote Imperial control. In consequence, when the Jews were driven out of one district, there was generally another willing to receive them, in consideration of some immediate monetary advantage. Thus, though there were few parts of the country which did not embark on a policy of exclusion at one period or another, there was no time, from the year 1000 onward (if not from Roman times), when Germany was without any Jewish population.

On the other hand, there was barely any intermission in the constant sequence of massacre. The example set in the first Crusade was followed with fatal regularity. When external occasion was wanting, the blood libel, or a charge of the desecration of the Host, was always at hand to serve as pretext. So long as the central authority retained any strength, the Jews enjoyed a certain degree of protection. On its decay, they were at the mercy of every wave of prejudice, superstition, dissatisfaction, or violence. In 1298, in consequence of a charge of ritual murder at Rottingen, a whole series of exterminatory attacks, in-

spired by a noble named Rindfleisch, swept through Franconia, Bavaria, and Austria. In 1336, a similar outbreak
took place in Alsace, Suabia, and Franconia at the hands
of a mob frankly calling themselves *Judenschläger* (slay-
ers of the Jews), led by two nobles nicknamed *Armleder*,
from a strip of leather which they wore round their arms.
The names of over one hundred places where massacres
occurred at this period were subsequently remembered.
Yet this was the merest episode in the history of German
Jewry.

It was in 1348 and the following year that the fury
reached its height. The Black Death was devastating
Europe, sweeping away everywhere one-third or more of
the population. It was the greatest scourge of its kind in
history. No natural explanation could be found.
Responsibility for it, as for any other mysterious visitation,
was automatically laid on the Jews. The ridiculousness of
the charge should have been apparent even to fourteenth
century credulity, for the plague raged virulently even in
those places, such as England, where the Christian population was absolutely unadulterated, and elsewhere the
Jews suffered with the rest, though their hygienic manner
of life and their superior medical knowledge may have
reduced their mortality. It was when the outbreak had
reached Savoy that the charges became properly formulated
in all their grotesque horror. At Chillon, a certain Jew
"confessed" under torture, that an elaborate plot had been
evolved in the south of France by certain of his co-
religionists, who had concocted a poison out of spiders,
frogs, lizards, human flesh, the hearts of Christians, and

consecrated Hosts. The powder made from this infernal brew had been distributed amongst the various communities, to be deposited in the wells from which the Christians drew their water. To this the terrible contagion which was sweeping Europe was due!

This ridiculous farrago of nonsense was sufficient to seal the fate of the community of Chillon, the whole of which was put to death with a refinement of horror. Hence the tale spread like wildfire throughout Switzerland, along the Rhine, and even into Austria and Poland. There followed in its train the most terrible series of massacres that had ever been known even in the long history of Jewish martyrdom. Sixty large communities, and one hundred and fifty small, were utterly exterminated. This was the climax of disaster for German Jewry, just as the great expulsions had been for England and France. Never again did they recover their previous prosperity or their numerical weight.

When the storm had died down, a large number of the cities thought better of the vows made in the heat of the moment never to harbor Jews again in their midst, and summoned them back again to supply the local financial requirements. The period which followed was one of comparative quiescence, if only for lack of victims. King Wenceslaus (1378-1400), however, initiated the short-sighted policy of the periodical cancellation of the whole or part of the debts due to Jews in return for some immediate monetary payment from the debtors. It was therefore impossible for the Jews to recover the position which their predecessors had held, and the hegemony of German Jewry passed, with the refugees, to the East.

There followed an interlude when the Jews of Austria, who in 1244 had received a model charter which guaranteed their rights and safety, enjoyed a certain degree of relative prosperity, succeeded as usual by intellectual activity and the emergence of a few scholars of note. This was ended by the revival of religious passions following the rise in Bohemia of the Hussite movement, an anticipation of the Protestantism which was to make its appearance one hundred years later. The Hussites did not show themselves by any means well-disposed towards the Jews. Nevertheless, the latter were suspected of complicity in the movement, and were made to suffer on that account. Every one of the successive expeditions sent to champion the cause of orthodoxy began its work, like the Crusaders of two centuries before, by an attack upon the various *Judengasse,* and massacre once again succeeded massacre. In 1420, a trumped-up accusation of ritual murder and Host desecration resulted in the extermination of the community of Vienna, a disaster long remembered as the *Wiener Geserah.**

For some years after, conditions continued precarious. The General Council of the Catholic Church which met at Basle from 1431 to 1433, in order to remedy the deplorable condition of ecclesiastical affairs, solemnly reenacted all past anti-Jewish legislation down to its least detail. Not long after, a fiery and eloquent, but strangely fanatical Franciscan friar named John of Capistrano, almost the embodiment of the anti-Hussite reaction, was commissioned to see that the policy of the Council was

Geserah in Hebrew means "evil decree."

carried into effect. Everywhere, from Sicily northward, anti-Jewish excesses followed in his train. At Breslau, in 1453, an alleged desecration of the Host led to a mock trial under his personal auspices. Forty-one martyrs were burned to death before his lodgings in the Salzring. All other Jews were stripped of their goods and banished, their children under seven years of age having previously been taken away to be brought up in the Christian faith. The example was faithfully followed in the rest of the province. Thus the Papal emissary passed on, attended by a constant procession of outrages, burnings, and massacres, toward Poland.

In the bewildering turmoil of slaughter and banishment which followed throughout Germany, down to the close of the Middle Ages and after, it is difficult to steer a clear path. The existence of one after another of the historic communities of a past age was brought to a violent end, a process which culminated in the expulsion of the ancient community of Ratisbon in 1519. Isolated handfuls continued to live here and there throughout the country. Larger aggregations were to be found in the semi-Slavonic territories on the eastern borders of the Empire. No important Jewish settlement in Germany proper, however, managed to protract its existence unbroken down to modern times, excepting that of Worms, and especially of Frankfort-on-Main, the mother-town of German Jewry, from which so much that was vital in the history of that country and of the world was ultimately to proceed.

XXI. THE CROWNING TRAGEDY

1.   Beyond the Pyrenees the social and economic degradation of the Jew was never completed as in other parts of Europe. Cultural activities continued undisturbed. Individuals rose to high rank in the financial administration, and sometimes enjoyed great favor at Court. Notwithstanding occasional local outbreaks, life and property were generally safe. In Castile alone, there were no less than three hundred communities. In the lesser kingdoms, Aragon, Portugal, Navarre, the proportion was equally high. It is true that the Jews were reckoned "serfs of the Royal Court," as elsewhere, but the yoke of serfdom lay lightly on their necks.

The Jews had been treated with especial favor by Pedro of Castile (surnamed by his enemies "the Cruel"). Under his rule (1350-1369) the communities of the country reached an influence never perhaps before attained since the *Reconquista*. Samuel Abulafia rose to the position of Treasurer of the realm, and the lovely synagogue which he built still stands at Toledo as a monument to his position, his affluence, and his taste. When a struggle for the throne broke out between Pedro and his bastard half-brother, Henry of Trastamara, the Jews (like the English under the Black Prince) warmly espoused the cause of the former. In the course of the civil war which followed, one prosperous *Juderia* after the other was sacked by Henry's wild troops and their wilder French allies. Ultimately, when Pedro was overthrown, the Jews suffered for their loyalty. To the fanaticism of the Church and the prejudice of the people there was now added the resentment of the sovereign. The new king made no secret of his feelings. For the first time in Spanish history, the repressive ecclesiastical policy, including even the wearing of the Jewish badge of shame, was more or less consistently enforced.

For the next few decades, ill-feeling continued to rise, especially at Seville. On June 6th, 1391, exacerbated by the fiery anti-Jewish sermons of the archdeacon Ferrand Martinez, a frenzied mob broke into the Jewish quarter. An orgy of carnage raged through the city. The number killed was estimated at thousands, few escaping except those who submitted to baptism. The example of violence spread like wildfire in that summer and the succeeding autumn, throughout the Peninsula, from the Pyrenees to the Straits of Gibraltar. In place after place, the entire community was exterminated. Outbreaks were averted only in the kingdom of Granada, the last surviving outpost of Moslem rule, and, thanks to the energetic measures taken by the sovereign in Portugal. The total number of victims amounted to more than seventy thousand souls.

The massacres were accompanied by a process which rendered them especially memorable. In the northern countries, throughout the age of persecution, it was usual for Jews to remain steadfast to the faith of their fathers at whatever cost, and they went to their deaths gladly rather than abjure it. But, in Spain conditions were different. Whatever the reason, for the first and only time in human

memory, the Jewish morale broke when put to the test.
Throughout the Peninsula, large bodies accepted baptism
en masse in order to escape death, led in some cases by
the wisest, wealthiest, and most prominent members of
their community.

When the storm had died down, Spanish Jewry found
its position radically changed. By the side of those, now
sadly diminished in numbers and in wealth, who had managed to escape massacre and still openly professed their
Judaism, there were now vast numbers of recent converts.
Some of them, perhaps, were sincere enough. It is sufficient
to mention in this connection, Pablo de Santa Maria, who,
as Solomon ha-Levi, had at one time been a Rabbi, but
subsequently rose to the dignity of Bishop of his native
Burgos, became a member of the Council of Regency of
Castile, and took the lead in baiting his former co-
religionists. But the vast majority of these "New Christians," as they were called, remained unaffected by the
superficial fact of baptism, though they feared to return
formally to their old faith. The ordinary citizens edged
away as they passed, with muttered curses. *Marranos,* or
"swine," they called them without much mincing of language. But the constancy shown by them and their descendants has redeemed the term in some measure from its
former deprecatory connotation, and endowed it with
associations of romance unique, perhaps, in human history.

2.   By painful degrees, the Spanish communities recovered in part from the catastrophe of 1391, impoverished,
numerically reduced, yet still unbroken. The lead in the

struggle against them was now taken by some of their former co-religionists who, with characteristic Jewish optimism, hoped to bring about a general conversion where the Christian efforts had so lamentably failed. Under the auspices of the Bishop of Burgos, a series of fresh edicts were issued. Meanwhile, at the instigation of the same evil spirit, Fray Vincent Ferrer, a fanatical Dominican friar, subsequently canonized, was traversing Castile from end to end preaching to the Jews and endeavoring to procure their conversion by fair means or by foul. In one place after another, he appeared in synagogues, with a Scroll of the Law in one arm and a crucifix in the other, while an unruly mob at his heels added force to his arguments. The result was another wave of mass conversions in 1411, during the course of which some whole communities gave way. Subsequently, this fiery missionary returned to Aragon, where he followed a similar procedure. Here he was assisted by the apostate Mestre Geronimo de Santa Fé (*Megadef*, "the blasphemer", as he was acrostically nicknamed by his former co-religionists). The latter persistently urged the anti-Pope, Benedict XIII, whose body-physician he was, to stage a disputation between representatives of Judaism and of Christianity upon the merits of the two faiths. The latter acceded, and the communities of Aragon and Catalonia were compelled to send representatives to Tortosa to champion their faith.

The ensuing debate, at which the Pope presided in person, was among the most notable of the Middle Ages. It lasted a year and nine months, and was spread over sixty-nine sessions. However, the result was a foregone conclu-

sion since, as usual, the truth of Christianity was postulated
as being beyond question, and freedom of speech on the
part of the attacked was rigorously suppressed. The only
tangible result was the publication by the Pope, soon, fortunately, to be divested of his last shreds of authority, of a
Bull of unusual severity, forbidding the Jews to study the
Talmud, to possess more than one poorly-appointed synagogue in each town, or to fail to attend at least three times
yearly the conversionist sermons instituted for their special
benefit. During the course of the Disputation of Tortosa
and after, the labors for the faith continued. Entire communities submitted to baptism in order to escape their
present miseries, and thirty-five thousand additional converts were said to have been secured during the course of
a very few years.

Meanwhile, there had grown up a new generation of
Marranos, born and educated within the church, yet as insincere in their Christianity as their fathers had been. They
would go to the priest to be married; they took their children to be baptized as a matter of course; they would attend mass and confession with the utmost punctuality. Yet,
behind this outward sham, they remained Jewish at heart.
They observed the traditional ceremonies, in some instances down to the least detail. They kept the Sabbath so
far as lay in their power, and from a height overlooking
any city it was possible to see how many chimneys were
smokeless on that day. Some went so far as to circumcise
their children. In most cases, they married only amongst
themselves. On occasion, they furtively frequented the
synagogues, for the illumination of which they sent gifts

of oil. They were Jews in all but name, and Christians in nothing but form.

Their social progress, on the other hand, was phenomenally rapid. In every rank of society, in every walk of life, New Christians were to be found occupying the most prominent positions and drawing the most lucrative revenues. The more wealthy intermarried with the highest nobility of the land. In Aragon, there was barely a single aristocratic family, from that of the king himself downwards, which was free from the "taint" of Jewish blood. Half the offices of importance at court were occupied by recent converts of more or less dubious sincerity, or else by their immediate descendants. The judiciary, the administration, the army, the universities, the Church itself, were all overrun by them. The populace, jealous at the progress of the Marranos, could see in them only hypocritical Jews, who had lost none of their racial characteristics, fighting their way into the highest and most lucrative positions in the country to the detriment of true Christians.

Once more, the pulpits throughout the Peninsula resounded to impassioned sermons, calling attention to the misconduct, not this time of the Jews, but of the "New Christians," and urging that steps should be taken to check them. Their position was almost identical with that of the Jews at the close of the previous century, and it expressed itself in a similar way. At intervals there were outbreaks of massacre and rapine, culminating in that of 1473-4, which swept the country from end to end. In more than one place, the municipal council passed a resolution forbidding any person of Jewish blood to live in the city henceforth. There was no parallel to this in Spanish history, excepting at the period of the anti-Jewish riots of 1391. There was, however, one significant difference. On that occasion, it had been possible for those attacked to save their lives by accepting baptism. Now, no such avenue of escape lay open.

3.   This was the state of affairs in 1474 when Isabella the Catholic ascended the throne of Castile. From the moment of her accession, the Queen's spiritual advisors urged her that the only manner in which the realm could be purified religiously, and so be rid of the troubles which were besetting it, was by the introduction of a special tribunal for the hunting out and punishing of heretics—the dreaded Inquisition. For a few years, her attention was monopolized by more pressing problems. Immediately domestic peace was restored, negotiations were set on foot with the reigning Pope, Sixtus IV, for the establishment of the Holy Tribunal. Ultimately, on November 1st, 1478, a Bull was issued euphemistically empowering the Spanish sovereigns to appoint three Bishops or other suitable persons above the age of forty, with full jurisdiction over heretics and their accomplices. On September 17th, 1480, after some additional negotiations and delays, commissions were issued to two Dominican friars to proceed to Seville and there to begin work. Early in the following year, a first auto da fè,* or Act of Faith, was held, six men and women of Jewish extraction being burned alive for the crime of fidelity to the faith of their fathers.

*Auto de fé is the Spanish spelling; the more familiar form, auto da fè.

This was the prelude to a long series of holocausts. Before long, similar tribunals were set up at a number of other centers throughout the Peninsula. They rapidly acquired an elaborate organization, Fray Thomas de Torquemada, himself of Jewish descent, becoming the first Inquisitor General. Lists were circulated containing minute signs (many of them grotesque) by which a Judaiser could be recognized: from changing linen on the Sabbath to washing the hands before prayer, and from calling children by Old Testament names to turning the face to the wall at the moment of death. The general population was enjoined, under the most severe temporal and spiritual penalties, to denounce any persons whom they suspected to be guilty of these or similar heinous practices. Before long, nearly thirty thousand persons are said to have been put to death by the Holy Tribunal, in addition to some hundreds of thousands who were penanced or sentenced to less savage punishments. With every year that passed, the Inquisition and its activities struck root deeper and deeper in Spanish soil, beginning the process which was to end only with the ruin of the country.

All these measures were manifestly inadequate, if the land was to be purged satisfactorily of the taint of disbelief. Professing Jews had meanwhile continued to live in Spain without disturbance. The position was, however, hopelessly illogical. A Marrano, Christian only in name, would be burned alive for performing in secret only a tithe of what his unconverted brethren were performing daily in public with impunity. It was impossible to attempt to extirpate the Judaizing heresy from the land while Jews were left in it to teach their kinsmen, by precept and by example, the practices of their ancestral religion. A trumped-up story of the martyrdom at Avila for ritual purposes of an unnamed child from La Guardia, said to have been perpetrated by Jews and *conversos* acting in conjunction, was taken as proof of the complicity between the two elements. Recent research has established the fact that the alleged victim never existed outside the imagination of a few fanatical clerics. Nevertheless, the Inquisition was stimulated to fresh efforts, and the episode provided a fresh weapon against the Jews, which Torquemada did not scruple to use. On March 30th, 1492, in their Council Chamber in the captured Alhambra, Ferdinand and Isabella appended their signatures to a decree expelling all Jews from their dominions, within a period of four months.

The news was received throughout the Peninsula with stupefaction. But the victims were not disposed to accept even the inevitable without a struggle. The outstanding figure among them at the time was Don Isaac Abrabanel (1437-1508), in whom all the glorious traditions of a former age seemed to be concentrated and revived. Since the days of Samuel ibn Nagdela, perhaps, Spanish Jewry had never known a more commanding and versatile personality. A prolific writer on philosophical and exegetical subjects, he was at the same time a financier of rare genius, who had formerly been high in the favor of the King of Portugal and was now serving the Spanish sovereign. When the Edict of Expulsion was issued he (in conjunction with one of his colleagues) is said to have sought an audience with their royal master and mistress, and offered a magnificent bribe if they would reverse their decision. As the latter were pondering over their reply, Torquemada burst from the arras behind the throne, and flung down a crucifix before them. "Judas sold his Master for thirty pieces of silver," he exclaimed, his eyes burning with the glow of fanaticism. "Now you would sell him again. Here he is: take him and sell him!"

Whether this was the cause or not, there was no wavering in the decision of the Catholic sovereigns. By the end of July, all professing Jews had to leave the kingdom. As they trudged along the dusty highways, in the summer heat, on the way to the frontier or to the seaports, musicians played jaunty airs before them, by order of the Rabbis, in order to keep up their spirits. The total number of the exiles is reckoned conservatively at over one hundred and fifty thousand souls.

4.   The disaster of 1492 was not confined to Spain. The terms of the edict of expulsion extended to the more remote possessions of the House of Aragon, notwithstanding the fact that the problem of the crypto-Jew—its titular pretext—was virtually unknown in them. These included, as well as Sardinia, with its ancient and flourishing community, the island of Sicily. Here the Jews had been established since the beginning of the Christian Era, as material relics still bear witness. Their general condition had never become so degraded as elsewhere. Their number at present did not fall far short of thirty thousand souls. All this carried no weight with the Spanish rulers, although the local authorities pleaded earnestly that they should recon-

sider their decision. Contemporary chroniclers tell us how, at Palermo, the inhabitants stood on the housetops to wave farewell to their old neighbors, as the boats which bore them disappeared in the distance.

A number of the exiles from Sicily and Spain sought refuge on the neighboring mainland, in the independent kingdom of Naples. They were headed by Isaac Abrabanel, who was once more summoned from a literary retirement to enter the service of the court. But they were followed first by the plague, and then by the French invasion of 1494, both of which took a terrible toll. Many, like the Abrabanel family, had to seek safety once again in flight. Ultimately, the kingdom passed under the control of Aragon. The outcome is easily imagined. In 1510, and again, more completely, in 1540, the Jews were expelled. Modern economists assert that even now some parts of the country have not fully recovered from the blow.

A handful of the refugees from the dominions of Ferdinand and Isabella directed their steps northward, to the kingdom of Navarre. In 1498, however, the joint sovereigns followed the example of their powerful neighbors, and decreed a general expulsion. So far were all avenues of escape cut off that the majority of the victims yielded to circumstances and accepted baptism. The few who remained constant crossed the Pyrenees into the south of France. Here, in those parts which were under the rule of the Counts of Provence, the edict of expulsion of 1394 had not been carried into effect. Yet, within a very few years, the remnant of the ancient French communities was driven hence also, and the glories of the age of Rashi and of the

Tosaphists were restricted to the tiny area about Avignon, subject to the Holy See.

The largest single body of Spanish exiles, some hundred thousand in all, had taken the obvious course, crossing the frontier into Portugal. Neither the native Jews on the one hand, nor the State Council on the other, were anxious to receive the influx. However, the ruling monarch, Joao II, actuated by anticipation of profit rather than a sense of humanity, thought otherwise. Only a handful, who could afford to pay heavily for the privilege were indeed authorized to remain permanently. On the other hand, all who desired, might enter the country on the payment of a poll-tax, on the understanding that they would not remain for longer than eight months. The conditions of this agreement were not fulfilled. Shipping was provided only tardily, and those who ventured on board were treated with the utmost cruelty, being disembarked, willy-nilly, at the nearest point of the African coast. All who remained behind after the prescribed period had elapsed, were declared to have forfeited their liberty, and were sold as slaves.

Not long after, João II, died. He was succeeded by his cousin, Manoel "The Fortunate" (1495-1521). Recognizing that those Jews who had not left the realm in time were guiltless, he restored them their liberty, and he even went so far as to refuse the gift which was offered him by the communities of the kingdom in gratitude for this generous action. But shortly afterward, considerations of public policy caused the young king to show himself in a very different light. Ferdinand and Isabella, who had united Castile and Aragon by marriage, had a daughter, Isabella.

If she became Manoel's wife, there was every prospect that their children would ultimately rule over the whole of the Peninsula. However, the Catholic sovereigns, who unreasoningly resented the reception of the Spanish refugees elsewhere, would consent to the match only on condition that the smaller country was "purified" of Jews as their own dominions had been. Opinions in Portugal varied, but the Infanta herself decided matters, writing that she would not enter the country until it had been cleansed of the presence of infidels. This was decisive. On November 30th, 1496, the marriage treaty was signed. Less than a week later, there was issued a royal decree banishing the Jews and Moslems from the country within a period of ten months.

Hardly was the ink dry on this edict when Manoel began to take the other side of the question into consideration. He recognized the value of the Jews as citizens, and was unwilling to lose their services. Moreover, he appears to have been genuinely anxious to save their souls, whether they were willing or not. The conclusion was obvious. For his own sake, for the sake of the realm, and for the sake of the Jews themselves, they must be driven to accept the Christian faith.

The parents were first struck at through the children, notwithstanding the fact that the clerical party stoutly maintained that the step meditated was uncanonical. In the spring of 1497, at the beginning of the Feast of Passover, orders were issued for all Jewish children between the ages of four and fourteen years to be presented for baptism on the following Sunday. At the appointed time, those who had not been brought forward voluntarily were seized by the officials and forced to the font.

Meanwhile, the date fixed for departure from the country approached. On their arrival in the capital, which had been fixed as the sole port of embarkation, the Jews were cooped up in an unbelievably narrow space, without food or drink, in the hope that their deprivations would open their eyes to the true faith. Those who still refused were closely guarded until the time-limit set for their departure from the country had elapsed. They were then informed that, by their disobedience, they had forfeited their liberty, and were now the King's slaves. By this means, the resistance of the majority was broken down, and they went in droves for baptism. Others were dragged to the font by brute force. The rest, still protesting, had holy water sprinkled over them, and were formally declared to be Christians.

Those persons who had been converted under such circumstances could hardly be sincere in their attachment to Christianity. They were similar in every respect to the Marranos of Spain, with the reservation that they comprised not merely the weaker brethren who had submitted to baptism in order to escape death, but, almost without exception, all the Jewish population of the country, the poor, the wealthy, the aristocratic, the ignorant, the learned, even the Rabbis. Crypto-Judaism, therefore, had in Portugal a greater tenacity than it had shown even in Spain. Moreover, for a long period, it could be practiced almost with impunity. It was not until 1531 that the Inquisition was introduced into the country; it was not until 1579 that the Holy Tribunal attained the same overwhelming authority which it enjoyed in the neighboring country.

There was thus nearly half a century in which the "New Christians" of Portugal could adapt themselves to the new conditions. In the meantime, they remained distinct from the mass of the population and the objects of a fanatical enmity, which the superficial change of religion had failed to modify. The outbursts of violence against them culminated in the horrors of the "Slaying of the New Christians" at Lisbon in April 1506, in which no fewer than 2,000 persons lost their lives. It was by these unwilling converts that the traditions of Iberian Jewry, with its records going back for fifteen centuries, were henceforth represented.

Thus the curtain fell upon the immemorial Jewish connection with the Iberian Peninsula. The western European stage of Jewish history, which had begun with the Middle Ages, ended with them, and now, once more, the center of gravity was to be found in the East.

BOOK FOUR

THE BREAK OF DAWN
(1492-1815)

XXII. RENAISSANCE AND REFORMATION

1.   In only two European countries, intimately concerned with his past, did the Jew remain a familiar figure in the dark epoch which began with the close of the Middle Ages. One was Germany, with the dependent territories on its eastern border; the other was Italy. In each case, the reason was similar. Political conditions, resulting in minute subdivision into numerous independent or semi-independent states, rendered concerted action in any matter of public policy a sheer impossibility. The Jews might be massacred, exterminated, or expelled in one state; but there was always another in the immediate neighborhood which was momentarily prepared to receive them.

Jewish settlements were now to be found in very few of the German cities which had harbored the great medieval communities. However, throughout the Empire, from Alsace to the borders of Poland, there were scattered groups, some of them of ancient establishment, enjoying a precarious tenure by virtue of an invitation from the City Council or the local ruler. They were always subject to the waves of unreasoning violence so especially characteristic of Germany. War, civic disturbance, the activities of some envenomed apostate, the momentary disappearance of a Christian child, continued to be regarded as ample cause for assault and massacre, sometimes followed by expulsion.

A typical figure of the age was Joseph, better known

as Joselman, of Rosheim, near Strassburg (1480-1554). A
man of the world and a ready speaker, he was appointed
by the communities of Lower Alsace in 1510 as their civil
representative (*Parnas uManhig*), ultimately acting in the
same capacity for the whole of German Jewry. He was not
a man of great means or superlative scholarship. But he
was the perfect type of the *shtadlan*—of the person, who,
at no matter what cost, devoted himself to the interests of
his co-religionists, untiringly watching the progress of affairs and quick to raise his voice when occasion arose. We
catch fugitive glimpses of him at the courts of the Emperors Maximilian and Charles V—lurking in the background at Imperial Diets; procuring from time to time
letters of protection; obtaining a decree whereby the business transactions of the Jews of the Empire were regulated
and put on a legal footing; on one occasion warning the
Emperor himself of a plot for the invasion of the Tyrol,
and thereby saving his life. If, with the advance of the
sixteenth century, conditions in Germany improved, the
former sequence of massacres being stemmed, and the
Jews being brought more effectively than hitherto under
the protection of public law, it is perhaps to Joselman of
Rosheim more than to any other individual that the responsibility is due.

An integral portion of the Holy Roman Empire was the
kingdom of Bohemia (from 1526 an appanage of the
house of Hapsburg), which was always within the German
orbit. Its Jewish communities were partly German in
origin, and wholly so in culture and in language; and, over
a period of many centuries, they shared the lot of their

co-religionists in the surrounding territories. The Jews, however, were never entirely uprooted from the country. The *Judenstadt* of Prague, constituting almost a city within a city, was able to develop its own life. Over many centuries, it was one of the most important Jewish centers in the Jewish world; and it is noteworthy as one of the few places in Europe with which their association has been virtually unbroken from remotest times to this day.

2.   In the southern part of Italy, as we have seen, the Jewish settlement had been brought to an end by Aragonese intolerance at the same time as the expulsion from Spain itself. It was thus only with the northern and central districts that the Jewish connection was continuous. As far as numbers were concerned, Italian Jewry never attained any great importance. However, its propinquity to the pivotal point of European culture, religion, and art, gave it a disproportionate prominence. Over a long period, the conception of the Jew, as entertained in more than one remote nation, was based upon the impressions brought home by visitors who had crossed the Alps on a religious or artistic pilgrimage. The importance of Italian Jewish history is thus out of all proportion to its numerical weight.

In a large part of the country, the Jew was legally restricted to the practice of money-lending. Merchants and manufacturers, indeed, were not unknown. But, in the mercantile republics of the north, their commercial rivalry was feared. It was hence only in the function of financiers that they could obtain admission to most places. A Jew who maintained a loan-bank for the benefit of the poor became an institution quite as necessary, and almost as usual, as the communal physician. The center from which these Jewish "bankers" operated was Rome and the neighborhood. From the fourteenth century, their numbers were reinforced by refugees driven over the Alps by the persecutions and expulsions which were taking place in northern Europe.

To see them flourishing through their shameless activities, sometimes proved too much for a zealous Catholic to bear. Accordingly, with the fifteenth century, there grew up an agitation for their replacement by public pawnbroking establishments conducted on a charitable basis. It was a natural corollary that the Jews were henceforth superfluous, and might be expelled. It happened more than once that they were summoned back after a few years, to supply by their skill what it had been found impossible to replace by mere enthusiasm. In many places, however, the movement brought about the end of a Jewish connection which had existed in some cases for centuries.

Yet, on the whole, the condition of the Jews in Italy was enviable. It was, perhaps, the only country of Europe in which persecution was never elevated into a system. Mob outbreaks, though they could not always be avoided, were rare, and in general strictly localized. The Blood Accusation (notwithstanding the notorious case of Simon of Trent in 1475) was never wide-spread, and generally failed to secure official sanction; and successive waves of refugees from France, Provence, Germany, and Spain were able to maintain a momentary foothold at least in various parts of the Peninsula.

3.   Notwithstanding the fact that the Italian Jew was restricted to occupations hardly conducive to the cultivation of the higher qualities, he could not fail, being a Jew, to develop his own intellectual life. This was deeply characteristic of the country. The distinctive feature of Jewish culture in Spain was its poetry and its philosophy; in France and Germany, it lay in the sphere of Talmudic studies. Neither of these branches was unrepresented in Italy. The outstanding characteristic here, however, was the constant action and reaction of secular and Jewish culture. There is a tradition of Jewish participation in vernacular literature dating back at least to the thirteenth century. On the other hand, Jews played an important part in the intellectual activity of the Renaissance.

Of this, the principal seat was Florence, where students would not hesitate to seek the aid of Jewish savants for the solution of any intellectual problem—not necessarily of a Hebraic nature—in which they were interested. Bearded Rabbis were hence familiar figures in the Florentine humanistic circles, when they were at the height of their reputation. The most important among them was Elijah del Medigo of Crete (1460-1497), equally distinguished as a physician, translator, and philosopher, who was tutor to the knight-errant of humanism, Pico della Mirandola, and instructed him not only in the method of Aristotle, but also in the mysteries of the Cabala.* In more than one rabbinic text of the period, one is amazed to have an intimate glimpse of the brilliant circle which was gathered about Lorenzo the Magnificent.

*See p. 258.

Florence was by no means the only center of such activity. Many a prelate, cardinal, or secular ruler had in his employment a versatile Jewish physician, whose interests extended far beyond the bounds of medicine. Cardinal Egidio da Viterbo was the Maecenas who patronized Elias Levita (1469-1549), the foremost Hebrew grammarian of his age, and who secured the translation of the Zohar * into Latin. Similarly, Jewish scientists engaged in investigations, and published their results, under Gentile patronage.

The active participation of the Jews in the Renaissance was exemplified by Don Judah Abrabanel (generally known as Leone Ebreo, d. 1535), son of the great Don Isaac. He was in touch with all that was most cultured in Italian society of his day, and his famous "Dialogues on Love" were amongst the most important philosophical productions of the sixteenth century. Conversely, the Renaissance made itself most strongly felt in Hebrew literature in the work of Azariah de' Rossi of Ferrara (1514-1578), author of *The Enlightenment of the Eyes,* which introduced the scientific method to Jewish studies, and made the Jewish reader familiar for the first time for centuries, with the Apocrypha and Philo. His example, however, was a solitary one, and the impending reaction delayed the rebirth of Jewish studies for many generations. History was long in making itself appreciated, but Italian-Jewish chroniclers of the sixteenth century like Joseph haCohen of Genoa, author of *The Valley of Tears,* and Gedaliah ibn Jahia of Imola in his *Chain of Tradition*

*See p. 259.

(called by his detractors a Chain of Lies), collected the material in a newer and more comprehensive fashion than had been known in past ages.

No Italian rulers showed themselves better disposed towards the Jews than the Popes of the Renaissance period, particularly those of the house of Medici, Leo X (1513-1521) and Clement VII (1523-1533). Enlightened beyond their time, and tolerant to a degree, they appreciated talent wherever it appeared; and they regarded even Jewish scholarship as an integral part of that intellectual life of which they were such passionate devotees. The acme was reached in 1524, with the appearance at Rome of a certain romantic adventurer named David Reubeni. The latter pretended to be the brother of Joseph, king of the tribe of Reuben, by whom he had been sent on a mission to the potentates of Europe to request their assistance against the Moslems. It may well be that this incredible story was the elaboration of a perfectly genuine errand on behalf of the indigenous Indian Jews of Cranganore, then hard pressed by their neighbors. In any case, his tale was believed implicitly. Accompanied by an exultant escort, he rode through the streets of Rome on a white horse to present his requests at the Vatican; and Clement proved so gullible as to give him letters of introduction to the various crowned heads.

Thereafter, he made his way to Portugal, where at the outset his success was no less pronounced, though eventually nothing materialized. His advent, however, caused great excitement among the Marranos; and one of them, named Diogo Pires, a promising young official, was so

stirred that he escaped from the country and declared his
allegiance to Judaism, under his ancestral Jewish name
Solomon Molcho. He studied the Cabala at Salonica and
Safed, aroused enthusiasm in the synagogues in Ancona
by his eloquent preaching, and sat at the gates of Rome
among the beggars and the maimed in order to fulfill in
his own person the rabbinical legends regarding the Messiah. Gaining access to the Pope, he communicated a
prophecy concerning a flood which was to devastate the
Eternal City not long after. The catastrophe punctually
took place (October 8th, 1530). Clement, correspondingly
impressed, extended the hospitality of his palace to the
heretic whom all the laws of the Church condemned to
death by fire; and when the inquisition finally became
aroused, delivered up a malefactor of similar appearance
to suffer in his place. It was only when the dreamer had
the temerity to abandon his refuge and go to Ratisbon
with David Reubeni to persuade the Emperor to adopt
their views that his luck deserted him, and he was burned
in Mantua as a renegade (March, 1532). In the end, Reubeni himself met a similar fate at a Portuguese auto-da-fè.

4.   The Jew had been quick to realize the potentialities of the new art of printing. By the beginning of the
year 1475, two presses were at work in Italy, one in the
far south at Reggio di Calabria, and the other in the
north at Piove di Sacco, not far from Padua. The former
completed the first dated Hebrew book. It was an edition
of the commentary of *Rashi* on the Pentateuch—a curious
illustration of the hold which the writings of that simple

French scholar had upon his people. Before long, there were Hebrew presses, generally directed by German immigrants, all over the country, especially in the north. The most important family concerned in this activity was that of Soncino, who produced nearly one-third of the total Hebrew books printed before 1500. Early in the following century, the supremacy in the printing art, as far as Hebrew books were concerned, passed to Venice. Here a Gentile enthusiast, Daniel Bomberg, founded a printing house which enjoyed a virtual monopoly in the Hebrew book-world for many years to come. Study, among the Jews, had always been regarded as a sacred duty. The invention of printing gave it an additional impetus, for henceforth every man, however poor, could boast his modest library. On the other hand, the diffusion of printed works in ever-increasing numbers from one or two centers tended to foster an increasing uniformity in Jewish life and to establish fixed standards of creed and practice which had hitherto been lacking.

North of the Alps, Hebrew literature owed its rehabilitation to a curious episode. A certain unscrupulous apostate named Johann Pfefferkorn, who had secured his release from imprisonment for common theft by embracing Christianity, showed his gratitude by attacking his old faith in a series of peculiarly scurrilous pamphlets. Notwithstanding, or perhaps by reason of his ignorance of the subject, he concentrated his venom upon the Talmud and Jewish literature in general. His attacks were assiduously taken up by the Dominicans of Cologne. Thanks to their exertions, Pfefferkorn was supplied with letters of introduction and dispatched to Vienna. Here he obtained from the Emperor Maximilian, in 1509, an edict for the destruction of all Hebrew books which contained assertions hostile to the Bible, or to Christian teaching. Thus armed, he proceeded to Frankfort-am-Main, by far the most important German Jewish community, where he immediately set to work so ruthlessly that even his clerical coadjutors were scandalized.

The Jews, on their side, made every exertion to defend themselves and to vindicate their literature from the aspersions cast upon it. The cudgels were taken up on their behalf by Johann von Reuchlin, one of the most famous German scholars of his day. During the course of a visit to Italy, he had encountered Pico della Mirandola, who had impressed upon him the importance of the Jewish Cabala as the key to the great verities of existence. Thus stimulated, Reuchlin had begun to study Hebrew. Accordingly, he joined issue eagerly. A Battle of Books started, which lasted for many years. Reuchlin, worsted before the ecclesiastical court at Mayence, appealed to Rome, where, in 1516, a favorable decision was finally elicited. Hebrew literature thus received official recognition as a mental discipline of independent importance. From this period dates the beginning of the long series of Christian Hebraists, who studied Hebrew literature for its own sake and not simply as a weapon for proselytization.

The reverberations of the dispute continued to reecho in Germany for some years. On the one side, behind Pfefferkorn, were ranged the obscurantists, bent on securing at all costs the perpetuation of the existing state of affairs.

With Reuchlin were the more enlightened scholars, profoundly influenced by the new intellectual currents. Eventually, the original motive was forgotten, and the dispute became merged in a movement wider and more significant by far, which was in the end, to change the face of Europe and to make a final, if not a fatal, breach in the fabric of the Catholic Church.

5.   The Reformation, in its early stages, had seemed likely to bring about some amelioration in the hard lot of the Jew. Luther, at the outset of his attack on the Papacy, had asserted that hitherto the Jews had been treated as though they were dogs, rather than men, so that good Christians, as a protest, might well have desired to become converted to this much-persecuted faith. There was little wonder, in his eyes, that the Jews had seen nothing to attract them in a system in the name of which they were made to suffer so greatly. Now that the Gospel was put before them in its purified, primitive form, he was convinced that their attitude would change; and he had high hopes that one of the most glorious results of his activity would be to secure the conversion of the house of Israel to the true faith. He was deeply disappointed when he discovered that this was not the case, and gradually, his attitude towards the Jews changed into one of profound hatred. His pen, when he wrote of them, appeared to be dipped in vitriol. He admonished his followers to burn their synagogues and to treat them without mercy; and, in a sermon preached shortly before his death, he urged the princes of Christendom to put up with them no longer,

but to expel them from their dominions. While his injunctions were not implicitly obeyed, the fact is that, long after his death, there was little to choose between Protestant and Catholic Europe so far as their treatment of the Jews was concerned.

The Catholic world, on the other hand, had little hesitation in ascribing to the adherents of the mother faith a considerable degree of responsibility for the Reformation. If it had been their influence which had brought about the disruption, it was plainly advisable to segregate them from Christian society, and to keep them more strictly subjected than had hitherto been the case. Accordingly, with the Counter Reformation, there began a darker age for the Jews of the Catholic world. Gone was the contemptuous tolerance which had characterized the Popes of the Renaissance. Its place was taken by a stern policy of repression, based upon the sombrest traditions of the Dark and Middle Ages. On this occasion, the enforcement was not temporary but remained in force without modification until a hurricane swept over Europe and levelled the old institutions.

The turn in the tide came with the middle of the sixteenth century, when Cardinal Caraffa, in whom the most fanatical aspects of the Counter Reformation were personified, became all-powerful at the Papal Court. A couple of the inevitable apostates followed precedent by denouncing the Talmud as pernicious and blasphemous. After a very summary inquiry, the work was condemned, and, in spite of the fact that it had been published under the patronage of so recent a pontiff as Leo X, it was consigned to the flames. In the autumn of 1553, on the Jewish New Year, all copies discoverable were burned publicly in Rome. The example was followed all over Italy with a ridiculous lack of discrimination, no exception being made in favor even of Hebrew texts of the Bible itself. Ultimately, greater moderation began to be shown, but only after the institution of a fantastically rigorous censorship, which has left its traces upon the vast majority of early editions.

Not much later, Cardinal Caraffa himself ascended the Papal throne, as Paul IV (1555-1559). Reaction now became triumphant. One of the first actions of the new Pope was to reverse the policy of his predecessors, who had permitted Marrano refugees from Portugal to settle at Ancona under their protection. Without notice, he withdrew their letters of protection, and ordered immediate steps to be taken against them. Twenty-four men and one woman, steadfast to the end, were burned at the stake. Others not so stubborn, were punished less drastically.

Even before these proceedings had been completed, the new Pope had initiated his general policy. On July 12th, 1555, he issued a Bull in which he renewed, down to its last detail, all the oppressive medieval legislation with regard to the Jews. They were henceforth to be strictly segregated in their own quarter (subsequently to be known as the Ghetto in imitation of the original Jewish quarter at Venice, founded in 1516 near the old *geto* or foundry) which was to be surrounded by a high wall and provided with gates, closed at night and on the major solemnities of the Christian year. They were excluded from the professions. Their commercial activity was restricted on all sides, none but the meanest occupations remaining open to them.

They were forced to wear their distinctive badge, in the form of a yellow hat. They were forbidden to own real estate, and had to dispose of all in their possession at whatever sacrifice. This all-embracing code was henceforth enforced with all possible strictness.

With the death of Paul IV in 1559, there was a momentary respite, and the Roman mob delighted itself by crowning the statue of the late Pontiff with one of the yellow hats which he had imposed on the Jews. Thereafter, down to the end of the century, the Papal policy varied, a peculiarly promising interlude occurring under Pope Sixtus V (1585-1590), under whom the traditions of his Renaissance predecessors seemed to be renewed. But, with his death, there was a return to the full obscurantism of the Counter-Reformation, and a series of regulations issued by Clement VIII from 1592 onwards finally ushered in the period of unrelieved darkness which was to last until the nineteenth century. Simultaneously, the Jews were expelled from all the minor centers of the Papal States, where communities had previously existed in more than one hundred places.

The Papal policy was more or less implicitly followed in the rest of the Catholic world, more particularly in the various Italian states, which continued to provide a model for half Christendom. Throughout the Peninsula, Ghettos came into being, and the Ghetto system was enforced down to its last petty detail. Thus, from the middle of the sixteenth century, Italy, the ancient paradise of the Jew, began for the first time to set the example of intolerance; and the Ghetto, in all its narrowness and all its degradation, became a feature of European Jewish life.

XXIII. THE LEVANTINE REFUGE

1.   Meanwhile, the center of gravity of the Jewish world had changed. When Christian Spain rid itself of the Jews, and they lost their last foothold in Western Europe, it was under the Crescent that they found a breathing space. Notwithstanding the vicissitudes through which they had passed, and the complete change in their environment, the refugees remained true in their new homes with pathetic fidelity to the traditions of the country which had spewed them out. All along the Mediterranean coast there was a succession of little islands of Iberian culture, maintained by the Jewish exiles in the midst of a strange land. This state of affairs, not unnatural at first, was perpetuated with unbelievable tenacity generation after generation. The culture of fifteenth century Spain, in a semi-fossilized form, continued to be preserved with the utmost loyalty among the descendants of the exiles. Centuries after the expulsion, Spanish travellers were amazed to meet in the Levant little Jewish children who had never seen Spain, but who spoke a purer Castilian than they did themselves. Christopher Columbus, could he have been resuscitated four centuries after his death, would perhaps have found himself more at home in the Jewish quarter of some trading center of Northern Africa or the Near East than along the quays of Seville.

Already at the close of the fourteenth century, the refugees from the outbreaks in Spain had awakened the communities of northern Africa to a new life. The former residents had no choice but to waive to the superior numbers, learning, and initiative of the new immigrants, and the authority of the Spanish Rabbis soon became generally acknowledged amongst them. After the expulsion of 1492, their numbers were immensely recruited. Along the northern coast of Africa, from Tangiers to Cairo, and inland to Mequinez and Fez, the refugees settled in tens of thousands. The sufferings which they underwent in the course of their readjustment were terrible. Many were despoiled at sea. Others were cast away on the coast, assaulted and murdered by the inhabitants, or sold into slavery. Their steps were consistently dogged by pestilence, famine, and fire. When they were at last permitted to settle down, they had to pay heavily for the privilege.

Even after, conditions were far from ideal, and the benevolence of the government was sporadic. The Jews found themselves fleeced periodically, arbitrarily, and unmercifully by their Moslem rulers—in this, at least, true counterparts of the monarchs of civilized Europe. Occasionally, there were ghastly mob outbreaks. From certain cities, considered of especial sanctity, they were utterly excluded. In other places, they had to live in a special quarter known as the *Mellah* which could conveniently be sacked at any interlude of popular unrest. They were forbidden to wear white or colored clothing, ultimately developing as their characteristic garb the long black gown and round skullcap still worn by their descendants.

Their position was hence always precarious. But, in practice, the Moslem governments showed that they believed at least in tolerance, and, like the Popes at Rome, they rarely or never resorted to the last extremity of expulsion. So long as the Jews could find a temporary resting-place, where they might live without disturbance, little else mattered to them, and they utilized their opportunities to the full. They were famous as artisans. They piled up fortunes at trade. As in a former age some attained great influence in the state, as financial agents, diplomats, physicians, interpreters, and (particularly in Egypt) mint-masters. They often acted as consuls for foreign powers. Thanks to their personal address and linguistic ability, they were sometimes appointed Ambassadors and Ministers Extraordinary to stolid Holland, condescending England, and even fanatical Spain. Over many a long century, the benighted Barbary States thus compared very favorably indeed, when tested by the touchstone of toleration, with the vast majority of the countries of Europe.

2.   By far the greatest number of the exiles of 1492 directed their steps further East, towards the central provinces of the Turkish Empire. That of Byzantium, during its protracted death-throes, had not perpetuated the gross fanaticism which had stained its earlier days. Its Jewish communities had continued to drag on a degraded and undistinguished existence, unenlivened over a period of many centuries by a single important event, or a single outstanding name.

The fall of Constantinople in 1453, which seemed to the Jews of the West one of those supernatural visitations which were to herald the coming of the Messiah, gave those of the East a new lease of life. Excepting for the payment of the poll-tax which was obligatory on all non-Moslems, they were subjected to few disabilities, and almost all walks of life were open to them. The Turks were essentially a military and agricultural people, despising a sedentary existence, and the trade of the Empire was thus left almost entirely to Jews, Armenians, and Greeks. The exiles from Spain accordingly found a warm welcome. "What! call ye this Ferdinand 'wise'—he who depopulates his own dominions in order to enrich mine?" the Sultan Bajazet is reported to have said, and he encouraged the immigration by every means which lay in his power.

Fresh communities were thus established, or the old ones revitalized throughout the Ottoman Empire. Many cities contained more than one congregation, which faithfully preserved the minutiae of the religious tradition of the Spanish province, or even city, from which its founders had come. With them the immigrants brought their language, their acumen, their fortunes, their knowledge. International trade throughout the eastern portion of the Mediterranean basin, lay very largely in Jewish hands. The expert Jewish artisans rapidly made a name for themselves, and introduced the methods and trade-secrets of Toledo or Segovia to the Levant. The troops and vessels of the Crescent were equipped with gunpowder and armaments manufactured by Jewish hands, and any increase of activity in the Jewish quarters of Adrianople or Brusa was assumed by foreign observers to presage an approaching sally of the Grand Seigneur.

The first, and most obvious place of settlement was Constantinople. In a short time, the Jewish community of this city grew to be the largest in Europe, comprising as many as 30,000 souls. But it was soon rivalled, and ultimately surpassed, by Salonica, which became, through Jewish enterprise, the greatest mercantile emporium of the Mediterranean. More Jewish settlers, and still more, flowed thither from every part of the Jewish world. Before long, it became a preponderantly Jewish city, as it was to remain for some four centuries. The non-Jewish population were in a distinct minority. Jews controlled its trade, its handicrafts, its industries, even its manual labor. Jewish fishermen supplied the city with a large proportion of its food, and Jewish porters discharged the vessels which arrived in the harbor with every tide.

3.   The Spanish immigrants in Turkey comprised not only a valuable mercantile and urban element, but also the only section of the population which had thorough experience of European conditions and knowledge of European languages. Hence, for the first time since the heyday of Moslem Spain, individual Jews began to play an important, and in some cases even a crucial part in international politics. It was seldom that the Sublime Porte did not have in its employment some Jewish physician—such as Joseph Hamon (d. 1518), one of the exiles from Spain, or his son, Moses (d. 1565), whose opinion it frequently consulted, and who was sometimes able to render great services to his co-religionists. In the second half of the century, a Jewish woman, Esther Chiera (d. 1592), stood high

in the favor of the Imperial harem, and was considered by foreign diplomatic observers to be one of the most influential persons at Court.

No case was more striking than that of Joseph Nasi, whose career reads like a page out of some exotic Jewish recension of the Arabian Nights. He belonged to an immensely wealthy Portuguese Marrano family of bankers, which, after well-nigh incredible adventures, escaped through the Low Countries and Italy to Turkey, where they threw off the disguise of Catholicism and reverted openly to Judaism. Nasi's subsequent career knew almost no check. He rose to high position at Court, so that for a time he was immensely influential in the Turkish Empire. His mother-in-law and aunt, Gracia Mendes, became known as the most benevolent and most adored Jewish woman of her day. His interest was solicited by every power in Europe. He was able to sway the election of a new king in Poland. He avenged himself on Spain by encouraging the revolt of the Netherlands. He repaid Venice for the indignities that his family had suffered at her hands by bringing about a declaration of war, in the course of which the Republic lost the island of Cyprus. He was created Duke of Naxos and the Seven Islands. At his palace of Belvedere, in Constantinople, he maintained an almost royal state. He was a munificent patron of letters, and maintained his own printing press for the publication of Hebrew works (an activity subsequently continued by his widow). Above all, he did not hesitate to use diplomatic means to protect his co-religionists abroad. No professing Jew in recent history had ever attained such power.

For a few years before Nasi's death, which took place
in 1579, his political influence was on the wane, and the
peace-party, under the Grand Vizier, gained the upper
hand. Yet there was no reaction against the Jews as a
whole. The former favorite was left in enjoyment of his
dignities, and the Vizier's physician became a power in the
state in his stead. This was a certain Italian Jew of German origin named Solomon Ashkenazi. His ability, his
linguistic attainments, and his tact won him golden opinions at Constantinople, where he had come to exercise an
influence comparable to that of Nasi, though less obvious;
so much so that the election of Henry of Valois to the
Polish crown in 1573 had partly been due to his exertions,
and his influence with the Venetian ambassador had secured
the withdrawal of an edict of expulsion issued against the
Jews of Venice two years before. In 1574, this much-
traveled physician was delegated Envoy Extraordinary to
the Venetian Republic—a mission which he performed to
the utmost satisfaction of his employers.

With the death of Selim II in 1574, the golden age
of the Jews in Turkey came to an end. The Ottoman Empire was showing signs of decay. The Turkish Jews lost
something of that international breadth which they had
shown in the generation which succeeded the expulsion
from Spain, and no longer produced statesmen of outstanding genius. We begin to read, at increasingly frequent
intervals, of lapses from the old standards; of sumptuary
laws, intended to mark out the Jews for contumely from
true believers; of persecutions at the hands of various
Pashas; of terrorization by the Janissaries. There was, how-

ever, no radical change in the policy of the government and no disaster on a larger scale. The Jewish people must always remember the Turkish Empire with gratitude because, at one of the darkest hours of its history, when no alternative place of refuge was open and there seemed no chance of succor, Turkey flung open its doors widely and generously for the reception of the fugitives, and kept them open.

4.   The names of the Jewish statesmen at the Turkish Court in the sixteenth century will always be remembered in connection with a gallant attempt which they made to restore the Jewish center in Palestine. The original settlement, in full decay after the abolition of the Patriarchate in 425, had been brought to an end by the devastations of the Crusades and of the Tartar invasion which had succeeded them in the middle of the thirteenth century. True, the country never lost its place in Jewish sentiment. Throughout the centuries, pilgrims had made their way thither, to pray at the tombs of the patriarchs, and sometimes to remain. Thus, for example, in 1211, no less than three hundred English and French Rabbis set out for the Holy Land. The father of the modern settlement, however, was Obadiah di Bertinoro, a saintly Italian scholar, famous for his commentary on the *Mishnah,* who arrived there in 1488. His strong personality, combined with his scholarship and his eloquence, led to his immediate acceptance as spiritual head of the community. In this capacity, he instituted regular courses of lessons, founded a *Yeshiba* for the study of the Law, brought charitable and benevolent institutions into

existence, suppressed corruption, and improved relations with the Moslem authorities. The ground was thus prepared for the numerical increase which was to take place a few years later.

On the expulsion from Spain, it was natural that many of the refugees, wandering about without an objective, turned their minds to the land which had been associated with their hopes and their prayers for so many centuries. Its Jewish population accordingly grew by leaps and bounds. Scholars and Rabbis, who had previously been reckoned amongst the greatest luminaries of Spain, Portugal, and Sicily, established themselves there in large numbers, accompanied by many members of their flocks. Communities of real importance were established, not only in Jerusalem, but also at Hebron, and above all Safed. So great was the influx of scholars that in 1538 a certain Jacob Berab considered that the time had come to reestablish Palestine formally as the center of Jewish spiritual life by restoring the ancient institution of rabbinical ordination, long in abeyance, and ultimately the Sanhedrin as well. This revolutionary suggestion aroused so great a wave of opposition that it had to be abandoned. The reintegration of Jewish life was as yet premature.

A less unworldly tendency was introduced into the Holy Land by the Duke of Naxos. He was the first person, perhaps, to envisage the restoration of Jewish Palestine by practical, as opposed to supernatural, means. Through his influence at the Sublime Porte he secured the grant of the city of Tiberias, which had long been in ruins. Not content with rebuilding it and its fortifications, he attempted to turn it into a manufacturing center by fostering the textile industry, in which the Jews of the Near East had long enjoyed supremacy. Mulberry trees in great numbers were planted; invitations were dispatched far and wide for artisans and professional men to come and settle in the new colony; and arrangements were made for the unfortunate Jews of the Papal States, in particular, to be transported from the growing miseries of their daily existence in the Duke's own ships. The latter's conceptions, however, were in advance of his time. Innumerable difficulties sprang up, which he was unable to surmount—sentimental, political, economic—and the experiment ended in failure.

5.   The most important of the new centers of Jewish life and scholarship was Safed, in Upper Galilee. At the time of the Expulsion, it contained a bare handful of Jews. A hundred years later, it supported no fewer than eighteen Talmudical colleges and twenty-one synagogues. But the disciplines here studied were very different from those of thirteen hundred years before, at the heyday of the Patriarchate. There had always flourished, by the side of the Talmudic studies which discussed how a man should act, a mystical tendency which endeavored to ascertain how he had come into being, and the nature of the unknown world. All of this lore was known as the *Cabala,* or tradition, and was handed down from generation to generation by word of mouth.

The persecutions of the Middle Ages made the Jews turn their minds more and more to the supernatural world, to counterbalance and compensate the vicissitudes of ordinary existence. In the thirteenth century, there came to light in Spain a work known, after its opening words, as the *Zohar*, or the Book of Splendor. This was, in form, a mystical commentary upon the Pentateuch, in the Aramaic language, replete with exotic speculations upon the origin of the Universe, the nature of the Godhead, the allegories contained in the Scriptures, and the hidden sense of every episode and precept. The fundamental conception was that the Law of God can contain nothing trivial, and that every verse, line, word, even letter or stroke, has some higher mystical significance, which can reveal to the initiated the very secret of human being.

The work purported to have been composed by the *Tanna,* Rabbi Simeon ben Jochai, in the second century of the Christian Era. Its opponents, on the other hand, neglecting the obvious antiquity of some passages, asserted that it was a modern fabrication, and even went so far as to indicate who, in their opinion, was responsible for the forgery. The truth, in all probability, lay mid-way between the two extremes; for the work, though perhaps a recent compilation, indubitably contained elements which went back to remote antiquity.

For the first couple of centuries after its publication, the Zohar and the Cabala in general did not exercise any very profound influence upon the life of the ordinary Jew, though they had passionate votaries in every land. With the expulsion from Spain, a new phase opened. It seemed obvious that this crowning disaster must be the darkest hour which presaged the dawn, heralding the final deliverance promised by the ancient Prophets of Israel. It was inevitable that more and more attention should now have been paid to the Zohar, in the hope that in its rhapsodies there might be some indication of the period when the Redeemer could be expected. Scholars of a mystical turn of mind directed their steps with one accord to Upper Galilee, where the action of the Book of Splendor was staged; where its saintly author had lived; and where his grave was still to be seen. Safed thus became what can only be described as a revivalist camp in perpetual being. The traditional Jewish life was lived with an intensity rarely equalled, coupled with a mystical bent which was all its own. The multitudinous precepts of the law were carried out meticulously, but with especial regard to the hidden esoteric meaning of each. Study centered around the Zohar rather than the Talmud, and the anniversary of the death of Simeon ben Jochai was celebrated by a pilgrimage to his reputed grave.

The new tendencies were personified and given a new direction by the activities of one man. Isaac Luria was born in Jerusalem, of a family of German extraction, in 1534. Becoming engrossed in the study of the Zohar, he adopted the life of a hermit. For seven years he lived in isolated meditation in a hut on the banks of the Nile, visiting his family only on the Sabbath, and speaking no language but Hebrew. The ascetic life had its natural result. He became a visionary, believing that he was in constant intercourse with the prophet Elijah, and that his soul was privileged to ascend to Heaven, where it was initiated into sublime doctrines by Simeon ben Jochai and the other great teachers who had adorned his circle. In the end, he removed to the "Holy City" of Safed, where a coterie of disciples, comprising some of the most elect spirits of the time, speedily gathered round him. Through them, he became known by the name of "Ari," or Lion, being the initial letters of the words *Ashkenazi, Rabbi Isaac*.

His personal fascination must have been extraordinary, to judge from the extent of his influence and the wealth of legend which gathered round his memory. Though he himself prepared nothing for publication, the notes of his discourses collected by his disciples, particularly Hayim Vital, a refugee from Calabria, soon circulated throughout the Diaspora, and had an enormous effect upon Jewish practice and the theory which inspired it. All the minutiae of observance, every letter of the prayers, every action of daily life, became infused with a new esoteric significance, occasionally bordering on superstition, but often beautiful, and sometimes profound. It was the most vital movement in Judaism which had come forth from Palestine since the days of the Second Temple.

6.   One of the most eager of the intent circle which hung upon the mystical utterances of the Lion of the Cabala in Safed was Joseph Caro (1488-1575). He was destined, however, to make his mark, not in mysticism, but in the more practical field. Already, at the close of the twelfth century, as we have seen, the great Maimonides had codified the traditional law as expressed in the Talmud. A little more than a century after, Asher ben Jehiel (1250-1328), an outstanding German refugee-scholar, whom the community of Toledo had taken as its spiritual leader, made

an abstract of the legal matter contained in each Talmudic tractate, as interpreted and supplemented by the later authorities. His son, Jacob ben Asher (d. 1340), had used this as the basis for a further code of the same methodical nature as that of Maimonides. This he called the "Four Rows" (*Arba Turim*).

Early in life, Joseph Caro had begun to write detailed annotations upon this work. It was, however, too voluminous, and by this time, hardly up to date. Accordingly, the sage of Safed composed an abridgement, supplemented by additions found in his own gigantic commentary. This he entitled "The Prepared Table" (*Shulhan Arukh*), indicating that the feast was spread, and that nothing remained for the guest but to help himself. It dealt clearly and methodically with the whole field of Jewish religious practice and jurisprudence in home, synagogue, counting-house, and law-court. The work, first published in 1567, attained an instantaneous reputation, being reprinted time after time, and spreading with phenomenal rapidity to every corner of the Diaspora. It became accepted as the final standard of Jewish law and observance. Even scholars had recourse to it rather than take the trouble of poring over the authorities upon which it was based. Commentaries, and super-commentaries, were written about it. Abridgements were drawn up for the benefit of those who could not spare the time to consult the original. Finally, even translations of the abridgements were made for such as were ignorant of Hebrew. Every trivial practice which the author had noted became sacrosanct. Every action of the Jew, from his rising in the morning to his lying down at

night; from his home to the synagogue; from the synagogue to his business, became defined, regulated, stereotyped, and occasionally devitalized.

With the decay of Jewish scholarship, there were many
communities (of the south of Europe and the Levant in
particular) where the study of the Talmud and the allied
literature now fell into rapid decline. All that was needed
as a guide to Jewish observance was Caro's code, and upon
it, together with the Zohar and the neo-mystical literature,
their studies were now centered. Talmud and Midrash,
Rashi and Tosaphoth, the medieval glosses, commentators
and codifiers—all this ripe literature of a former age was
abandoned in an increasing degree. In northern Europe,
however, there was yet a sturdy body on which traditional
values still retained a strong hold—Poland, the second
haven, where, in that dark period which succeeded the
close of the Middle Ages, Jewish life found a refuge and
a breathing space.

XXIV. POLAND (TO 1648)

1.   Jews had been settled in Eastern Europe, in the lands immemorially associated with the Slavonic peoples, from a very early date. Archaeological evidence shows that they were to be found in some numbers as early as the first century of the Christian Era in the Cimerian Bosphorous, now known as the Crimea. Pious inscriptions in the Greek language demonstrate that, even in this remote spot, obedience to the traditional Jewish law was implicit. As the years passed, the area of settlement extended, notwithstanding the competition of Christianity: and by slow degrees, the influence of Judaism began to impress itself on some of the semi-barbaric tribes and kingdoms of the region.

The most important of these were the Khazars, a mixed people, with a strong Mongolian strain, which occupied a territory comprised in what is now the Ukraine, between the Caucasus, the Volga, and the Don. For a period of two hundred years, they were one of the most important of the independent states which lay to the north of the Byzantine Empire. Early in the eighth century, Bulan, the ruling prince, recognized the merits of Judaism and formally adopted it as his religion. His example was followed by many of the aristocracy. One of his descendants, Obadiah, was especially memorable for the zeal with which he propagated the faith, constructing synagogues and inviting foreign scholars to settle in the country. The governing classes became thoroughly Judaized, their example being followed by many of the ordinary people: though, in accordance with the traditional Jewish principles of tolerance, followers of other religions were left undisturbed. Throughout the golden period of the Khazar state, it was considered essentially Jewish. Its heyday, however, did not last for long. In 965-969, the Prince of Kiev invaded the country and overran the greater part of it in successive campaigns. For half a century longer, independence continued to be maintained in the Crimean area, until in 1016 a short-lived alliance between the Russians and Byzantines conquered this last outpost.

2.   The history of suceeding centuries in Eastern Europe is obscure. We read of intolerant Greek abbots and bishops, of occasional riots and massacres, of Jewish merchants from the west—sometimes even from as far afield as Spain—pushing resolutely inland, of Rabbis of international reputation established at Novgorod and Kiev, of the gradual extension of the area of settlement northwards, into what is now Poland, of Jewish traders and tax-gatherers and even mint-masters, who actually struck coins bearing Hebrew lettering.

The invasion of the Tartars in 1240-1 was a turning point in the history of Eastern Europe generally. Russia itself was conquered by the barbarians, who subsequently accepted the religion of Islam. For centuries to come, the country was outside the bounds of civilized Europe, and our knowledge of the conditions of its Jews at this period is, in the main, based on conjecture. Poland, indeed, was not conquered. However, in 1241, there took place the first of a series of invasions which devastated the whole country, and reduced the principal towns to heaps of smoking ruins. When the incursions ceased, conditions were desperate. The middle class, never strong, had all but disappeared. Industry and commerce were non-existent. Accordingly, the Polish sovereigns, from the middle of the thirteenth century, set about a considered policy of attracting merchants and craftsmen from Germany.

Among the Germans, and after them, there came also large numbers of Jews, similarly attracted by the economic potentialities of the new field of enterprise. There had, indeed, been a tendency to migrate eastward from the Rhineland ever since persecution had become endemic in Germany, from the beginning of the period of the Crusades: and this factor became increasingly strong as time went on. King Boleslav the Pious, in 1264, issued a model charter of protection and liberties for the Jews, securing them freedom of opportunity as well as security from molestation. Under the auspices of this, the settlement grew apace. Just as the German immigrants introduced handicrafts and industry into the country, so the Jews opened up fresh avenues of commerce and provided the necessary finance. What proportion of the Jewish population of the country they actually constituted can never be ascertained. But in any case (in precisely the same manner as the refugees from Spain in the Balkans after the Expulsion of 1492) they were able to impose their superior culture upon their indigenous brethren. The latter adopted German costume, standards of culture, methods of study, and even language. In consequence, the vast majority of the Jews of Russia and Poland, whatever their immediate origin, as well as many of their descendants in other lands, still speak the Middle High German dialect which these immigrants brought with them.

Though the rulers of the country were generally friendly to the Jews, confirming or developing Boleslav's policy, the population was not invariably so. Jealous merchants on the one hand, and fanatical ecclesiastics on the other, resented their privileges. The Christian immigrants from Germany had introduced with them the intolerant standards of their own home. Clerical synods clamored for the enforcement of the repressive legislation of the Lateran Councils. In the middle of the fifteenth century, the fanatical John of Capistrano, embodying the reaction against the Hussites, was as successful in stirring up anti-Jewish feeling and excesses in Poland as he had been elsewhere along his path.

Yet, by comparison with neighboring countries, conditions appeared attractive, while economic opportunity still abounded. Accordingly, the current of migration from western Europe continued. Casimir the Great, in 1354, under the influence, it was said, of his lovely Jewish mistress, Esther, ratified and extended the provisions of the Charter of Boleslav the Pious, of a century earlier. Every facility was given to the Jews for carrying on their business activities. They were authorized to rent estates even from the nobility and the priesthood, or to hold them in mortgage. In order to secure impartiality, cognizance of disputes in which they were concerned was reserved to the

Crown. In 1388, a similar Charter of privileges was secured by the Jews of Lithuania, conditions in which (notwithstanding a temporary expulsion in 1495) remained very similar to that of their co-religionists in the larger country with which, from 1501, it was united.

Even when the age of terror in Germany had ended, Polish rulers continued to encourage the Jews. Local excesses recurred at not infrequent intervals. At some of the larger places, Cracow, Lublin, Posen, there were Jewish quarters, with their walls, gates, and warders, in the full German or Italian style. Occasionally, there would be some legislative enactment against the Jews. But, on the whole, they could count upon the royal protection; there was general, if not invariable, security for life, limb, and property; and economic opportunity above all, left to flow in its own channels, was far wider and more ample than elsewhere. For long generations, therefore, Poland continued to appear in the light of a land of promise for the Jews of northern Europe, and to receive a perpetual accession of new settlers—refugees escaping from massacre, young men seeking opportunity, merchants from as far afield as Italy or the Balkans. In 1500, the number of Jews in the country is estimated to have been only 50,000 souls; a century and a half later, it had risen to half a million. Just as the expulsion from Spain concentrated the majority of Sephardic Jewry in Turkey and its dependencies, so, from the beginning of the sixteenth century, the overwhelming mass of Ashkenazic Jewry—the remnants of the communities of medieval England and France and Germany, with others from further afield—became concentrated in Poland and

the surrounding Slavonic territories. It is from them that
the majority of the Jews in the world today are descended.

3.   Polish Jewry was not by any means confined to
the sordid occupations followed by its forefathers or by contemporaries in the adjacent countries. There was a very
large mercantile class, engaged in every branch of commercial activity. Many were interested in handicrafts and manufacture. They half-monopolized the great fairs in which
Polish commerce was centered. Wealthy Jews were found
as tax-farmers; they administered the excise and tolls; they
were frequently employed as financial agents for the sovereign. Some leased and exploited the landed property of
the nobility, or the Crown domains. They were familiar
all over the country as stewards and administrators of the
great estates. Communities, or isolated individuals, were to
be found in almost every hamlet.

Nothing was more characteristic of Polish Jewish life
than the remarkable degree of self-government which it
evolved. In 1551, Sigismund Augustus, the last king of
the house of Jagello, issued an edict permitting the Jews
of his realm to elect their Chief Rabbi and lawful judges,
answerable only to the king, with authority to exercise
jurisdiction in all matters concerning Jewish law. This
measure has rightly been described as the Magna Carta of
Jewish self-government in Poland, for it set the seal of the
royal approval upon the natural urge of the Jew of past
ages to rule himself according to his traditional jurisprudence.

The outstanding feature of Polish economic life was the

succession of great fairs held yearly in various centers. Hither streamed the Jewish merchants from every corner of the country. What was more natural than that, on coming together, they discussed questions of common interest, and adjudicated on matters which were in dispute between one community and another? Ultimately, it was discovered that these gatherings afforded an admirable opportunity for apportioning the amount which each *Kahal* or community was to contribute towards the collective burden of taxation. As a matter of course, this convenient arrangement was backed up by the royal authority, and by slow degrees the *Vaad,* or Council, became omnipotent in Polish Jewish life. At the beginning, its authority extended over the whole of Poland and Lithuania. The Grand Duchy, however, had a distinct fiscal administration of its own, and it was thus natural that its Jewish communities broke away and formed a separate organization (1623). That of Poland eventually became known as the Council of the Four Lands, or Provinces (comprising Great Poland, Little Poland, Podolia, and Volhynia) of which the kingdom was composed.

The Council, at its prime, was virtually the Parliament of Polish Jewry, with authority nearly as absolute as that of any legislature. Plenary meetings were held each year, not only at the Spring Fair at Lublin, but also at that in the early summer at Jaroslav, in Galicia. During the sessions of the Polish Diet at Warsaw, the Council would send an agent, or *Shtadlan,* generally a *persona grata* at court, to watch over Jewish interests. Internally, its authority was absolute. Besides apportioning taxation, it would assist in

enforcing royal edicts; it passed sumptuary laws, to enforce moderation in dress and social life; it did all that
lay in its power to prevent undue competition; it super-
vised education; it acted as a court of appeal, and decided
on matters which were in dispute between one congregation and another. All the Council's regulations, however
trivial, could be enforced, if the necessity arose, by the
power of excommunication, which was backed up by the
authority of the State. Nowhere, since the decay of the Jewish center in Palestine, had a more complete approach to
autonomy existed.

4.   As has almost always been the case in Jewish life,
learning followed in the wake of numbers. The intellectual
hegemony of German Jewry had slowly passed eastward,
together with its center of gravity. In the early part of the
fifteenth century, Austria and the surrounding territories
boasted outstanding scholars. In the succeeding period, the
pride of place was occupied by Prague. Hence came, to be
Rabbi in Cracow, the famous Rabbi Jacob Pollak (d. 1541),
the first important figure amongst Polish Jewish scholars.
His name is especially associated with the curious method
of Talmudic study which had originated in South Germany, and goes by the name of *pilpul*. This can only be
described as a species of mental gymnastics centering upon
the text of the Talmud. The method was futile, wasteful,
and from certain points of view, even pernicious. But the
minds of those trained in it became preternaturally sharpened, and as the process went on, generation after generation, it produced in Polish Jewry a standard of intelligence,

a mental adaptability, and a degree of acumen which has probably known no parallel.

The pilpulistic method was perfected by Shalom Shakna (1500-1559) of Lublin, one of the Chief Rabbis appointed over the Jews of Little Poland in 1541. His son-in-law, Moses Isserles of Cracow (1520-1572), was regarded as one of the outstanding Talmudists of his day, questions being addressed to him from every corner of the Jewish world. It was his annotations upon Joseph Caro's *Shulhan Arukh* which adapted that compendium of Jewish practice for the use of northern Jewry. An opposite tendency was represented by his contemporary and friend, Solomon Luria of Brest-Litovsk and subsequently of Ostrog (1510-1573), who reverted to the fountain-head of Jewish tradition, the Talmud, the obscurities of which he endeavored to elucidate in his classical *Sea of Solomon*. In subsequent generations, other scholars continued to maintain the tradition, and Poland became known as the home of the Talmud, just as Safed was that of the Zohar.

But the outstanding feature of Polish Jewish scholarship was not the prominence of its exponents so much as the level of excellence attained by the average pupil. Nowhere else was higher education so widely diffused or brought to such a pitch of perfection. No town lacked its *Yeshiba*, or Talmudic Academy; no household was without its students; and to maintain a learned son or son-in-law was the ambition of every father. This was the ideal in Polish Jewry in the sixteenth and seventeenth centuries, and it resulted in the training of an educated laity, such as even the Jewish world had perhaps never before seen.

XXV. LIFE IN THE GHETTO

1.   The canon of the Third Lateran Council of 1179, which forbade Jews and Christians to dwell together, was long enforced only sporadically. In most lands, the Jews continued to live where they pleased, and non-Jews had little compunction in having houses in the middle of the "Jewry." The places where there existed a formal Jewish quarter, enforced by law and rigidly shut off from the rest of the city, were in a small minority. Least of all was the regulation obeyed in Italy, under the eye of the Popes. Their actual example, so different from their precept, was at hand for all to follow. In 1516, however, the Venetian Republic ordered the segregation of the Jews of the city in a special quarter, formerly known as the *Ghetto Nuovo*, or New Foundry. A little later, the *Ghetto Vecchio,* or Old Foundry, was added to the district. Hence the term *Ghetto* spread throughout Italy, where the Jewish quarters, compulsorily established in the second half of the sixteenth century and in subsequent years, became known officially by this name.

In the south of France, the parallel institution was known as the *carrière des juifs*; in Germany and the adjacent territories as the *Judengasse* or *Judenstadt.* Despite the difference in nomenclature, nevertheless, the general system, whether in Italy, France, Germany, Poland, Bohemia, was everywhere similar; and it is worth the pains to examine, in greater details, this typical setting of European Jewish life and the conditions to which it gave rise.

It must not be imagined that the institution appeared to those who suffered by it in the same harsh light in which it does to us. In most cases, it is true, they fought fiercely against its establishment. But it soon became apparent that the Ghetto walls, though originally intended to keep the victims in, were no less useful in keeping their enemies out. It is significant that the gates were furnished in many cases with bolts on the inner side for use in emergency. Moreover, with an insight rare in the oppressed, the Jew realized that segregation, however humiliating it might be, tended to act as a powerful preservative of racial solidarity and culture. Thus we find the amazing paradox that, at certain places in Italy, an annual feast-day was instituted, and long observed, to celebrate the establishment of the Ghetto.

The entrance was through a low archway, provided with massive doors. It was under the custody of Christian gate-keepers, paid at the expense of their victims. In larger cities, there was a second entrance, similarly guarded, at the far end; but, though this provision was occasionally neglected, it was expressly forbidden to have more than two entrances. After nightfall, it was considered a serious crime for any Jew to be found outside the Ghetto, or any Christian within it. This latter precaution was actuated by regard for the purity of race as well as of belief; for intercourse between adherents of the two faiths was considered to be little less serious than incest, and was punished as such. The Ghetto gates were similarly kept closed, and its inhabitants utterly segregated, on the major solemnities of the Christian year, until the recital of Mass.

The hardship was not, however, so great as might be imagined. True, in some places, the Jewish quarter consisted of no more than a single narrow lane or courtyard. In many cases, however, in Rome, Venice, Lublin, or Prague, a whole labyrinth of streets and alleys was to be found, constituting a real town within a town. The street nomenclature within these ancient quarters still gives testimony to the nature of the life which once pulsated within them, as essentially Jewish as the inhabitants themselves.

In Frankfort, each house had its own sign, from which the families living in it often took their surnames; and the Rothschilds, the Adlers, and the Schiffs have made familiar, throughout Western civilization, nomenclature derived from the sign of the Red Shield, and the Eagle, and the Ship, in that famous *Judengasse*, the greatest in all Germany.

One obvious difference would immediately strike the visitor, the greatly superior height of the houses. The extent of the Jewish quarter was rarely increased, and the only expedient to accommodate the rapidly growing population (the Jew was notoriously prolific, and his standard of living relatively high) was to anticipate that adopted centuries later, under the most modern circumstances, in America. Instead of the lateral expansion forbidden to him, he sought relief in a vertical direction, by the addition of story upon story to the already rickety buildings. From a distance, indeed, it seemed sometimes as though the Jewish quarter of the city, towering high above the rest, was

actually constructed on rising ground. But the construc-
tions were often more audacious than solid: and it not
infrequently happened that they collapsed under some
unusual strain, converting the celebration of a marriage or
a betrothal into an occasion for general mourning. Similarly,
outbreaks of fire were peculiarly dangerous in the Ghetto,
utter destruction sometimes taking place before help could
be brought from outside; and Frankfort, Nikolsburg, and
Verona, long remembered conflagrations which were, in
their way, no less disastrous, though on a smaller scale,
than the Great Fire of London itself.

The overcrowding led to another important development.
The Jew, prohibited by law from owning real estate, was
unable to purchase his house outright even in the Ghetto.
There was thus no check upon the rapacity of the Gentile
landlord, and no security for the tenant, who would be
ejected without notice immediately a higher rental was
offered. The solution of this difficulty was found in an
adaptation of the ancient Jewish law of *Hazakah,* or pro-
prietary right. This established, under the most severe social
and religious sanctions, a sort of tenant-right in favor of
the actual occupant, which secured him against overbid-
ding on the one hand, and hence against exploitation on
the other. Nobody was permitted, under any circumstances,
to bring about the expropriation of the lessee, or to offer
a higher rental than that actually paid. Occupation thus
became almost equivalent to proprietorship. The property-
right could be disposed of by gift or by purchase, devolved
by heredity from father to son, and was frequently included
in the dowry of a daughter; but, as long as the rent was

paid, tenure was safe. Thus *juz gazaga* (as, with a curious hybrid form, it was termed in Italy) was recognized, in many cases, even by the civil authorities. It is a striking instance of the innate adaptability of the Jewish law to the most diverse circumstances, as well as a remarkable anticipation of expedients resorted to in modern days in the urban centers of contemporary Europe and America.

2. The Ghetto walls were not considered in themselves a sufficient guarantee to prevent the contamination of the faithful by the leaven of Jewish unbelief. They were reinforced by the Jewish badge: first imposed by the Lateran Council of 1215, but consistently enforced only from the sixteenth century. In Italy, at this period, it invariably took the form of a hat of distinctive color—yellow or red. In Germany, the badge retained the primitive form of a yellow circle, which had to be affixed to the outer garment above the heart. The heaviest penalties were enforced against those who dared to stir abroad from the Ghetto without their distinctive mark; sometimes, indeed, it had to be worn even within it. Only in the case of those who were setting out on the perils of a long journey were the regulations relaxed. We know what a wave of lamentation and of protest was originally aroused by this supreme indignity, which put Jews on the same footing as prostitutes, and how sedulously individuals exerted themselves to be released from its provisions. But, ultimately, it appears to have become a point of pride; and the ultraconservative continued to wear it, as the distinctive Jewish garb, even when its enforcement had fallen into desuetude.

Frequently, the badge of shame was the Jew's only touch of color. Not that he was averse to gaudy and even extravagant clothing. He was prone, indeed, to err in the reverse direction, especially where his women-folk were concerned. Since this trait was considered a direct incentive to Gentile cupidity, if not enmity, there was enacted in almost every place a whole series of sumptuary laws, which regulated the costume of the Jew from his headwear down to his shoe-buckles, and limited, above all, the amount of jewelry which might be worn. Similar restrictions governed private festivities, such as those which took place in honor of a marriage, a circumcision, or a betrothal, stipulating the sort of sweetmeats which might be handed round, the number of the guests, the nature of the various courses, and even the gifts which might be presented by the bridegroom to his bride.

There was hardly any limit to the tale of indignities to which the Jew was subjected, especially in the Papal States. Many famous communities, such as that of Venice, existed down to the eighteenth century on a precarious tenure under an agreement lasting for only a short period of years, continually modified and sometimes not renewed. Each year, the leaders of the down-trodden *Universita degli Ebrei* of Rome had to pay homage to the Pope by the presentation of a Scroll of the Law, which the Vicar of God would return contemptuously over his left shoulder, with a derogatory remark. Contributions were exacted for the upkeep of the House of Converts, to which their children might be snatched away for baptism at any moment, under the flimsiest pretext: the reported wish of a renegade relative, or a mock ceremony performed with ditch water by a superstitious nurse or a drunken ruffian. From the seventeenth century, outrages of this sort became more and more common, owing to the spread of the superstition that eternal felicity would be assured to any person who secured the baptism of a single Jew. Small wonder that Jews were forbidden under severest penalties from approaching the House, lest they should tamper with the newly-imposed faith of the inmates.

To prevent any semblance of authority, the Jew was forbidden to ride in a carriage, or to employ a Christian servant, or even have some kindly neighbor perform for him the service of kindling a fire upon the Sabbath day. Throughout Germany the Jews, like cattle, had to pay a special toll or *Leibzoll,* when they crossed the frontiers of the innumerable petty states, or entered any city. From place after place they were excluded, or admitted only during the day. When they appeared in the law-courts, the oath had to be taken *more judaico,* according to a special, degrading formula, and to the accompaniment of an obnoxious ceremonial. War was even waged upon their books which were confiscated, censored, or burned, without compunction. In a large part of Italy, indeed, the possession of the Talmud was a criminal offense, and early specimens of Hebrew printing are frequently disfigured by unsightly expurgations made by some friar better endowed with zeal than with a sense of proportion. During the whole of Eastertide, from Holy Thursday onward, the gates of the Ghetto were kept rigorously closed, and no Jew dared to show his face in the streets. Each year, at the Carnival

season, especially fattened Jews, stripped almost naked, had
to run a race down the Corso at Rome for the delight of
the populace—a privilege shared with the women of the
town. At the slightest pretext, the race was declared null,
and had to be repeated on another day. This supreme indignity was abolished only in 1668, though the special
tribute instituted to compensate for it continued to be paid
for nearly two hundred years after. Worst of all (in obedience to Nicholas III's Bull of 1278, confirmed by Gregory
VIII in 1577 and 1584), the Jews were forced at regular
intervals to attend conversionist sermons, at which their
ears were examined lest they should have been plugged
with cotton wool, and officials armed with canes effectively
prevented the obvious expedient of slumber.

It was Germany, however, which, with ruthless logic
combined with fiendish ingenuity, brought the repression
implicit in the Ghetto system to its climax. Up to a certain
point, Jews might be useful to the city or the state; but,
beyond this, their presence was superfluous, and hence resented. Official license of residence was generally given for
a specified number of households, which might not be
exceeded on any pretext. By natural process, the population tended to grow. Births could not be controlled by any
legal enactment. But weddings could, and the number of
families kept down by this means. In many places, therefore, rigorous control was established over Jewish marriages. Only the eldest child of the family was allowed to
take himself a wife and to build up his own home: or else
marriage permits were issued in strict proportion to the
number of deaths. In any case, no Jew was allowed to

marry without official license. Thus, the most sacred and most fundamental right of human beings was denied to that section of the human race which perhaps valued it most. South of the Alps, this infamous system never applied: but, to the north, it retained its force in many parts, long after the Ghetto itself had passed away.

The liberal professions were closed to the Jews (though, in the happy island of Corfu, they were permitted to engage in Law). So was almost every other occupation and handicraft. They were not allowed to sell new commodities of any sort; though they were grudgingly permitted to deal in second-hand wares, this becoming a typical occupation down to our own days. It is not surprising, under the circumstances, that they had recourse to ingenious subterfuges, such as introducing an insignificant tear into a perfectly new article of clothing, so as to render it technically second-hand. To enter the textile, or any other industry, was to invite protest from rivals, generally followed by suppression by the government. It was only in tailoring and shoe-making that they were generally permitted to engage without interference: though they were not allowed to sell their wares direct to the consumer. Not being allowed to open shops outside their own quarter, they were driven into peddling, which, in time, they almost came to monopolize. The Jewish itinerant huckster, pack on back, was an integral feature in the rural scene, by the eighteenth century, all over Europe not excepting the remotest English counties.

It was not possible to exclude the Jews, with their natural acumen and their wide-spread foreign connections, from trade in jewelry and precious stones; and in many places they exercised a virtual monopoly in this. Moneylending and pawnbroking, like dealing in second-hand commodities, was imposed on them from above. In many Italian cities especially (Venice was an outstanding example), they were under the legal obligation to maintain establishments for this purpose, for the benefit of the poor of the city, as an essential condition of the tolerance which they received. In those places where the restrictions were less strenuously enforced, economic life was organized much as it was among the Gentile population. From early times there were at Prague, for example, four Jewish guilds—those of the butchers, goldsmiths, tailors, and shoemakers. In the larger cities of Poland (as, indeed, had been the case in ancient Alexandria or Jerusalem) each guild or occupation had its own synagogue; and the visitor to Lublin may still inspect those formerly maintained by the coppersmiths, tailors, clerks, and porters.

Notwithstanding all restrictions, the profession of medicine continued to be followed, as in all former and subsequent ages, with especial enthusiasm. Frequently it was combined with the Rabbinate: indeed, it was customary for young men to combine their medical studies at the University of Padua with attendance at the famous Talmudical academy of that city. Thither flowed needy students, athirst for knowledge, from all the teeming Jewries of Poland—to end, in some cases, as body-physician to the Grand Vizier at Constantinople. The Jewish doctor was not indeed permitted to practice his art on the person of true believers. Nevertheless, in time of emergency the eye of faith was sometimes dimmed. Crowned heads and prelates continued to consult their convenience, rather than canon law, when they appointed their medical attendants: and the yellow hat of the Hebrew practitioner was not too closely scanned as he entered the house of some dying patrician, or was hurriedly escorted over the threshold of the Vatican itself.

3. The Ghetto constituted in the fullest sense an *imperium in imperio*. It was only in his collective capacity that the Jew had any connection with the government, which barely recognized his existence as an individual. The community (*Judengemeinschaft, università degli ebrei*) represented the inhabitants of the Ghetto in their collective capacity: its duly appointed delegates (*massari, baylons,* or *Parnassim,* as they were variously called) being entitled to act for it juridically and politically. It must not be imagined that the organization was essentially democratic. At its head, by the side of the wardens, stood a small administrative council. This was generally elected by a larger body, comprising all the major contributors to communal taxation, who formed a secondary council for the decision of important business. The proletariat, under this system, had no voice whatsoever in the internal regulation of communal affairs. In the south of France, and other places under strong Spanish influence, the community (other than paupers) was divided into three sections according to their wealth, each having an equal voice in the administration, a system which obviously gave an utterly disproportionate voice to the moneyed classes.

Upon the communal government, as thus constituted, devolved the duty of raising the heavy taxation which was exacted by the government year by year from the whole body of the Jews. Added to this were the internal expenses of the community as a whole—the maintenance of the synagogue, the relief of the poor, the upkeep of the burial-ground, and the payment of the various officials. The latter included not merely those intimately connected with religious life, such as the Rabbi, at last become a salaried official, but also such functionaries as the secretary, the beadle, the *Schulklopfer,* who roused the faithful for service, the *shochet* or slaughterer, the postman, and the scavenger. In addition, there had to be found the salary of the gate-keepers of the Ghetto, in whose appointment the Jews had no voice, and with whose service they would gladly have dispensed.

The heavy sums necessary for all these expenses were raised by a graduated tax on capital or on income, sometimes on both. In a narrow circle, in which each man was not only the other's neighbor but also his business competitor, strict inquiry was an obvious impossibility; and, in the main, the assessment was left to the individual conscience. The conditions governing the system, which differed greatly from land to land, and from city to city, were frequently printed, especially in Italy, for the better guidance of the contributors. A special sermon, stressing the needs of the community and the obloquy of evasion, was in some places prescribed as an additional encouragement. The only sanction in case of disobedience or fraudulence was excommunication. Under the circumstances of Ghetto life, this spiritual and social penalty held fears greater than any physical punishment could have done, and was seldom ineffective. Nevertheless, it was sometimes found impossible to raise the disproportionately heavy sums imposed; and in the eighteenth century more than one community, including Rome itself, was reduced to actual bankruptcy.

Largely in consequence of its fiscal autonomy, the governing body of the community became omnipotent within the walls of the Ghetto. To it, all edicts were entrusted for execution; on it devolved the maintenance of order and the responsibility for the good conduct of the individuals. On the other hand, it was empowered to adjudicate in matters of dispute: and it was in a position to appeal to the government to get its wishes carried out, to suppress opposition, or to secure the exclusion of unwelcome strangers. It regulated, in a word, the whole of the internal life of the Ghetto, occasionally over-riding the Rabbi himself. In Prague, the Jewish court, known as the *Meisterschaftsgericht,* was especially strongly organized, enjoying the fullest governmental authority, and it even had its own prison to punish the recalcitrant and to enforce its sentences. Prague, too, had its own Jewish town-hall, or *Rathhaus,* erected by the famous philanthropist, Mordecai Meisel, at the beginning of the seventeenth century; with its clock-tower and the famous clock, the dial of which bore Hebrew instead of Roman lettering. In this, perhaps, the Bohemian capital was unusually fortunate. But most large Ghettos had their communal offices, their bathing-establishments, their hospitals, and their inns—all, in fact, that a self-contained township could require.

4.   The center of the Ghetto life was, of course, the synagogue. Externally, this was necessarily plain and unpretentious to a degree. Not only was there the fear of exciting Gentile cupidity, but even as late as the eighteenth century, there was constant surveillance to see that the Jewish place of worship was not enlarged beyond its earlier limits, or exceeded neighboring Christian churches in height. In the Papal States, it was forbidden to have more than one synagogue in each town—a provision which the community of Rome ingeniously evaded by constructing five under one roof to accommodate the various traditional "rites", Roman, Sicilian, Castilian, and the rest. Universally, the synagogue was known as the "school—*schul* in Germany, *scuola* in Italy, *escolo* in the south of France. As a matter of fact, this was originally applied to the Jewish *community* (much as we speak of a "school" of porpoises, or of the "Saxon School" at Rome), being used with reference to the *building* only at a later date. The application is nevertheless symptomatic of the role of the synagogue in Jewish life as a center, not only of worship, but also of study.

Though the religious tradition was everywhere fundamentally the same, each community in the course of time developed its own peculiarities. There were communities in the north of Italy which preserved the old French rite brought across the Alps by fugitives in the fourteenth century, and there was at least one in the south of Germany which maintained the Roman rite introduced by Italian merchants in the sixteenth. Many a place had its own special fasts, in commemoration of some local disaster, or its special *Purim* (with its record, sometimes, written in imitation of the biblical book of Esther) to record the deliverance of the community from a modern Haman. Thus, at Frankfort, they still celebrate, year by year, the anniversary of the fall of the demagogue Vincent Fettmilch, who drove them out of the town after a brutal attack in 1616, and at Padua they kept up till recently the *Purim del Fuoco* in thankfulness at their escape from a conflagration in 1795.

By the side of the synagogue—before it almost, in the consideration in which it was held—came the school itself. This was always given pride of place in the Jewish scheme of life: and, in this respect, the Jew of the Ghetto period did not fall short of the ancient ideals of his race. The smallest place had its educational institutions, frequently under the charge of some pious association formed for the express purpose. A community of less than a thousand souls would maintain a Free School which could serve as a model for today. All expenses were defrayed by voluntary contributions, nothing being expected from the parents. The elements of the vernacular were taught, as well as of Hebrew. The number of teachers, and the size of the classes, were carefully regulated. Most astonishing of all, the poorer pupils actually received free meals, and there was a distribution of boots and clothing each year at the beginning of the winter. At some places, there were special schools for girls. The universality of education is barely equalled in any country of the Western world even at the present time.

Besides education, no conceivable species of well-doing

escaped the care of one or the other of the many pious fraternities which abounded in the Ghetto, for the Jewish conception of religion was broad enough to embrace almost every sphere of social life. There were numbers of associations with purely spiritual objects—fasting and confession and midnight prayer, in order to avert the Divine wrath, and to hasten the coming of the Redeemer. Alongside these were others for study and adult education and charitable works. There was an association to help women in childbed, and an association to admit male babies into the Covenant of Abraham. Brides were dowered by one fraternity, and prisoners solaced by another. In the great maritime ports, Venice, Leghorn, Hamburg, and the rest, there were special bodies which saw to the ransoming of Jewish travelers captured and sold into slavery by the Knights of Malta or the Barbary Corsairs. At every stage of want or necessity, the unfortunate could confidently expect succor from his neighbors, in one capacity or another. When a man fell ill, the fraternity for visiting the sick came to comfort him; when he died, one fraternity looked after the mourners, while another saw to his burial. Only in the Papal States were these activities curtailed, since there it was forbidden to escort the dead to their last resting place with the customary dirges, or to erect any sort of memorial over their graves.

5.   Yet these manifold religious and communal activities did not monopolize the Ghetto scene. Within that little world there was a Jewish society, with its own life, its own interests, its own diversions. There were the same

petty enmities and the same jealousies to be found as in any other human circle, the same romances, the same comedies, the same tragedies of existence. Even a species of foreign intercourse was afforded by the hostelry which existed for the entertainment of strangers; though the general spirit of hospitality which prevailed, particularly when some wandering scholar appeared, must have jeopardized its prosperity.

In many ways, the life was as characteristically Italian, or German, or French, as that of the great world outside. The artistic spirit of the country penetrated the Ghetto to a marked degree. The synagogues were constructed by the most eminent architects of their day, and notwithstanding their unpretentious exteriors, no pains were spared to make them places of aesthetic inspiration. Objects of ceremonial use were elaborately chased, not always by Jewish artists. The brocades hung before the ark and the mantles for the Scrolls of the Law, embroidered by the matrons with their own hands in the long winter evenings, were of the finest. The most skillful silversmiths were employed to manufacture the trappings for the Scrolls and the lamps which swung from the roof. The Sabbath lamp which was kindled in every home on Friday evening was often of precious metal. The craft of the illuminator was kept alive in the Ghetto long after it had begun to decay in the outside world. The *Haggadah* liturgy for the eve of Passover was written and illustrated by hand many centuries after the invention of printing: and its tradition was continued in woodcuts and copper-plate engravings for those who could not afford greater luxury. The scroll of Esther was similarly favored, and the artistic abilities of the Ghetto were lavished upon representations of the ten sons of Haman strung up on the gallows, in illustration of the enthralling story. In Italy, especially, the marriage contract was richly illuminated, sometimes with an excess of ornament.

It was characteristic of the innate Jewish conservatism that in many countries (Poland and Turkey are outstanding examples) the language spoken by the Jews among themselves was a foreign one, introduced by the original refugees from Germany on the one hand, or from Spain on the other. Even where the vernacular was in everyday use the admixture of tongues, inevitable among Jews, naturally resulted in borrowing occasional words in common parlance from one language or another, especially from Hebrew. To this were added, in consequence of close inbreeding, certain peculiarities of pronunciation and expression. The result was the creation of a number of characteristic Jewish dialects. In addition to the familiar Judaeo-German, and Judaeo-Spanish, there were also Judaeo-Italian, and, in the south of France, Judaeo-Provençal. All these were frequently, in the first two cases, almost invariably written, and even printed, in Hebrew characters. In the memoirs of an educated German Jewess of the seventeenth century, one finds an admixture of nearly thirty per cent pure Hebrew, and the proportion is not exceptionally high. The same hybrid dialect would be employed from time to time, with an even higher smattering of the Holy tongue, in recording communal business, and drawing up new regulations. There was a vast popular literature, ballads, translations, homilies, legal hand-books, for the women and others whose attainments were unequal to the full sublimities of traditional lore.

Social life was ample. The Purim season, each year, saw buffoonery and masquerades, and sometimes a fair. The Ghetto of Prague, on this occasion, would be thronged with hundreds of girls in festive garb, who were entertained in whatever house they entered. Even the students allowed themselves some relaxation, and elected a Lord of Misrule, who flouted the Rabbi himself. The elaboration of the story of Esther and Mordecai gave rise to what was known as the *Purimspiel*, developing into a rudimentary drama. Itinerant play-actors went from place to place giving representations of this, or of scenes from the lives of the Patriarchs. Weddings and banquets were enlivened by professional jesters (*Schalksnarren* in Germany), the broadness of whose witticisms sometimes scandalized devout opinion. There were musical societies, which did not always concentrate their attention on synagogal harmony. Births, marriages, and other notable occasions would be saluted in a flood of verses. The pageants and processions which the Jews arranged in celebration of a royal visit or some similar event were famous. The wealthy ladies of the Ghetto had their salons, and the wealthy householders their private courses of study, to which they invited their friends. Dancing, though eyed askance by the more pious elements, was regarded on the more festive occasions of the religious year, at least, as a meritorious duty: and in Italy, the teaching of that art was long regarded as one of the duties of a Hebrew tutor. Jewish instrumentalists, whose services were called upon more especially on the occasion of weddings, enjoyed no small fame in the outside world.

6.   The Ghetto was thus a microcosm which faithfully reflected every aspect of the outside world, while giving it a pronounced Jewish tone. Some observers, indeed, have attempted to vindicate it as an institution, pointing to all that it achieved for the development and the preservation of the essential Jewish standards of life. Some professional lauders of that which is past profess even to look back on it with regret, as a lost bulwark against assimilation. To a certain extent, this is true. Yet there is another side of the question. One tends to judge the Ghetto too much from its formative period, when the traditions of an ampler and freer life were still strong, and before the policy of exclusion had become absolutely effective. In its later stages, Ghetto life was more restricted, more monotonous, and more dreary. Persons of the highest intellectual ability were condemned to pass the whole of their lives in self-contained communities, seldom numbering more than a couple of thousand souls all told, and cut off so far as was humanly possible from all intercourse with the outside world. One must imagine such communities, too, as living under the worst possible physical conditions, huddled up, indescribably over-crowded, in insalubrious quarters in the heart of great cities, egress from which, excepting between sunrise and sunset, was forbidden by law.

The results were what might have been imagined. The circle of human interests was intolerably confined. Life became indescribably petty. There was a superlative degree of

inbreeding, both physical, social, and intellectual. Keen in-
telligences were wasted by dealing with trivial themes.
That which was meant for mankind was confined to a
single bleak street. The intellectual fecundity which can result only from the constant fertilization and cross-fertiliza-
tion of human intercourse became impossible. By the time
that the Ghetto had been in existence for a couple of centuries, it was possible to see the result. Physically, the type
of Jew had degenerated. He had lost inches off his stature;
he had acquired a perpetual stoop; he had become timor-
ous and in many cases neurotic. Degrading occupations,
originally imposed by law, such as money-lending and
dealing in old clothes, became a second nature, hard to
throw off. His sense of solidarity with his fellow-Jews had
become fantastically exaggerated, and was accompanied in
many cases by a sense of grievance against the Gentile who
was responsible for his lot. As a counterblast to the attempt
of the authorities, and indeed of the whole world, to re-
press him, the Jew was driven to evasion; and sharp practices, at one time understandable, retained their hold in
some cases when the original justification had passed.

The economic consequences were no less deplorable. Pauperization rapidly increased, the systematic blocking of opportunity making recovery almost out of the question. The
well-to-do emigrated to places where life was more ample,
leaving behind them as a burden on their fellows those
least qualified to fight the battle of existence. During the
course of the eighteenth century, beggars became a social
menace. In Germany they are reckoned to have numbered
one-tenth of the whole population; while in certain places

in Italy one person out of three was in receipt of public relief in one form or another.

Even from the Jewish point of view, he had degenerated.
He had begun to lose his sense of proportion. Every item
in the traditional scheme of life was now sacrosanct, and
had attained equal importance in his eyes. The most trivial
tradition was of equal weight with the most fundamental
ethical teaching. Superstitions were on the increase, and
in some cases acquired semi-religious sanction. Simultaneously, Hebrew scholarship was on the downward grade.
The study of the ancient texts became more and more
mechanical, so that the production of outstanding scholars
even in the purely rabbinic field became increasingly rare.
After two centuries of Ghetto life, the institution appeared
to be doing its work, and the repression of the Jew was
nearly complete.

XXVI. THE DAWN OF LIBERTY

1.   The heroic period of European history which was
ushered in by the Renaissance saw the Jew (as has been
shown in preceding chapters) at a universal disadvantage.
There was one region only where Jews were in a position
of equality with the general population. This was the Iberian Peninsula. Since the close of the fifteenth century, the
open practice of Judaism in Spain and Portugal had been
an offense punishable by death. The Inquisition had been
kept busy, endeavoring to root out this most unspeakable
of crimes. At frequent intervals, it staged Acts of Faith, or
autos-da-fé, which counted amongst the most magnificent
spectacles which contemporary Europe could show. In
these, before the eyes of thousands who had streamed in
from the surrounding countryside, condign punishment
would be inflicted upon harmless individuals whose loyalty
to the Holy Catholic Faith was suspected. In the vast majority of cases, the victims were the so-called Marranos, descendants of Jews who, in spite of all dangers, remained
faithful in the secrecy of their homes to the tenets and, so
far as was possible, to the practices of their old faith.

Down to the very last days of the Spanish and Portuguese Inquisitions, at the close of the eighteenth century,
crypto-Jews continue to provide a very high proportion of
the victims. Thereafter, the record becomes blurred and
indistinct. However, in our own days, a traveler in the

remote hill-country in the north of Portugal was amazed to discover a number of Marrano communities, still paying lip-service to Christianity while faithful at heart to Judaism; and one of the most romantic episodes of recent history has been the movement which has sprung up among them for reidentification with the people and the creed from which they were so ruthlessly torn away four and a half centuries ago.

Judaism, then, however much it was proscribed and whatever dangers were inherent in its practice, was a very real force in the Peninsula. It was notorious that a very large proportion of those descended from Jews adhered at heart to the faith of their fathers. They were to be found in every conceivable walk of life, from beggars to statesmen, from playwrights to revenue farmers, from cobblers to explorers. They almost controlled Portuguese commerce. They established banking-establishments of European influence and reputation. The faculties of the universities were crammed with persons of Jewish blood, who were vaunted as the greatest intellectual luminaries of Portugal until the time came to haul them to the stake. Half of the most illustrious physicians of the day were Marranos. They frequently entered, for security's sake, it was believed, into the Church, in which some of them attained high rank.

Thus, while in all the rest of the world the Jew was considered an inferior being, conditions in Spain and Portugal were different. No declared Jew was indeed admitted in the country. But there was a vast body of persons known to be Jewish at heart, but against whom no definite evidence

was forthcoming, who were on terms of perfect equality
with the rest of the population. They spoke the same
language. They followed the same occupations. They
lived in the same quarter. They dressed in the same
fashion. Their way of life was outwardly identical, down
to the least detail. They bore the high-sounding Gothic
names which their ancestors had assumed at baptism. In
the very fullest sense of the word, they were Spaniards,
or Portuguese, marked off from the rest of the population
only by virtue of their descent and of their religious beliefs.

2. Ever since the close of the fifteenth century there
had been a constant stream of emigration from the Peninsula on the part of the New Christians, eager to reach
some spot where they might profess their ancestral religion
in public. Their objects, indeed, were notorious, and expatriation on their part was categorically forbidden by law.
Yet evasion was always possible either by flight or on the
plea of urgent business abroad, or, more characteristically
still, on the pretext of pilgrimage to Rome. Accordingly,
almost from the moment of the mass baptisms in Spain,
the Mediterranean ports became filled with Marrano refugees who had fled in order to return to Judaism. With the
Forced Conversion in Portugal, the tide became increasingly
strong. Throughout Turkey, North Africa, and Italy, the
existing congregations became reinforced by Portuguese refugees: often men of learning and deep piety who had
been involved, despite themselves, in the disaster of 1497.
At some places, indeed, the Portuguese Marranos arrived
in such large numbers as to be able to found their own

congregations by the side of those already in existence.

A part of greater importance in history was played by that section who turned their steps in the opposite direction. The prosperity of the Mediterranean world, as a matter of fact, was on the wane. America had been discovered. The tide of commerce, navigation, of wealth, and of Empire, was transferred to the Northern Seas. The position of Spain and Portugal in world commerce at this time was vital, in view of the fact that both the new continent in the far West, and the new routes to the treasure houses of the East, had been discovered through their efforts—assisted, it may be added, by the scientific skill and the financial enterprise of their Jewish subjects. Every important mercantile center of northern Europe contained, therefore, at this time a Spanish and Portuguese trading colony of greater or less importance, in which the "New Christians" occupied a commanding position. The ultimate history of these varied. Some faded away or were absorbed in the surrounding population. Others maintained a dual existence for many generations. Others, again, who had the good fortune to discover themselves in a more tolerant environment (generally under the rule of one of the vigorous Protestant powers of the North), were able to cut short the intervening period, and to organize themselves into open and undisguised Jewish communities without great loss of time.

The most important of these colonies was that in the Low Countries. Ever since the early part of the sixteenth century, Marrano settlers had made their way in small numbers to Antwerp, the most important seaport in the north of Europe, at this time under Spanish rule. The revolt of the Netherlands put an end to its predominance, its commercial supremacy being usurped by Amsterdam. This city became henceforth the principal Marrano place of refuge.

An ancient legend, which need not be discounted in all its details, gives a most romantic origin for the Amsterdam community. In the year 1593, we are told, a brother and sister, Manuel Lopez Pereira and Maria Nunez, whose parents had suffered from the persecutions of the Inquisition, set sail from Portugal with a large party of Marranos, in the hope of finding some haven of security. The vessel was captured on its journey by an English ship, and brought into port. An English noble, fascinated by Maria's rare beauty, solicited her hand. Queen Elizabeth, hearing the story, expressed a desire to see the prisoner. Captivated by her loveliness, she drove with her about London, and gave orders for the vessel and all its passengers to be set at liberty. In spite of this, Maria would not accept the tempting offer which she had received. "Leaving all the pomp of England for the sake of Judaism" (as the old record puts it), she pursued her way to Amsterdam with her companions. Here, in 1598, they were joined by her mother and other members of the family.

The activities of these recent arrivals from the Peninsula, titularly Christians as they were, could not escape attention for long. It seemed obvious that they were holding Catholic services, at that time forbidden, and perhaps even conspiring against the newly-established government. On the Day of Atonement, the unwonted attendance resulted in drastic steps being taken. The whole party was arrested, and dragged off for examination. They were as yet entirely ignorant of Dutch, and their difficulty in expressing themselves increased the suspicions against them. However, one of the leaders of the little group happened to be familiar with Latin, and had the inspiration of explaining himself in that language. He made it clear that the assembly was not one of Papists, but of followers of a religion persecuted by the Inquisition even more ferociously than Protestantism: and he pointed out the great advantages which might accrue to the city if the New Christians of the Peninsula were encouraged to establish themselves in it. His appeal, either to humanity or to interest, was convincing. The prisoners were released forthwith; the position of the refugees was regularized; and the colony grew with astonishing rapidity, throwing out offshoots to The Hague, Rotterdam, and elsewhere.

Meanwhile, a similar succession of events had been taking place in Hamburg, where Portuguese Marranos were to be found in small numbers from the closing years of the sixteenth century. They remained, however, titular Catholics, and thus doubly aroused the ire of the Protestant population. A petition was accordingly presented to the Senate to expel these strangers from the city. The Lutheran academies at Frankfort and Jena, appealed to for their opinion, recommended that the Jews be received, under certain restrictions, in order that they might be won over to the love of the Gospel. In consequence, in 1612, the Senate formally authorized the Jewish settlement.

The third great center of commerce in Western Europe, and hence of Marrano settlement, was London. A colony of secret Jews which had established itself here, had been broken up as early as the reign of Henry VIII. Another was formed under Queen Elizabeth. In 1609, the Portuguese merchants in London who were suspected of Judaizing, were expelled from the country, and the venture came to an end. Nevertheless, by slow degrees, new settlers arrived to take the place of the old ones. By the period of the establishment of the Protectorate, a little colony existed once more in London, with one or two veritable merchant-princes at its head.

The popular attitude towards them had meanwhile begun to alter. The Puritan mind regarded the Jews with favor as the ancient people of God. The more sanguine hoped, moreover, that the newly-purified forms of Christianity would convince them of the truth of the Gospel, where the Church of Rome had so miserably failed. Cromwell, himself, on the other hand, had the insight to realize the commercial importance of the Marrano merchants, whose information he had found invaluable in political matters, and whom he thought an ideal instrument for fostering English trade.

There was living in Holland at this time a mystically-minded Rabbi of Marrano birth, Menasseh ben Israel (1604-1657), whose fecund, shallow, fertile pen had won him an unexampled reputation in the Christian world. Prolonged meditation had convinced him that the completion of the Diaspora, by the introduction of the Jews into England, was a necessary preliminary to the great Messianic deliverance to which all humanity looked forward. It was with him that Cromwell opened up conversations. After some time, Menasseh was invited to London to conduct negotiations personally; and a great conference of statesmen, lawyers, and theologians was convened at Whitehall at the end of 1655 to discuss the matter in all its aspects. The deliberations, indeed, were inconclusive: but the sympathy of the government was sufficiently obvious for the London Marranos to throw off the mask. Their position was still highly irregular. The Resettlement had not been authorized: it had been connived at. It was a typical English compromise, inconsistent, illogical, but unexpectedly satisfactory as a working arrangement.*

At the same time, Marrano settlements had been formed in several of the French seaports, notably Bordeaux and Bayonne. The country was Catholic, and officially in sympathy with the policy followed in Spain and Portugal. Declared Jews were, indeed, unable to settle there. Marranos, on the other hand, might immigrate without interference, so long as they continued to call themselves Christians; and there was no over-meticulous supervision of their conduct. It was about 1730 that the hollow formality which had prevailed for two centuries was abandoned, and the New Christians of southern France were at last officially recognized as Jews. Closely connected with these colonies on the Atlantic seaboard were the Marrano communities encouraged by the Grand Dukes of Tuscany in the Free Ports of Pisa and Leghorn, the only places in Italy where the Ghetto system was never introduced, and

* It has recently been discovered that the decision of the Council of State on June 25th, 1656, authorizing the establishment of a Synagogue in London, had mysteriously been hacked out of the records, presumably by some enemy of the Jews.

where the Jew was allowed to attain the proper stature of
a man. Similarly in the overseas possessions of Holland
and England, particularly in the West Indian islands, a
little nexus of small communities grew up.

3.   It was to these places, above all, that the tide of
the Marrano migration was directed from the beginning of
the seventeenth century. Hardly any rank or calling was
left unrepresented. There were scholars, professors, authors,
priests, friars, physicians, manufacturers, merchants, soldiers, poets, statesmen. A number of them were raised to
the nobility, while the Spanish and Portuguese sovereigns
did not scruple to have themselves represented in the Low
Countries or at Hamburg by declared infidels. The members of the Marrano Diaspora were thus, in a very real
sense, the first modern Jews.

The importance of these settlements, with their offshoots
as far afield as India and America, was extraordinarily significant from every point of view. In the economic sphere
they played a vital part. From the beginning of the seventeenth century they formed a commercial nexus which
has few parallels in history. They controlled a good part
of the commerce of Western Europe. Trade in coral, sugar,
tobacco, and similar colonial commodities rested largely in
their hands. From the middle of the seventeenth century,
Jews of Spanish and Portuguese origin were prominent
figures on every important Exchange. They were partly
instrumental in the establishment of the great national
banks. The transference of the center of the world's commerce during this period from southern to northern Europe

is not the least important of the achievements which the Inquisition helped to bring about.

In Jewish life, similarly, the influence of the Marranos was very marked. Those who went to join existing settlements naturally became assimilated in all things to the condition of those whom they found there. But the pioneers who came to fresh countries, and founded their own communities, were in a different position, and could be treated on their own merits. They had been accepted, in the first instance, as foreigners. They could not very well be excluded subsequently because they turned out to be not Papists, but Jews. It would have been ridiculous to create a Ghetto in order to segregate persons whose society was sought and whose opinion was valued by the wisest and noblest in the land, or to distinguish, by a badge of shame, men who were admittedly the leaders of the intellectual and commercial world of their day. To admit them to full citizenship, indeed, was hardly to be thought of. But whereas hitherto such privileges as the Jews enjoyed merely qualified an utter servitude, such restrictions as now persisted were the exceptions which proved the rule of complete liberty. The circumstance of the Marrano settlement is thus the key to the remarkable paradox that those European lands, such as England and Holland, where conditions had till now been most adverse, and where exclusion had been rigid, were the first to treat the Jew with real tolerance.

On the heels of the Marranos came Jews from other countries, less attractive superficially, who automatically enjoyed the privileges which their polished forerunners

had gained. Almost immediately after the arrival of the
Marranos to Amsterdam, a German influx began; and,
before the middle of the seventeenth century, a congregation was formally organized. This rapidly established offshoots in the other important cities of the United Provinces
and soon attained an unquestionable supremacy in Dutch
Jewry in point of numbers, if not of wealth. Similarly, in
London, the establishment of an "Ashkenazic" community
dates from the last decade to the seventeenth century, from
which date its increase was phenomenally rapid. It was
thus through the Marranos that Western Europe became
opened up to Jewish migration, and that Jewish communities of a new type emerged to serve as a nucleus and as a
model in the new age which was about to dawn.

4.   Eastern European Jewry was, meanwhile, reaching
its hour of crisis. In 1648, the Cossacks of the Ukraine,
under the hetman Chmielnicki, rose against the oppression
of their Polish masters, whose political and economic
tyranny they deeply resented. In all of this, in their eyes,
the Jews were implicated. Their religion was even more
hateful to the Greek Church than the Roman Catholicism
which the Poles professed and endeavored to impose. Jews,
moreover, acted as stewards of the Polish nobles' estates, as
collectors of the taxation, as administrators of the revenue,
as lessors of the forests and the inns and the mills. Accordingly, the Cossack hatred against them burned even more
deeply than their detestation of the Poles. Throughout the
country, massacres took place on a scale and of a ferocity
which beggared anything which had been known in Eu-

rope since the time of the Black Death; and the horrors were accentuated by the refinement of ingenuity shown in the tortures by which they were accompanied. In every city or township which was entered, a veritable holocaust took place, in many instances the Poles betraying their Jewish neighbors in the mistaken hope of saving their own lives.

This was only the beginning of a whole series of similar waves of violence which completely broke the pride of Polish Jewry. In 1654 the Czar of Russia took the Cossacks under his protection, and invaded Poland; and, as the cities of White Russia and Lithuania capitulated, the Jewish residents were either exterminated or expelled. Simultaneously, Charles X of Sweden was invading Poland from the west, bringing fire and sword in his wake. The total toll of Jewish lives taken between 1648 and 1658 was estimated at no less than 100,000 souls. But still the period of tribulation was not at an end. There followed a protracted series of local disturbances, of petty persecutions, of ritual murder libels—the latter, in such numbers as to lead to an appeal for protection to the Pope himself, who, after an elaborate inquiry, declared the wretched story to be entirely without basis. Finally, in 1768, lawless bands of "Haidamacks" or rebels rose again in the Ukraine, and perpetrated atrocities rivaling those of one hundred and twenty years earlier.

The cumulative effect of all this was the complete ruin of Polish Jewry. The center of Jewish life, such as it was, moved northwards, never reestablishing itself in Podolia and Volhynia as firmly as had been the case previous to

1648. The resolutions passed at successive sessions of the Council of the Four Lands reflect the straits in which the country found itself. Taxation progressively increased. Sumptuary laws restricted the outlay on family festivities and even the number of weddings, and a score of regulations expressed the general grief at the recent tragedy.

Hardly less important were the repercussions outside Poland. The whole of Europe became familiar with penniless refugees, fleeing from the Cossack terror. With the recurrent disasters in Poland, and in face of the impossibility of economic recovery, what had been originally the merest trickle of emigration, and in 1648 became a sudden overflow, developed into a steady stream. The walls of the Polish reservoir were broken down. From the close of the eleventh to the close of the fifteenth century, the tide of Jewish migration had been directed eastward, from France and the Rhineland and Spain towards Turkey and Poland. The equilibrium remained fixed for approximately a century and a half. With the Chmielnicki massacres, the swing of the pendulum recommenced, and a second wave in a westerly direction set in. This was to continue in a varying intensity for nearly three centuries, and was not to be stemmed until it had succeeded in recasting completely the distribution of the Jews throughout the world.

5.   Meanwhile, even in Germany, fresh types had been emerging. After the close of the Thirty Years' War, there had begun to develop in that country a new variety of state virtually independent (for the power of the Empire had dwindled almost to vanishing point), strongly central-

ized, maintaining an elaborate organization, and looking to France as its model. The monarchs of these new absolutisms recruited their instruments wherever they could, even in the *Judengasse*. In time of war a Jew was generally irreplaceable as purveyor to the forces; in time of peace, he was invaluable as administrator of the finances. At every turn he was useful to provide a loan for the royal or Grand Ducal exchequer, materials of peace or war for any new enterprise, or jewels for the court favorites. Thus almost every German state, whether it tolerated the Jews or not, admitted one or two *Hofjuden* (Court Jews), for the personal service of the monarch and his entourage.

The history of German Jewry during the period under review is punctuated by such figures. There was Jacob Bassevi (1580-1634) of Prague, the first Jew to be raised to the ranks of the nobility; Samson Wertheimer (1658-1724) of Vienna, Chief Factor to the courts of Vienna, Mayence, the Palatinate, and Treves, who was responsible for the Austrian commissariat during the War of Spanish Succession; and Joseph Süss Oppenheim (d. 1738), better remembered as "Jew Süss," who, for a short time before his tragic fall, was omnipotent at the court of Württemberg.

In addition to these emancipated Court Jews, upon whom there was no restriction, and who exercised, in many instances, an influence fully as great as any Christian of similar rank, there came into existence in Germany numerous so-called "protected" and "tolerated" Jews—jewelers, craftsmen, engravers—who were similarly accorded special privileges for a more or less limited period, and freed from the restrictions imposed upon the generality of their co-religionists. Below all of these was the proletariat, cooped up in its *Judengasse,* marked off by a distinctive badge, forced to pay special tolls, confined to the most degrading occupations, and limited in the most sacred and intimate human rights.

At intervals, down to a comparatively late date, reaction might momentarily triumph in a manner more reminiscent of the twelfth or thirteenth century than of the dawn of modern times. Thus, in 1670, the influence of an Empress of Spanish birth and Jesuit upbringing brought about the temporary expulsion of the Jews from Lower and Upper Austria. Similarly, in 1745, on the excuse of a charge of treason made against their co-religionists in Alsace, the Jews of Bohemia, and more particularly the famous community of Prague, were condemned to banishment. At this stage, an event unprecedented in European history took place. The semi-emancipated Jews of London and of Amsterdam bestirred themselves in the matter. Thanks to their efforts, the English and Dutch governments made diplomatic representations to the Empress, begging her, on humanitarian grounds, to reconsider her decision. The episode indicated that the Jews, however much degraded, were at least men to whom the ordinary standards of humanity should apply, and on whose behalf the civilized governments of the west were prepared, if the occasion demanded, to exert mild pressure.

6.   It had been a commonplace among the Rabbis since ancient times that the Messiah was to come to redeem his people at the darkest hour before the dawn, when gen-

eral conditions seemed to be blackest. Time after time some
unprecedented wave of disaster had appeared to fulfill
these conditions, and Messianic pretenders had never been
lacking to fill the vacant role. No circumstances, however,
seemed to correspond more closely to all that was expected
of "the pangs of the Messiah" than the middle of the seventeenth century. Throughout the world, political conditions
were peculiarly disturbed. The fires of the Inquisition were
still defiling the pure heavens of Spain and Portugal. The
recent wave of massacres at the hand of Chmielnicki and
his hordes in Poland and the Ukraine—by far the greatest
disaster of its sort in recent history—had filled Europe with
penniless refugees and brought home the magnitude of the
catastrophe. In addition, the Cabbalists of Safed, meditating
day and night upon the date and nature of the final deliverance, had made this the principal pre-occupation of every
householder.

There was living at this time in Smyrna, in Asia Minor,
a young man in his early twenties named Sabbatai Zevi
(b. 1626). He had come profoundly under the influence
of the Cabbalistical school. His companions noted with
respect how he mortified his body with repeated flagella-
tions, and bathed constantly in the sea, both in summer and
winter. His appearance was unusually imposing, and his
personal fascination strong; and gradually he came to be
looked up to with a reverence which approached awe.
Ultimately he became convinced that he, and no other,
was the Messiah so long awaited, and on his return from a
visit to Jerusalem in 1665, he publicly proclaimed himself
as such. Letters were sent broadcast throughout Europe,

Asia, and Africa announcing the good tidings. Everywhere
the approaching deliverance was hailed with jubilation.

The frenzy of the masses knew no bounds. Prayers were
offered up in all the synagogues on behalf of "Our Lord,
King, and Master, the Holy and Righteous Sabbatai Zevi,
anointed of the God of Israel." There was a wave of peni-
tence and ascetic exercises. Children of tender years were
united in wedlock, so that they might beget bodies into
which the few remaining unborn souls might enter, the
last impediment to the Redemption being thereby removed.
The merchant-princes of the community of Amsterdam,
men whose signatures would have been good for almost
any amount on the Bourse, prepared a petition to forward
to the Pretender, assuring him of their implicit faith in his
mission.

Thus encouraged, Sabbatai set out on an indeterminate
errand for Constantinople. As he disembarked, he was
arrested by order of the Grand Vizier, and thrown into
prison. This setback made no difference in the eyes of his
admirers, for was it not inevitable that the Messiah should
suffer tribulations before his final triumph? In consequence,
he maintained an almost royal state even in prison. He
went from one extravagance to another, the climax being
reached when he abrogated the fast of the Ninth of Ab,
intimating that it was henceforth to be observed as a major
feast, in commemoration of his birth.

At last the patience of the Turkish authorities was exhausted, and they summoned him to Constantinople. Here
Sabbatai was brought before the Sultan, who blandly placed
before him the alternatives of apostasy or death. With

a pusillanimity which is the only disappointing feature in an otherwise harmonious career, the pretender chose the former. Donning the white turban of a true believer, in place of his Jewish headgear, he publicly proclaimed his belief in Islam, and left the Sultanic presence as a royal pensioner.

The most remarkable part of the whole episode was still to follow. Belief in the pseudo-Messiah's claims was not shaken even by this negation of all for which he had previously stood. Throughout the world, bands of devoted adherents continued to assert his claims. Their hero himself discreetly encouraged them, continuing to consort with his admirers, and to practice mystical rites in their company. After his death, in 1676, many of his adherents, who had followed him into Islam, transferred their allegiance to his putative son. Down to the present day their descendants, under the name of Domneh, still maintained their identity in Salonica and elsewhere. Outwardly, they are strict Moslems; but, in the privacy of their homes, they perpetuate their own curious, mystical rites, recalling the glamorous episode of three centuries ago.

Elsewhere the ferment continued in a different form. Wandering prophets and mystics continued long after to preach belief in the Messiah who had renounced Judaism. Many Rabbis of the utmost scholarship and piety were suspected of cherishing a secret allegiance to him; and learned circles were convulsed over a long period of years, nearly a century later, by a dispute between Rabbi Jacob Emden (d. 1776) and Jonathan Eybeschütz (d. 1764), who was accused by the former of having introduced allusions

to Sabbatai Zevi in certain mystical amulets of which he
was the author.

In the east of Europe especially, there remained large
numbers of persons who maintained a mystical belief in
the Messianic current. In the second half of the eighteenth
century they found a rallying point in a certain Podolian
adventurer named Jacob Leibovicz (known as Frank),
who claimed to be the reincarnation of Sabbatai Zevi and
his successors. His adherents were soon to be numbered
by thousands. The alleged licentious manners of the new
sect resulted in their excommunication by a rabbinical
synod, which prohibited the study of the Zohar, on which
the Frankists depended for their very existence, until matu-
rity. The innovators retorted by proclaiming themselves
Zoharists, at war with the Talmud and the Rabbis, and they
presented a semi-Trinitarian confession of faith to the local
Christian authorities. The result was a trumped-up disputation in the fullest medieval tradition, after which the
Talmud was condemned and thousands of copies publicly
burned. Ultimately, the Frankists went over *en masse*
to the dominant faith, proving as questionable Christians
as they had been Jews.

7.   A more remote effect of the Messianic stir was the
birth of Hassidism. The revivalist movement in Poland
permeated all sections of society, until it touched a simple
Podolian limedigger, Israel ben Eliezer (1700-1760). The
new leader, a tender-hearted mystic of rare personal fascination, taught that piety was superior to scholarship, and
that it was the prerogative of any man, however ignorant

and however poor, to attain communion with his God.
Man could derive no advantage from the mortification of
the flesh; it was by spiritual exaltation and complete aban-
donment of self that the gulf between earth and heaven
could be bridged. On the other hand, there existed certain
Righteous Ones (*Zadikkim*) who were very close to the
Almighty, and whose intercession might sometimes sway
His immutable will.

Gradually the little band of disciples who gathered round
the Master of the Good Name (*Baal Shem Tob*)* as they
termed him, grew into many thousands, who adopted the
name of *Hassidim* ("the Pious"). A revivalist movement
swept through the Jewish masses of Eastern Europe. Prayer-
meetings were established at which feasting and ecstasy
and song were considered of greater importance than mechanical recitation of the liturgy. After the founder's death,
the conception arose of the presence, in a few chosen families, of special merits which passed down by hereditary right
from one *Zadik,* or Righteous One, to another, all able to
act as intermediaries between man and God. Dob Baer, of
Mezdyrzecz (1710-1772), adapted the new doctrines to the
taste of the more scholarly elements, among whom it henceforth began to make increasing headway. By 1772 the
movement had reached Lithuania, and a secret Hassidic
meeting-place was formed at Vilna. This at last brought
the traditional party, with the approval of Elijah ben Solomon, the *Vilna Gaon,* the last of the rabbinical giants of
the heroic age, to take drastic steps and to issue a formal
edict of excommunication against all who followed the new

*In abbreviation, *Besht.*

movement. It goes without saying that this measure proved ineffectual to stem the tide.

For some years to come, eastern European Jewry was divided between *Hassidim* and *Mitnagdim*, or "Opponents." When the din of battle faded, however, a new spirit pervaded both sides. The *Hassidim* now recognized the importance of the traditional order of things, and counted Rabbis of outstanding ability amongst their numbers. The *Mitnagdim* had become tolerant, and their conceptions were perceptibly influenced by the warm humanity of their erstwhile opponents. Thus Hassidism was prevented from developing into a sect, and its adherents, now to be numbered by the million, remained within the Jewish fold. Its advent had, nevertheless, made an enduring difference to Judaism, the poetical element which it had reinforced, while its hold among the lower, more impressionable and less learned classes, who felt the need for some mystical constituent in their daily life, was enduringly strengthened.

The pseudo-Messianic movement of the seventeenth century, with its subsequent ramifications, thus marked the end of an epoch. The Jews of the West were utterly disillusioned. Their pride was touched, and it took them long to recover from the blow. Never again was a pseudo-Messiah, relying upon supernatural powers, to obtain universal credence. In Eastern Europe, on the other hand, while the giants of the Talmudic scholarship were dwindling, a new brand of Judaism was arising to which, for the first time, scholarship was unnecessary. From more than one point of view the Jewish Middle Ages were definitely on the wane.

XXVII. THE FALL OF THE GHETTO

1.   By the second half of the eighteenth century the rifts in the Ghetto walls were becoming manifest. The western countries of Europe had not introduced the institution after the Jews began to resettle in the seventeenth century. In Italy, excepting in the Papal States where an edict of 1775 recalled the worst aberrations of the Middle Ages, conditions were slowly ameliorating. In enlightened states like Tuscany, no great objection was raised if a few individuals lived outside the Ghetto, the gates of which were not closed with such punctuality as hitherto. As far as Germany was concerned, the *Judengasse* no longer retained their predominance. Privileged persons were beginning to be admitted to the Universities and to mix in polite society, and the "protected" Jews of cities like Berlin were more to the fore, and enjoyed greater influence than those who still lived, under the old obscurantist regime, in Frankfort and elsewhere.

The new position of the Jew in German society was typified by, and at the same time received a powerful impetus from, Moses, son of Mendel, or Moses Mendelssohn (1729-1786). Born at Dessau under typical medieval conditions, he had humped his back and sharpened his intellect by inordinate poring over the rabbinical texts. In 1743 he had gone to Berlin having to pay the special toll incumbent upon every Jew before being allowed to enter the gates.

Here he picked up mathematics, Latin, and a smattering of modern languages, and he became successively tutor, book-keeper, and, finally, manager in the establishment of a wealthy Jewish manufacturer. In 1761, to the general surprise, he won a prize awarded by the Prussian Academy of Sciences for the best essay on a certain abstruse metaphysical subject. The achievement was all the more noteworthy in view of the fact that one of the two unsuccessful candidates was none other than Immanuel Kant.

Mendelssohn was henceforth a made man. The wealthy Jews of the Prussian capital took him to their bosom. Lessing made him the model for the central character in his *Nathan the Wise.* All the communities of Germany looked up to him with adoration. His pen was placed unreservedly at their service, and a series of works in flawless style appeared, in which, like another Philo, he endeavored to reconcile Judaism with all that was most fashionable in contemporary thought.

Emboldened by all this, he made a deliberate attempt to introduce new standards into the spiritual and literary life of the *Judengasse.* The new era was started by the publication of his famous edition of the Pentateuch, with a translation into excellent German and a collaborative modern commentary in pure Hebrew. By this achievement, the uncouth Judaeo-German dialect, hitherto in almost universal use, was, as it were, split into its component parts. The translation initiated the vernacular literature of the German Jew, which, in the course of the next century, was to attain classical dignity. The commentary broke through the exclusive Talmudic horizons which had hitherto hemmed in German-Jewish life, and thereby gave a powerful spur to modern Hebrew letters. Mendelssohn's disciples, collaborators in the pioneer literary periodical known as *haMeassef* (The Gatherer), and known after it as *Meassefim*, further developed the tongue of their fathers as a literary vehicle. Thus they initiated, so far as the northern countries were concerned, modern Hebrew prose, poetry, essay, and drama. The Jewish Free School, opened in Berlin in 1781, put Mendelssohn's educational ideals into practice, and his collaborator, Naphtali Hartwig Wessely (1725-1805), the most gifted Hebrew poet of his day, conducted a tireless propaganda in favor of their universal adoption.

In the political sphere the reactions of Mendelssohn's example were immediate. The "Enlightened Despots" of the age began to realize that the barriers between Jew and Gentile were not insuperable. Joseph II of Austria, influenced largely by the suggestions of Moses Mendelssohn's Christian friend, Christian Wilhelm von Dohm, for the civil emancipation of the Jews, led the way. In his famous *Toleranzpatent* of January 2nd, 1782, his ideas received their fullest expression. While there was as yet no question of Jews being placed on civil parity with Christians, the principle was laid down that their disabilities were to be removed gradually and that they should be encouraged to mix in the life of the general population. Six years later an edict was issued ordering every Jew to adopt a proper, recognizable surname, instead of the biblical patronymic which had hitherto sufficed in most cases. Special commissions were appointed to supervise the procedure. If any

individual hesitated or demurred, some name was created
for him and registered out of hand—often with intention-
ally ridiculous results, still perpetuated by their unfortunate descendants. These reforms were all the more important in view of the fact that the Partition of Poland in 1772,
which assigned Galicia to Austria, had enormously increased the number of the Emperor's Jewish subjects.

The example was followed elsewhere. In Alsace in 1784
the *impôt du pied fourchu* (toll of the cloven foot), hitherto payable by Jews and cattle at every *douane,* was abolished, as far as the former were concerned, by Louis XVI,
who, a few months later, issued Letters Patent which did
away with some other major abuses. In Tuscany the Grand
Duke Leopold II included the Jews in the scope of his
sweeping reforms, though he did not entirely abolish their
disabilities.

2.   In the midst of these pious experiments burst, in
1789, the bombshell of the French Revolution. The enjoyment by the Jews of the same privileges as other citizens
was a natural corollary of the Declaration of the Rights of
Man. Nevertheless, they had so long been considered a
race apart that many months elapsed before this elementary
piece of logic could obtain general support, notwithstanding
the impassioned pleas of demagogues like the Abbé Gré-
goire. The Portuguese Jews of Bayonne and Bordeaux,
followed by those of the former Papal States, made out a
cause for themselves as being the Jewish aristocracy, and
secured emancipation on January 28th, 1790. This did not,
however, affect the vast majority in Alsace, concerning

whom there were protracted discussions. At last, during one of the last sittings which preceded the dissolution of the National Assembly, the deputy Duport suddenly forced the question. His motion was carried almost without opposition. Thus, for the first time in the history of modern Europe, the Jews were formally admitted equal citizens of the country of their birth.

In the succeeding period, in every place to which the armies of the young Republic penetrated, they brought the new gospel of the equality of all men, with its corollary of Jewish emancipation. In Holland, full citizenship was accorded in a constitutional manner by the National Assembly, under the pressure of the French Envoy on September 2nd, 1796, and, in the following year, for the first time probably in history, Jews were elected members of the Legislature. More dramatic by far was the change effected in Italy. Here, as the French forces entered one sun-drenched city after the other, the gates of the Ghetto were broken down, and the Jews summoned forth to the pure air of the outer world, to enjoy all the privileges of other human beings. In Venice, the gates of the Ghetto were removed and burned, amid great popular jubilation, on July 10th, 1797. In Rome, the deliverance took place in February, 1798. Everywhere, the Jews formed part of the new municipal governments, and were even granted commissions in the National Guard.

Much the same, though somewhat slower, was the progress of events in Germany. In the Rhineland, as in Italy, emancipation came in the first warm flush of enthusiasm which followed upon the French irruption. A similar process followed in those parts of the country which came under French influence as the result of subsequent campaigns. In the Kingdom of Westphalia, formed under the titular sovereignity of Jerome Bonaparte in 1807, the Jews were soon placed on the same footing of equality as in France. In Frankfort, Jewish disabilities were removed in 1811, after the payment of a very ample composition for the annual protection-tax hitherto exacted. Full equality was similarly granted in the Hanseatic towns after their annexation to France. In the other German states under French influence, limited emancipation was granted.

Even in Prussia, the Jewish population of which had enormously increased in consequence of the second and third partitions of Poland, in 1793 and 1795 respectively, there was a perceptible amelioration after the French Revolution. This culminated in 1812, in the course of the national consolidation which preceded the War of Liberation, with a grant of complete emancipation, governmental offices only remaining closed to the Jews. The only important state where marked vestiges of the old regime still prevailed was Austria, where even the reforms introduced by Joseph II tended to become a dead letter under his successors.

3.   With regard to the Jews of the French Empire proper, the organizing genius of Napoleon Bonaparte led to an important series of experiments. As he passed through Strassburg on his triumphant return from the Austerlitz campaign, he was assailed by the population of Alsace with complaints against the Jews, upon whom they

blamed all their misfortunes. In consequence of this, he determined to summon a representative assembly, which should make an authoritative pronouncement as to the position of the Jew in the modern state, and revive "that civic morality lost during the long centuries of a degrading existence." Only, where another ruler would have thought in terms of a Rabbinical Assembly, Napoleon's grandiose ideology could conceive nothing less than a revival of the ancient Sanhedrin, for fifteen centuries nothing but a memory.

It was in July, 1806, that the preparatory Assembly of Notables met in Paris. Needless to say, this body gave satisfactory replies, erring only on the side of over-obsequiousness, to the twelve inquiries officially submitted to it. Immediately after the conclusion of its sessions, in the following February, the Sanhedrin, fastidiously modeled on its ancient Palestinian prototype, was convoked to give its findings religious sanction. After seven sessions, occupied in the main with formal business, this body voted without discussion upon the recommendations of the Assembly of Notables, and passed them as laws. The tenor of the whole was summed up in a clause to the effect that the Jew considered the land of his birth his Fatherland, and recognized the duty of defending it. To this succinct summary of the Imperial ideal, those present replied in a truly Napoleonic fashion, rising as one man in assent with the cry *Jusqu'à la mort*. Other clauses embodied a declaration against the practice of usury and a full recognition of the incumbency upon the Jew of the matrimonial laws of the State.

The position as far as Jewish law was concerned was thus settled. The same genius which brought into being the Code Napoléon now set about reorganizing the communities of the Empire with the same thoroughness. By an order promulgated from Madrid in 1808, every department containing two thousand Jews or more was to establish its "consistory," comprising ecclesiastical and lay members. A central committee, consisting of three Grand Rabbis and two lay members, was established in Paris, with general control over the local organizations. Thus the Jewry of the French Empire was organized in a hierarchy of mathematical symmetry which still prevails.

Whatever the merits or demerits of the Napoleonic Sanhedrin and the subsequent reorganization (and it is frequently regarded with good reason as having set the footsteps of French Jewry upon the pathway of assimilation) there can be no doubt that it was a fine stroke of diplomacy, and captured the imagination of the Jews far beyond the boundaries of the French Empire. On the invasion of Poland, Napoleon found himself greatly assisted by gabardined, ringletted local Jews, who rendered his forces every assistance which lay in their power. "The Sanhedrin is at least useful to me," he is reported to have said. But sectional sympathy was powerless to avert the final cataclysm, and the fall of the First Empire, in the Armageddon which succeeded the retreat from Moscow, threw European Jewry once again into the melting pot.

BOOK FIVE

THE NEW AGE
(1815-1935)

XXVIII. REVOLUTION *and* EMANCIPATION

1.　　The representatives of a score of European powers, assembled in Vienna in 1814 and 1815, spent long months attempting to patch together the political framework which had been shattered a generation before, on the outbreak of the French Revolution. Even the Jews, for the first time in diplomatic history, sent their delegates to watch the negotiations, for it was obvious that their interests were likely to be profoundly affected. A proposal, that they should be confirmed in the rights granted them during the period of French supremacy, obtained powerful support. An attempt was accordingly made to establish in the new Germanic Confederation a uniform liberal policy, similar to that in force in Prussia since 1812. In the Act of Confederation adopted by the German governments, a clause was inserted to the effect that, pending legislation to regularize their position, the Jews should continue to enjoy all privileges granted to them in the various states. The reactionaries, however, artlessly secured the substitution of the innocuous word "by" for "in." Thus the undertaking was rendered completely valueless, as any signatory could plead that the emancipation effected under foreign influence had not been granted "by" the states themselves.

The gate was thus left ajar, if not open, for reaction to enter. During the course of the next decade, the question of Jewish status in the newly-reorganized Free Cities assumed international importance. Bremen and Lübeck went so far as to expel the Jews settled there in recent years. In other states, no uniform status prevailed, the systems in force ranging from an almost full emancipation to segregation in a semi-medieval sense. Large areas, comprising some of the most important cities of the country, refused to admit permanent settlers under any conditions.

In Italy, the reaction was even more pronounced. Universally there was a more or less complete return to the unenlightened system of the eighteenth century. In the States of the Church, an attempt was made to re-introduce the Ghetto system to the last detail, down to and including the wearing of a distinctive badge. In many places the gates of the Jewish quarter, destroyed and burned in the first flush of revolutionary enthusiasm in 1797, were again set up.

In 1819, to the accompaniment of cries of *Hep! Hep!* (the initials of *Hierosolyma est perdita,* and traditionally the anti-Jewish watchword of the period of the Crusades) sanguinary excesses against the Jews took place throughout Germany. Promising young men like Ludwig Börne and Heinrich Heine, despairing of ever making their way in a hostile world as Jews, cynically accepted baptism, while continuing to preserve throughout life a nostalgia for the environment of their younger days.

Yet, however drastic the reaction, there was in most places a subtle difference between the old regime and the new. Before the close of the eighteenth century, the restrictions upon Jewish life had been universal, and opportunities were the exception. Now, opportunities were widespread, though they were still qualified by restrictions. The Jew was no longer an inferior, degraded being, marked off from his fellow-humans by dress, by language, by occupation, by interests. He had breathed the free air of the outside world. He had known what it was to mix with the rest of mankind on an equal footing. He had attained the status of a man at least. All that remained for him was to attain the status of a citizen.

In his exclusion from this, he was not alone. The era in question was one of general reaction. Throughout Europe, in the preceding period, men had learned to know and to admire constitutional government, and the introduction of Parliamentary institutions was regarded as the panacea for every ill and the goal of every liberal striving. The emancipation of the Jew would be incomplete without the extension to him of those constitutional rights which the rest of the population hoped to attain for themselves. Hence, the Jews of Central Europe flung themselves heart and soul into the revolutionary movements of the nineteenth century, which finally resulted in the destruction of alien domination and the establishment of constitutional governments from the Baltic to the Mediterranean, and from the Danube to the Rhine: and the triumph of constitutionalism, as they had hoped, was ultimately accompanied everywhere by emancipation.

2.   As far as Germany was concerned, the struggle for Jewish rights entered into a new phase in 1830 under the leadership of Gabriel Riesser, a magnificent orator and

organizer, who was one of the heads of the constitutional party in the country. Thanks to his advocacy, Jewish emancipation became a plank in the platform of German liberalism. The headway which it made was very slow, but the direction was unmistakable. In 1833, full civic equality was accorded the Jews of Cassel. Brunswick followed suit in the following year, and Prussia, in a modified degree in 1847. In the revolutionary wave of 1848, the Jews throughout Germany took a prominent part, confidently hoping that success would bring emancipation in its train. In the reforming wave which followed, state after state granted a liberal constitution, and everywhere the new code contained a clause removing Jewish disabilities. Almost simultaneously, the Austrian and Hungarian diets, mindful in the latter case of the fact that a regiment composed of Jewish soldiers had taken up arms under Kossuth, carried motions in favor of emancipation for the Jews.

A period of reaction followed, in which the new constitutions were either withdrawn or else rendered nugatory. The new-won Jewish rights, indeed, were seldom cancelled, but, in practice, they were considerably circumscribed. Yet, in most cases, they remained on paper, and in the hearts of the liberal leaders, as an integral part of the constitutional system, and, when the interlude of reaction was over, they automatically reappeared. Thus there was full and final emancipation in Baden in 1862, in Saxony in 1868, in Austria and Hungary by the Ausgleich of 1867. When the North German Federation was formed in 1869, a clause was adopted abolishing all restrictions, of whatever nature, incurred by reason of religious opinion. The German Imperial Constitution of 1871 embodied the same principle, which thus became extended to the few provinces which had not yet fallen into line. Thus, the emancipatory movement in Germany, begun when Moses Mendelssohn gained a foothold in Berlin society, was completed.

Elsewhere in Europe, the process was closely paralleled. France had never known a return to the repressive system which had obtained under the old regime. After 1830, indeed, Judaism, like other religions, received a State subvention. The case was identical in Holland and Belgium. In Denmark, the Jews obtained extensive rights in 1814, were admitted to municipal offices in 1837, and achieved full emancipation in 1849. In Switzerland, as late as the middle of the century, intolerance was so extreme that most cantons refused to admit the Jews even temporarily. This obscurantism resulted in a diplomatic struggle which lasted over a long period of years; for neither England, France, nor America was disposed to sign any arrangement with a country in a large part of which their Jewish subjects would not be permitted to settle or to trade. One by one, however, the various legislatures adopted a more liberal policy, the last falling into line in 1866.

In the various phases of the *Risorgimento* in Italy, the Jews were meanwhile playing an exceptionally important part. The Roman Republic under Mazzini, the Venetian Republic under Manin (himself of Jewish descent), the various enterprises of Garibaldi, owed more proportionately to the Jews than to any other section of the Italian people. In 1848 the liberal government of the Kingdom of Sardinia, which was assuming the lead in the struggle for the unity of Italy, enfranchised its Jewish subjects. This measure, elaborated and completed by successive legislation, was one of the few enduring fruits of the Year of Revolutions. As Sardinia expanded, this remained one of its fundamental institutions. Lombardy, Tuscany, Venice, the Papal States, all in turn were added to the dominions of the House of Savoy, and Jewish disabilities automatically crumbled. At last, in 1870, Rome itself was seized, to become the capital of United Italy. Thus a slavery which had lasted for three hundred and fifteen years came to an end, and the oldest Jewish center of the Western World was enabled to look forward to a new lease of life.

If, in England, progress was somewhat slower, the reason is to be found in the fact that the disadvantages from which the Jews suffered were so slight. Their social emancipation had been complete almost from the beginning. The Jew lived where he would, could enter almost any walk of life, and mixed freely with Gentile society. It is true that popular prejudice was not altogether absent, and when, in 1753, an innocuous measure was introduced to facilitate the naturalizing of foreign Jews (the so-called "Jew Bill"), the agitation against it rose to such dimensions that it was soon repealed.

In 1829, on the triumph of the movement for Catholic emancipation, an agitation was begun for similar legislation in favor of the Jews. On its second introduction, in 1833, the Bill was passed by the House of Commons; but it was rejected by the Lords, with monotonous regularity in one session after another. Meanwhile, the Jews were successively admitted to the Bar (1820), to the Shrievalty (1835), and to other municipal offices (1845). One or two outstanding individuals were raised to the dignity of knighthood; while Benjamin Disraeli, a baptised Jew, proud of his race (to which he lost no opportunity of referring) attained a dominant position in the counsels of the Tory Party. Minor disabilities were removed by the Religious Opinions Relief Bill of 1846, whch left their exclusion from Parliament the only serious grievance of which English Jews could complain.

Time after time, from 1847 onwards, Baron Lionel de Rothschild was sent to Westminster as their representative by the electors of the City of London, but the continued opposition of the Lords prevented the passage of legislation which would have enabled him to take his seat. Finally, in 1858, a compromise was reached, each House being allowed to settle its own form of oath. Twenty-seven years later, the son of the protagonist in the struggle was raised to the peerage as Lord Rothschild, being the first professing Jew to receive that honor: and he was allowed to assume his place in the Upper House as a matter of course.

3.   In eastern Europe, ostensible progress was slower. From the beginning of her history, Russia had been the least tolerant of European powers. During the embryo period of the Czardom, in the fifteenth and sixteenth centuries, a sporadic movement for conversion to Judaism, widely spread amongst certain elements in the population, was repressed with blood and fire. The rulers of the seventeenth century, such as Peter the Great, had been somewhat

more favorably inclined, but the succession of Empresses who succeeded them were at one in their fanaticism, if in nothing else. Catherine the First in 1727, Anne in 1739, and Elizabeth in 1742, all issued edicts expelling the Jews from Little Russia. Successive partitions of Poland, however (1772, 1793, 1795), put the lion's share of that unfortunate country in Russian hands. Thus it came about that the European country which had hitherto shown itself least disposed of all to welcome them now ruled over the largest section of the Jewish people, equalling if not outnumbering all others combined.

The declared policy of the Czars, from the outset, was therefore to confine the Jews to the newly-acquired western provinces, the so-called "Pale of Settlement," and to prevent them from spreading to other parts of the Empire. The well-meaning Paul I (1796-1801) and Alexander I (1801-1825) had indeed seemed to envisage ultimate emancipation. They did their best to encourage handicrafts and agriculture; they admitted Jews, in a limited proportion, to municipal offices; and they encouraged the establishment of Jewish schools infused with a "modern" spirit. The object was, confessedly, to facilitate the absorption of the Jew in the general population. Under the circumstances, it is not surprising that those for whom the reforms were intended remained impervious.

In the last years of his reign, the liberalism of Alexander I had given way to a reactionary panic. This continued under his successor Nicholas I (1825-1855). Rendered nervous by recent developments in neighboring countries, he set himself to isolate his country from the rest of the world, and to prevent any infiltration of Western institutions, Western ideals, and above all, Western liberalism. That the Jews would be made to suffer more than any other section of his subjects was a foregone conclusion. The treatment to which they were subjected, and the special regulations devised to crush their spirit, had no parallel in history. Of the legal enactments concerning the Jews published in Russia from 1649 to 1881, no less than one half, or six hundred in all, belong to this one reign. An Imperial ukase of 1827 extended conscription to them for the first time, with the proviso that the period of service was to be twenty-five years, beginning in some cases from the age of twelve (subsequently from that of eight). Yet even this ruthless measure failed in its object, and the steadfastness shown by some of these child-sufferers ("Cantonists" as they were called) constitutes a touching chapter in the history of Jewish martyrdom. By the *Statute Concerning the Jews* of 1835, the Pale of Settlement was yet further narrowed down. Jews were excluded from all villages within fifty versts of the western frontier. Synagogues were forbidden to be erected in the vicinity of Churches, and a strict censorship was established over all Hebrew books. Later, the Jews were expelled from the towns as well as the villages of the frontier area. Special taxation was imposed on meat killed according to the Jewish fashion, and even on the candles kindled on Friday night.

With the accession of Alexander II (1855-1881), it seemed as though a new era was dawning. The old ideal of excluding foreign conceptions and institutions was reversed, and an attempt was made to secure the industriali-

zation, and with it the westernization, of the country. The
special regulations governing the conscription of the Jews
were repealed forthwith. The whole Empire was opened
up to wealthy merchants, university graduates, and
mechanics. Jews were admitted to the legal profession, and
even to the judiciary. All this did not in fact amount to
much. But the moral effect was more important by far.
Russian society as a whole began to manifest a more tolerant attitude. The process of Russification, no longer imposed so ostentatiously from above, began to make rapid
progress. If the Jews were far from enjoying the ideal
status of their co-religionists in Western Europe, it must be
remembered that the idea of the Constitutional Monarchy
and of parliamentary institutions had barely begun to
make progress in the Empire of the Czars. But, in those
days of liberal enthusiasm, few persons doubted that this
would ultimately be the case, and that the Russian Jews
would then enjoy the same opportunities, the same rights,
the same privileges, as their fellow-countrymen and as free
men all the world over enjoyed. The process might be long
and weary, but its completion was assuredly only a matter
of time.

4.   One of the factors which had made Jewish
emancipation inevitable was the important part which individuals were playing in the new economic and intellectual order. The House of Rothschild dominated the world
of finance. This was however, only one of many families
which attained a position of first importance in this sphere
(it is enough to mention the Péreires, the Goldsmids, the

Sassoons). Jews entered every branch of commerce and
industry, some of which (like tailoring) they almost controlled. In professional activity and public life, conditions
were identical, and there was no sphere to which the Jew
did not penetrate, and in which he did not distinguish
himself. There were illustrious Jewish statesmen, writers,
actors, musicians, scholars, scientists, physicians, philosophers, playwrights, soldiers, in almost every country before the nineteenth century had closed. The break-up of
the Ghetto was succeeded with astonishing rapidity by the
rectification of its untoward influences upon the Jewish
physique. The former stoop was lost, the sallow com-
plexion became less and less common, open-air life obtained an increasing hold, and inches were added to the
average stature.

The age when Jewish scholarship was confined to the
study and elaboration of the standard rabbinical texts was
now obviously past. Just as the Jew himself had come out
of the Ghetto and widened his field of interests until they
embraced everything human, so, it was felt, Jewish scholarship must come out of its isolation, and be re-interpreted
in modern terms. Moses Mendelssohn, in his translation
of the Bible half a century before, had pointed the way;
and the tradition remained centered above all in the country in which he had lived and worked. A simple scholar
named Leopold Zunz,* irritated at an attempt of the Prussian government to suppress the "innovation" of vernacular sermons in the synagogue, published a work in 1832,

*The dates of persons mentioned in this section who flourished during the
last hundred years, are omitted.

Die gottesdienstlichen Vorträge der Juden, in which he
showed that the homiletical address in the language of the
country was, in fact, an institution of immemorial antiquity. The volume still remains a storehouse of Jewish
lore, to an extent rarely paralleled in a pioneer work. But
it was more significant as the attempt to apply modern
critical methods and standards to the study of the problems
of Hebrew literature. It was to this that the study of the
Science of Judaism, or *Jüdische Wissenschaft,* as it is
generally termed, owed its origin.

Not content with this achievement, Zunz devoted himself in a succession of further volumes to research in the
Jewish liturgy and synagogal poetry. He found worthy coadjutors. Moritz Steinschneider, the prince of Hebrew
bibliographers, explored the treasures of the libraries of
Europe, made them accessible to the learned world by his
catalogues and articles, and demonstrated the immeasurable debt which western culture owes to the Jewish translators of the Middle Ages. The first history of the Jews
since the close of the Bible, with the exception of one or
two medieval chronicles and elementary Protestant experiments, was that of Isaac Marcus Jost, published in the
eighteen-twenties; but it was soon superceded by the
monumental work (1853-1870) of Heinrich Graetz, based
upon original sources in a bewildering variety of languages,
which retains its fundamental importance even to the
present day.

Outside the political boundaries of Germany, though
within the orbit of the Austrian Empire, Hebrew continued to serve as a medium of scholarship, though its method

was modernized. The Galician Nahman Krochmal attempted to formulate a philosophy of Jewish history, which he envisaged as a series of Hegelian waves of rise and decline faithfully reflecting every main tendency in the general world, in his *Guide to the Perplexed of Our Time;* while Solomon Rapoport, in a series of penetrating essays, recreated personalities and movements of the Talmudic and post-Talmudic epochs. In Northern Italy, Samuel David Luzzato, of Padua, an omniscient scholar and collector, who would be perhaps better remembered had he confined his work to a single field, together with Isaac Samuel Reggio, of Gorizia, combined the immemorial traditions of Italian Jewish culture with the new conceptions which had come to life in Germany. German-born or German-trained scholars carried the ideals of *Jüdische Wissenschaft* to Paris, London, and elsewhere, though it was long before they struck root beyond the bounds of the German-speaking world. The laboratories for the new science were the various Theological Seminaries, thoroughly modern in method and intention, which began to be set up at this period. The earliest was established at Padua, in 1829; the example being speedily followed in almost every other important country.

Even in Russia, the intellectual revival, or rather readjustment, was paralleled. There, however, its nature was entirely different. Whereas among the enlightened groups of the West it took the form of the presentation of a modernized Jewish scholarship to European circles through the medium of the vernacular, among the masses of the East it lay in the introduction of secular literature to Jewish circles through the medium of Hebrew. The movement was called that of the *Haskalah,* or enlightenment. The activities of the German *Meassefim* had indeed aroused a sympathetic echo in Eastern Europe, and the periodical from which they took their name had a long series of imitators. A few devoted literateurs began to produce a succession of works through which they hoped to introduce the fine flower of European culture to their Hebrew-speaking coreligionists. Essays, poems, brochures, scientific works, finally even novels, began to be published in comparative profusion, in the tongue hitherto regarded as essentially and exclusively "holy."

Hebrew, thus rendered malleable once more, was allowed to wander beyond the purely scholastic sphere and the stilted rabbinical phraseology; and the foundations were laid for a cultural revival which was ultimately to attain imposing dimensions.

Three or four names only need be mentioned in illustration: Isaac Baer Levinsohn, essayist and philosopher, the father of the movement; Judah Loeb Gordon, the first modern Hebrew poet; Abraham Mapu, the founder of the Hebrew novel; and Perez Smolenskin, who led an abortive revolt against what he regarded as obscurantism. Parallel but slightly posterior to the Hebrew revival was a Yiddish one, producing a few poets and novelists of real genius, who depicted the life of the Jewish masses of the Russian pale, and perhaps culminating in Solomon Abramovitch, better known as Mendele Mocher Seforim (Mendele the Bookseller), or in Shalom Rabinovitz (Shalom Aleikhem), the great Yiddish humorist.

5.   It was not to be imagined that the modernizing tendency could fail to affect spiritual life. The traditional religious practices, that began to be evolved over twenty centuries before, had easily been reconciled with the spirit of the Ghetto, but they appeared somewhat incongruous to a generation which was doing its best to steep itself in European life. Accordingly, *pari passu* with Jewish emancipation there had been a movement for religious "reform." Israel Jacobson (1768-1828), financial agent for Jerome Bonaparte, King of Westphalia, and President of the consistorial organization established by him, was its pioneer. He had established, in 1801, at Seesen, near the Harz mountains, a boarding-school where Jewish and Christian boys might be brought up on mutual toleration and amity. In 1810, he opened a synagogue where an organ was introduced, German prayers were heard as well as Hebrew, and the confirmation of adolescents of both sexes was practiced.

On the fall of the Kingdom of Westphalia, when these innovations were automatically swept away, Jacobson removed to Berlin. Here he and Jacob Herz Baer, father of the composer Meyerbeer, installed services in their homes according to the new style. The reactionary Prussian government, however, objected on principle to anything in the way of novelty in whatever sphere, and had these private conventicles closed. Eduard Kley, one of the young men who had preached at the services, shortly after became headmaster at a Jewish school in Hamburg, where he gathered round him a small group of persons with views similar to his own. Thus, the first Reform synagogue was founded (1818), and a new prayer-book, comprising a number of changes, was published for use in its worship.

By slow degrees, the Reforming element began to take up a more extreme attitude on many other matters of doctrine, ritual, and practice. What had begun as a movement for superficial reform in synagogal worship developed into a general revolt against the traditional forms and against Talmudic Judaism as a whole. The old ceremonial was discarded. The whole of the rabbinical structure was repudiated. In place of the Messianic idea in the old sense, there sprang up a new conception—that of the "Mission of Israel," which could be accomplished only in dispersion. Reform found its apologists in scholars like the radical Samuel Holdheim, who preached a conception of Judaism entirely divorced from nationality, and officiated at a Berlin synagogue in which the Sabbath was transferred from Saturday to Sunday. He found a whole-hearted collaborator in Abraham Geiger, the philosopher of Reform, who elaborated a theory of an evolutionary Judaism, constantly changing and constantly renewing itself, in accordance with the conditions of each succeeding generation.

The movement was not, of course, confined to Germany. As early as 1836, its influence began to be felt in London, where a Reformed Congregation was organized in 1840, and a more extremist movement, under the name of "Liberal Judaism" sprang up under the leadership of Claude Goldsmid Montefiore, a couple of generations later. German immigrants brought the new ideas to America where, by the middle of the century, Reform Judaism in a radical sense had established a stronghold.

The evolution of Reform naturally drove the other wing to reconsider its position. Samson Raphael Hirsch, Rabbi at Frankfort, formulated a philosophy of strictly traditional Judaism which, without surrendering one whit to modernity, could satisfy the modern mind no less than that of Holdheim or of Geiger. Between the two extremes, a "conservative" element was able to modernize synagogal worship and to accommodate itself to prevailing standards, without fundamental alteration of the liturgy or the abandonment of any essential practice.

6.   With the new era, a deep cleavage began to manifest itself between the Occident and the Orient. The western countries, especially England, France, and Germany, with the new-born United States of America beyond the seas, now led mankind, in science, in art, in literature, and in all else that made for human advancement. It was in these lands that the Jews had entered most intimately into general life, and in which their emancipation first became a reality. Other countries of Europe, Russia, Italy, or the Balkan States, were backward in this as in every other respect. The day would surely come, however, when the benefits of civilization, and of Parliamentary institutions, would be extended to them also; and Jewish emancipation, physical and intellectual, would automatically follow. In the background there loomed the Moslem world, straddling across Asia and North Africa, where the process might ultimately be repeated, though at a much slower rate.

In the meantime, it fell to the lot of the emancipated

Jews of Western Europe to assume the tutelage of their brethren, to obtain diplomatic intervention on their behalf in case of persecution, and to fit them for emancipation by means of education. Similar works, of course, had to be done among the immigrants from less happy parts established in London or in Paris, who still needed assistance in order to relieve them from penury and to qualify them for citizenship. An admirable network of charitable organizations was established for the purpose of alleviating their distress and supplying their intellectual requirements, and it was a recognized point of pride that though the community contributed its full quota to ordinary taxation, no Jew was ever allowed to become dependent upon public relief.

It was the Damascus Affair of 1840 which initiated the new era in foreign affairs, and confirmed Occidental Jewry in its position of leadership. On February 5th of that year, Father Thomas, Superior of the Franciscan Convent at Damascus, mysteriously disappeared, together with his servant. By means of the bastinado, a sort of confession was extorted from a poor Jewish barber to the effect that a ritual murder had been meditated. In consequence, several members of the community were arrested and put to the torture. A general massacre seemed imminent.

When the news reached Europe and America, public opinion was deeply stirred. Meetings of protest, attended by Christians as well as Jews, were held at the Mansion House in London, as well as in New York and Philadelphia. Sir Moses Montefiore (who had been Sheriff for the City of London upon the accession of Queen Victoria,

when he had been knighted) proceeded to the East together with Adolphe Crémieux, the famous French lawyer, and Solomon Munk, the well-known Orientalist. At
Alexandria, they obtained an order without difficulty from
Mehemet Ali, Governor of Egypt, for the release of the
survivors. In Constantinople, the delegates were received
in audience by the Sultan, from whom they elicited a
firman, unconditionally acquitting the accused persons,
pronouncing the ritual murder a gross libel, and confirming the inviolability of the persons and property of Jews
throughout the Ottoman Empire.

The return journey of the Delegation was like a triumphant procession. Never before had any Jews achieved
a success on behalf of their people so outstanding, so public, or so far-reaching. Everywhere, prayers, deputations,
public addresses, greeted the returning heroes, who remained until their deaths the idols of the Jewish world.
Montefiore and Crémieux were continually called upon
whenever persecution threatened in any quarter of the
globe. The former especially, never turned a deaf ear, and
the figure of the stately patriarch, who remained active
almost to the end of his phenomenally long life, became as
familiar in the courts of Russia and Roumania as in
the Jewish quarters of Palestine and Morocco.

In 1858, another wave of indignation swept through
Europe by reason of the kidnapping at Bologna (still under Papal rule) of a seven-year old Jewish child, Edgardo
Mortara, on the pretext that he had been submitted to
some sort of baptismal ceremony by a servant-girl six
years previous: and the indefatigable Montefiore went in

person to Rome to obtain the rectification of the outrage. The Pope, however, remained adamant, and Edgardo Mortara was brought up in the dominant faith, ultimately attaining some distinction in the Church. This fresh *cause célèbre* resulted in the organization in Paris, under the auspices of Crémieux, of the *Alliance Israélite Universelle.* This organization had as its object the defense of Jewish rights whenever they were attacked, and the diffusion of Occidental education and ideals—as the event showed, of a notably Gallic tinge—among the less advanced Jewish communities of the world. The Franco-Prussian War of 1870 naturally diminished the universality of the appeal of this body. Accordingly, an organization with similar objects, the Anglo-Jewish Association, was formed in England in 1871, to be imitated by the *Hilfsverein der deutschen Juden* in Germany some time later. The advance of civilization, and the activities of these bodies and others like them, it was hoped, would ultimately succeed in ameliorating the lot of the down-trodden Jews of Eastern Europe, Asia, and Africa. It was under this conviction that Jewry prepared to confront the last decades of the century.

A XXIX.

ANTI-SEMITISM *and the* NEW DIASPORA

1.   Disillusionment, alas, was in store. There had been in all countries reactionary elements which opposed Jewish emancipation tooth and nail, and acquiesced in it even now only reluctantly. At the close of the nineteenth century it was impossible to base such feelings upon religious prejudice as had hitherto been the case. The opposition, therefore, took on a new aspect. With regard to Judaism it was sneeringly tolerant; but it transferred the basis of the prejudice from essentially religious to essentially national grounds. The anti-Semites, as they came to be called, insisted not only that the race to which the Jews belonged was distinct—which was probably true—but also that it was inferior, which, in view of Jewish eminence in art, literature, science, business, politics, and general life, was demonstrably absurd. They were scientifically distinguishable, it was asserted, by a lower cranial capacity; and they were inferior physically and intellectually to their fellow-citizens of the Aryan, and more especially of the Teutonic or Nordic stock—"the fairest blossom on the human tree."

The movement, in its new form, owed its inception to the year 1873, when the wave of over-speculation, which had followed in the wake of the Franco-Prussian War, resulted in the inevitable crash; and popular resentment found its scapegoat in the only section of the speculating

347

minority easily distinguishable from the rest. For some time the agitation was restricted to the gutter-press. In 1878, however, Bismarck, the German Chancellor, who had climbed to power with Liberal support, made a political *volte-face*. Allying himself with the reactionaries, he now set about a ruthless attempt to stem the tide of democracy.

The Jews, indebted to Liberalism for their emancipation, had been prominent upon that side in politics, and had provided it with more than one outstanding leader. This in itself was sufficient to win the Iron Chancellor's resentment, and he had no scruples in reverting to the immemorial policy of making the Jews serve as whipping-boys. In support of his new policy, the Court Preacher, Adolf Stöcker, formed what he called the Christian Socialist Workingmen's Union, in reality bourgeois, reactionary, and diametrically opposed to the best teachings of Christianity. In the forefront of its programme was the restriction of the Jewish "domination" in business, in society, and in politics. The movement was eagerly joined by unprogressive middle-class traders, who resented the commercial competition of enterprising Jews; by aristocrats who regarded them as intruders; and even by scholars, who vigorously championed the superiority of the "Teutonic" race above all others.

Thus, the anti-Semitic movement was born. For a few years it gathered force. Books reviling the Jews poured out in an unending stream from the printing-presses. Deputies delivered inflammatory speeches in the Diet. On April 25th, 1881, the Chancellor received from the newly-organized anti-Semitic league a petition demanding, among other things, the disenfranchisement of the Jews. This document bore the signatures of no fewer than 255,000 persons. To accede openly to such requests, at the close of the nineteenth century, was out of the question. Nevertheless, a number of the discriminations demanded were already being acted upon quietly by the authorities. It was all but impossible for any Jew, without submitting to the formality of baptism, to obtain a commission in the army, a Chair in any University, or an important office under the State. Popular passions found their expression in anti-Jewish rioting in many parts of the country, and attacks were made upon persons of Jewish appearance in the streets of the capital itself. More than once disenfranchisement was debated in the Prussian Diet, while the relations between the Jews and their neighbors continued to be embittered by an unending series of inflammatory publications.

The movement was not confined to Germany. It soon spread to the Dual Monarchy of Austria-Hungary, where it was fanned by a ritual murder trial, in full medieval style, at Tisza-Eszlar in 1882. In the same year there was held at Dresden the first of a series of international anti-Semitic congresses, at which fantastic restrictions against the Jews were demanded.

Even France, the home of Jewish emancipation, was not immune. Matters here came to a head in 1894, when Alfred Dreyfus, an Alsatian captain attached to the French General Staff, was accused of betraying military secrets to the German government. As a matter of fact, the whole affair was patently the result of an intrigue against the Republic, in which the French anti-Semites and the clerico-royalist faction were intimately concerned. Nevertheless, to the accompaniment of a wild anti-Jewish campaign in the press, in the streets, in the Chamber, their victim was tried before a court-martial and found guilty. On January 5, 1895, loudly proclaiming his innocence, he was publicly degraded on the Parade Ground in Paris, and sent to Devil's Island to serve a sentence of life imprisonment. Subsequently, it was brought to light that the famous "bordereau" in Dreyfus' handwriting, upon which the case against him had depended, was a forgery by a certain Esterhazy, a dissipated major in German pay. The clamor against the condemnation increased, the tone being set by Emile Zola's famous appeal *J'accuse*. The whole of France was divided into two camps, Dreyfusard and anti-Dreyfusard. Colonel Henry, of the General Staff, committed fresh forgeries to bolster up the accusations, and took his life when his action was discovered. Nevertheless, it was only in 1899, after a Liberal ministry had entered into office, that Dreyfus was brought back to France for re-trial. A council of war, sitting at Rennes, condemned him once more; but so obviously unfairly that the President of the Republic granted a free pardon. Later, the Court of Appeal quashed the verdict, and the innocence of Dreyfus was proclaimed to the world.

2.   In Western Europe, the new anti-Semitic movement had been on the whole academic in character. In Russia, on the other hand, the niceties of distinction between theory and practice were unappreciated. A great

part of the pseudo-intelligentsia looked to Germany for inspiration in all matters, and regarded the new doctrines as modern scientific gospel. On March 13, 1881, the Emperor Alexander II, was assassinated. This was ample to give the reactionaries the upper hand; and, within a few weeks, the fury of hell was let loose against the unfortunate Russian Jews.

On Wednesday, April 27, 1881, a dispute about the Blood Accusation in a tavern at Elisavetgrad, in the government of Kherson, served as pretext for the outbreak of a riot. All that day and the next the fury raged unabated. Deeds of incredible barbarity were perpetrated under the eyes of impassive officials, and in some cases even with the cooperation of the soldiers of the garrison. The example spread like wildfire, being followed on an especially large scale at Kiev (May 8th-9th) and Odessa (May 5th-19th). By the autumn, outbreaks had occurred at no fewer than one hundred and sixty places in South Russia. Instead of taking steps to punish the culprits, the Russian government attempted to solve the problem to which the attention of the world had been called, by embarking upon a determined policy of repression against the victims. In May 1882, there were promulgated the infamous "May Laws," by which the Jews were excluded from all villages and rural centers even in the Pale of Settlement. In its subsequent interpretation, moreover, the code became even more severe, serving to restrict all movement and to cripple trade. By an ignoble quibble, towns of as many as ten thousand inhabitants were classed as villages, and their Jewish population expelled.

With the passage of years, conditions showed no signs of amelioration. While on the one hand resenting the fact that the Jews refused to merge themselves into the national pattern, the government put all manner of obstacles in the way of their assimilation, on the plea that once they entered into Russian life they would dominate it. Meanwhile, there was a constant series of expulsions from the rural districts, as well as from the interior of the country. Jewish women were allowed to live in the great cities, and thus enjoy the benefits of a university education, only if they held the "yellow ticket" of a prostitute.

The Russian example was followed, though generally without its most violent manifestations, in Roumania. From the seventeenth century, there had been a more or less continuous stream of immigrants from the border-districts of Poland to the Danubian provinces of Moldavia and Wallachia (at that time part of the Turkish Empire). By the middle of the nineteenth century, when Roumania attained her independence, they numbered some 200,000 in all. The Treaty of Berlin in 1878, conferred full independence on the country, conditional upon the concession of equal rights to all subjects, irrespective of religious differences. This provision was ingeniously evaded by the plea that all Jews, though subject to military service and to every other civic duty, were, in fact, aliens, however many generations their ancestors before them might have been settled in the country. Recurrent intervention on the part of the signatories to the Berlin Treaty were treated with contempt. As in Russia, the Jews in Roumania were subjected to special legislation, deprived of equality of opportunity, and on occasion, subjected even to physical violence.

The liberal movement in Russia, in 1905, forced a shadowy constitution upon the Czars. The reactionaries now organized themselves under the name "Genuine Russians," with terrorist branches, popularly known as "The Black Hundreds," in the principal provincial centers. Antagonism to the Jews, whom they identified with everything that made for progress in the state, was an integral part of their programme. After the summer of 1882, the pogroms, as these attacks were called, had remained a more or less distant menace for over twenty years. On April 19, 1903, there was a fresh outbreak at Kishinev, which outdid in sheer savagery any of those which had preceded it, and obviously took place as a result of semi-official encouragement, if not organization. It was only after the conscience of Europe had been shocked by three days' continuous rioting, accompanied by much bloodshed, that orders arrived from St. Petersburg to restore peace. In 1905, there was a further outbreak. Within a period of four years, massacres were perpetrated in no less than two hundred and eighty-four Russian towns, and the total number of victims was estimated at 50,000. In 1911, a poor Jewish laborer, Mendel Beilis, was arrested in Kiev on the preposterous charge of having murdered a Christian child for ritual purposes. In spite of the notorious fact that a well-known hooligan had been responsible for the crime, Beilis, and with him, in a sense, the whole of the Jewish people, was put on trial. The case dragged on for two years, to the accompaniment of a wild anti-Semitic campaign throughout the country; and when finally the unhappy prisoner

was acquitted for lack of evidence, it was in such a way
as to cast discredit and suspicion on his co-religionists as a
whole. The greatest agglomeration of the Jewish people,
numbering over one-half of the Jewish population of the
world, was reduced to a condition of misery, of rightless-
ness, of insecurity, of degradation, which recalled the
traditions of the Middle Ages at their worst.

3.   For the martyred Jews of Eastern Europe (many
of them uprooted from their homes by the "May Laws"
and cooped up, on the verge of destitution, in vast Ghettos)
existence in their native country had become a nightmare.
Their only hope lay in flight. With every fresh outburst of
pogroms, a new wave of refugees made its way to the
frontiers, fleeing for their lives. Every road which led to
the borders, every train bound westward, every ship which
sailed from the harbors, was choked with exiles. For the
next thirty-three years, the new exodus continued without
interruption. The movement of population was greater in
magnitude than any which had preceded it in Jewish history; and it was more important in its consequences than
anything since the Jews first set foot in Europe, in the dark
mists of antiquity.

In the neighboring countries of Germany and Austria-
Hungary, permeated with anti-Semitism, the strangers
were eyed askance. In Roumania, conditions were little
more tolerable than in Russia; and that country, far from
receiving the refugees, added perceptibly to their numbers.
The vast mass pushed on westward towards the Anglo-
Saxon countries, the only parts of the world which were

as yet free from dangerous manifestations of anti-Semitic
feeling, and where, moreover, dazzling economic opportunity seemed open.

In England, the face of communal affairs was revolutionized by the Russian-Jewish influx, which attained impressive dimensions. In London, where the greater number
settled, largely in the old center in the East End, the Jewish population rose within twenty-five years from 47,000 to
150,000. Throughout the rest of the country, the old communities were reinforced, and new ones established. The
general diffusion of cheap clothing, cheap boots, cheap
furniture, was given an enormous impetus as a result of
their energy. But, at the same time, the influx was eyed
not altogether sympathetically by some elements in the
population. The agitation culminated in the Aliens Immigration Act of 1905, which stemmed, though it did not
stop, the incoming tide. Conditions were very much the
same in the overseas dependencies of Great Britain—Aus-
tralia, South Africa, and especially Canada—where large
numbers similarly found a home and galvanized the Jewish communities which existed before their arrival into a
new life.

4.   The English scene was imitated, on a scale larger
by far, in the United States of America. Here, the Jew was
no stranger. The epoch-making enterprise of Christopher
Columbus in 1492 was very largely a Jewish, or rather a
"New Christian," undertaking. It was made possible by a
loan which was advanced by a Marrano, to whom the first
report of the great discovery was addressed. Among its

patrons were several other persons of similar origin, as were several of the expedition's personnel. Luis de Torres, the interpreter, who was baptized on the day before the expedition sailed, was the first European to set foot in the new land, and is worth recording also as the first to make use of tobacco.

The Marranos of Spain and Portugal were quick to realize the potentialities of the New World, and to transfer themselves thither. Soon they were to be found in every province. It was not long before they were followed by the Inquisition, which, after some little preliminary activity, became established in Mexico in 1571, and elsewhere in the Spanish dominions not long after. Nevertheless, the numbers of the secret Jews in the New World grew; and, when in the first half of the seventeenth century, the Dutch conquered the Portuguese colony of Brazil, open communities were formed in its principal cities.

The Dutch rule was of short duration. In 1654, the capital, Pernambuco, was forced to capitulate, and its community was dispersed. The refugees were scattered throughout the New World where, in those places under English and Dutch rule, free from the fatal shadow of the Inquisition, they formed a network of little settlements. All through the West Indies—at Jamaica, Curaçao, Barbados, and elsewhere, as well as on the adjacent mainland—Jewish communities were established which, for a couple of centuries to come, played a very important part in economic life.

Late in the same year (1654), a small party of refugees arrived in New Amsterdam. Here, by the express order of the Dutch West India Company, they were allowed to remain, so long as "the poor among them do not become a burden to the Company or to the community, but be supported by their own Nation." Hence, this most distant outpost of the Marrano Diaspora, periodically reinforced from Europe or the West Indies, spread to the neighboring regions. By the second half of the eighteenth century, there were communities, looking to London and Amsterdam for spiritual guidance, scattered throughout the American colonies—in New York, Newport, Philadelphia, Savannah, Charleston, and elsewhere. Their outstanding members were engaged in the import and export trade. Of Aaron Lopez, of Newport, it was said that "for honor and extent of commerce, he was probably surpassed by no merchant of America." Some were ship-owners; and it was a Portuguese Jew, Lucena, who first introduced the manufacture of spermaceti, then invaluable for the manufacture of candles, into North America.

In the War of Independence, the Jews played an important part. Numbers of them adhered to the Non-Importation agreement. The names of Francis Salvador, "scalped by the Indians"; Major Benjamin Nones, one of Lafayette's romantic Frenchmen; Jacob Franks, Benedict Arnold's aide-de-camp before his treachery; and Haym Salomon, an immigrant Polish Jew who showed remarkable gifts in the realm of finance, exemplify the sympathy of the Jews with the cause of liberty. On the other hand, the Hart and Pollock families of Newport, and Rebecca Franks, the toast of the famous *meschianza* (the ball given by the British officers before Evacuation at Philadelphia), indicate that they were capable of appreciating the constitutional point of view as well. As in England itself, the Jews of colonial America had been subjected to few disabilities; and the original constitution of the United States, with its stipulation that no religious test should be required as qualification for any public office or post of trust, virtually completed their Emancipation.*

Even before the War of Independence, the original Marrano stock of the Jewish community in the United States had been diluted by new arrivals of German and Polish origin. When peace was restored to Europe after the Napoleonic Wars, the tide of immigration increased enormously. New synagogues were opened in rapid succession in New York, and small communities sprang up all over the Middle West. The majority of the newcomers were from Central Europe. Their natural desire to better themselves economically was a factor less potent than the acute discomforts to which they were subjected through the reenforcement of the anti-Jewish code, particularly the limitation of marriages, which still prevailed in many places. After the stirring events of 1830, and especially of 1848, the trickle developed into a stream, and a better class of immigrant began to arrive. Men of culture and substance, who had participated in the revolutionary movement of those years, or who were disappointed at the wave of reaction which subsequently set in, turned their faces in increasing numbers to the new continent, where equal

*Even in the United States full emancipation unaccountably lagged, locally at least. It did not become a fact in Maryland until 1825, after a prolonged struggle, while the last remaining minor disabilities were not removed in North Carolina until 1868 and in New Hampshire until 1877.

constitutional rights and economic opportunity were open to all.

Among the abiding results of the Gold Rush was the extension of the area of Jewish settlement to the Pacific coast. At every incipient city and township, there was a little body of Jews; general merchants, or sometimes mere peddlers, who painstakingly covered every mile of the surrounding territory with their packs or carts. Slowly these became organized in rudimentary congregations. By the period of the Civil War, the immigrants were becoming fully incorporated in American life. Ten thousand Jews were enrolled with the armies in the field, on the one side or the other; and a Jewish lawyer of rare ability, Judah Philip Benjamin, served the Confederate government with distinction successively as Attorney-General, Secretary of War, and Secretary of State. Even at this period, there was a sprinkling of Polish and Russian Jews, who had founded their own religious organization in New York as early as 1852. In culture, in wealth, in numbers, and in influence, however, the German Jews had unquestioned supremacy.

Under the circumstances, the new German spiritual tendencies struck root rapidly in the country. As early as 1824, a small band of enthusiasts in Charleston, fired by recent reports from Europe, had seceded from the congregation and organized a short-lived "Reformed Society of Israelites." With the later immigrants, some element of Reform was assumed as a matter of course. Enthusiastic Rabbis of the new school, who had found opposition at home too strong, saw unrivalled opportunities for giving expression to their views in the great Republic of the

West; and, in Isaac Mayer Wise, Rabbi at Cincinnati from 1854, the progressives found not only a vigorous spokesman, but also an organizer of unusual ability. Largely through his influence, Reform Judaism became deeply rooted in America; and radical innovations (such as the supplementary Sunday service), which were exceptional in their land of origin, became comparatively frequent. The last quarter of the nineteenth century saw Jews of German origin, and an interpretation of Judaism which harked back to Holdheim and to Geiger, dominating American Jewish life.

5.   This was the state of affairs when the outbreak in the spring of 1881 initiated the Age of Pogroms in Russia. It was the period of the labor famine in America, when the continent absorbed each year hundreds of thousands of poor immigrants from every corner of Europe. With a dramatic suddenness, the infection spread to the crowded Ghettos of Russia, Poland, and Roumania. The eyes of every Jew were turned to the new land beyond the Atlantic, where there was freedom from violence, where there was equal opportunity for all, where the very streets appeared, to distant observers, paved with gold. Between 1881 and the close of the century, over 600,000 Jewish refugees had landed in the American ports. The new series of pogroms which started at Kishinev sent another half-million to join them in less than five years. By 1903, the Jewish population of the country, which thirty years before had barely exceeded 250,000, had risen to one and a half million; a quarter of a century later, this figure was more than doubled.

The new arrivals naturally tended to concentrate at New
York. Here, where up to 1825 one small synagogue could
suffice the whole community, there were living a century
later no less than 1,750,000 Jews, comprising nearly one-
third of the whole population of the city. At no other time
in the whole course of Jewish history had so many Jews,
or anything remotely approaching that number, either absolutely or proportionately, been concentrated together at
one spot. An attempt by some American Jewish leader
(headed by the prominent banker and communal worker,
Jacob H. Schiff, a founder of the American Jewish Committee), to divert the port of entry to Galveston (Texas), and
thus extend the area of Jewish settlement, met with only a
qualified success; and the Eastern States continued to receive the vast majority of the new arrivals. Outside New
York, communities which would in any other country
have been considered of first importance, sprang up in
Chicago, Boston, Baltimore, Cleveland, Philadelphia, and
elsewhere. The American process was repeated, as was
only natural, across the Canadian border, where great
agglomerations were to be found in Toronto and
Montreal.

As in England, the newcomers, in an inordinately high
proportion, entered the tailoring and allied industries, in
every branch of which they came in a short time to exercise a virtual monopoly. Through their means, the industry was subjected to minute sub-divisions, and its overhead
charges hence greatly reduced (the so-called "Boston
System"). In cabinet-making, tobacco-working, the fur industry, and similar callings, Jews were equally prominent

and efficient. Exploited mercilessly at the beginning by their employers—frequently their own co-religionists—they evolved before long a very strong Trade Union organization. The Amalgamated Clothing Workers of America, which was preponderantly Jewish, attained a membership of nearly 200,000, and it was rivalled by the International Ladies' Garment Workers' Union. The two are memorable for the revolution effected through their means in the hygienic conditions in workshops, hitherto unspeakably foul and unsanitary. This, however, was not achieved until general strikes in the so-called "needle industries" in 1890 and 1892, had caused wide-spread misery.

But an agglomeration of millions of persons cannot be confined to one or two spheres of activity. Before long, the newcomers had entered almost every branch of industrial enterprise. There were agricultural settlements, supported by philanthropic organizations, in one or two states. Within the first generation, the sphere of activity was extended to cover the professions. The children of the original immigrants, sometimes themselves born beyond the ocean, became prominent lawyers, physicians, journalists, authors, actors, painters, sculptors. The newly-established cinematographic industry gave ample scope for their initiative and adaptability; and they were of the utmost importance in it, whether as producers, actors, or managers.

The East Side of New York, like the East End of London, became the seat of a curious alien cultural world. There were whole streets, or even areas, in which nothing but Yiddish was heard. Newspapers in the same language, modeled as closely as possible on the standards of American journalism, were published in a steady profusion to satisfy their intellectual needs. The Yiddish theatre attained a momentary importance in New York which it had never had in Warsaw. The children received a rudimentary Hebrew education in hundreds of *Heders,* and a smaller number of *Talmud Torahs,* the methods and general atmosphere of which were transplanted bodily from the Pale of Settlement. Old acquaintances from any one province, or city, or township, would band themselves together to establish their own synagogue, or prayer-hall, or friendly society, with the result that within the New York Ghetto there was a host of minor divisions, according to place of origin. There were synagogues of every degree of orthodoxy, reflecting the local atmosphere of every important community in Russia, Poland, and Roumania. Greybeards studied the law, in the traditional singsong, in innumerable stuffy Bethels. Master-tailors amassed fortunes, and moved to fashionable districts; and, in the mire outside, the descendants of great Talmudists pushed barrows, endeavoring to earn a few coppers to keep body and soul together. It was a vast melting-pot, into which all sorts and conditions of men were poured, and where they were merged and tried and moulded—no man yet knew into what.

XXX. A NEW WORLD

1.   The European War, which broke out in the summer of 1914, and was ultimately to involve almost every nation in the world, marked in many ways an epoch in the history of the Jewish people. The wave of emigration from Eastern Europe, which had gone on at such a phenomenal rate since 1881, was automatically checked. The tide of battle on the eastern front, as it swept backwards and forwards, overwhelmed time after time the old Polish provinces, on either side of the frontier, in which such vast masses of the Jewish people lived. What with the inevitable havoc of destruction and with ruthless deportations, often inspired by obvious anti-Semitic prejudice, many communities were completely destroyed, while thousands of families were reduced to destitution.

These sufferings were negligible when compared with what followed in the aftermath. In Russia, the Czars paid at last the penalty of centuries of misrule, and in the spring of 1917 a revolution took place in St. Petersburg. One of the first actions of the new government was to proclaim the principle of equality for all, irrespective of race and of belief. A new, perhaps a golden era seemed to have dawned for Russian Jewry. Yet, within a very short time, the movement took a new turn. On November 7th there occurred the momentous Bolshevik revolution, which dethroned the moderates and placed the destinies of the

country in the hands of the Soviets, or Councils of Workmen and Peasants. Before long, the country was plunged
into the throes of civil war. By the one side, the Jews
were accused of being subversionists, and by the other of
being counter-revolutionaries; and whenever either temporarily triumphed, it was they who were treated as the
scapegoats for past reverses.

Conditions were worst in the Ukraine, where an attempt was made to establish an independent republic under the Hetman Petlura—a worthy successor to
Chmielnicki. The new state was invaded in turn by
Bolsheviks and reactionaries, ill-armed and ill-disciplined,
and at one only in their determination not to lose any
opportunity which offered for Jew-baiting. When the disorder seemed to have died down, a fresh bid was made to
overthrow the Bolshevik regime by a "White" army under
the Czarist General Denikin, whose name is associated
with the worst atrocities in Jewish history since the Middle
Ages. In almost every town and village, there took place a
whole series of pogroms, which made the outbreaks of
pre-war days seem by comparison no more than displays of
boisterous spirits. The dead numbered over a quarter of a
million; while as many more fell victims to the deprivations and disease which followed in the wake of the
armies. Those who remained alive were utterly destitute.
The example of disorder proved infectious; and elsewhere
in Eastern Europe—in Hungary, Poland, Roumania—
similar riots took place, though on a smaller scale, in the
disturbed period which succeeded the conclusion of major
hostilities, in the autumn of 1918.

2.   When the turmoil of battle had died away, it was obvious that the condition of the Jewish people had become fundamentally altered during the past ten years. In 1914, the great mass of the world's Jewry was living in the Russian Empire. This was now split up, so that, out of a total of a little more than five millions in the territories formerly subject to the Czar, more than one half were assigned to the new republic of Poland. Here, as in the other states which owed their birth to the recent upheaval, equality of rights and opportunity was nominally safeguarded to all, without distinction of race or religion, by the "Minority" clauses which, largely owing to the efforts of the various Jewish delegations at the Conference of Paris, had been embodied in the successive Peace Treaties. The same was the case in Lithuania, Latvia, Esthonia, Czecho-Slovakia, and above all, Roumania, which, through the annexation of a large part of Hungary, had now doubled its Jewish population.

For the lethargic Sephardic Jewries of the Near East, the War of 1914-18 similarly constituted a landmark. They had not indeed suffered to any great extent in the actual hostilities. Nevertheless, the tide of nationalism which followed the peace affected them most adversely. Turkey began reorganizing itself as a national state, and could no longer tolerate in its midst heterogeneous bodies, alien in culture, in religion, and in speech, as it had done throughout its former history. Very similar was the position in Greece, which had acquired the thriving port of Salonica after the Balkan War of 1912. After the restoration of peace in the Near East, the government methodically set about converting this important center into a Greek city. In consequence of the systematic blocking of opportunity, the Jewish population began to dwindle, absolutely as well as relatively, with the result that the Jewish majority which had existed for many centuries diminished into a definite, though not insignificant, minority. Thus, the importance of the Sephardic communities of the Levant, which had been created in the aftermath of the expulsion from Spain in 1492, began to decline with increasing momentum; and well-informed observers imagined that they were in sight of final and definite decay.

The greatest body of Jews to be found in any one country of the world was now that settled in the United States of America. The tide of immigration checked by the war was never allowed to resume its former proportions, and ultimately became insignificant. Yet, as the result of natural growth, added to the unprecedented immigration of pre-war years, the total Jewish population here now exceeded 4,000,000. They were by far the most wealthy, as well as the most numerous section of the Jewish people. But for the support which they so lavishly poured out for the relief of their kinsmen in Eastern Europe from 1914 onward, the measure of the latter's disaster would inevitably have been greater still. Over a long period of years, it was to America that the eyes of Jewry throughout the world looked for assistance when any new enterprise was on foot.

With the cessation of immigration to the United States, the area of Jewish settlement began to spread; though (owing to legislative restrictions) the post-war movements of population were on a smaller scale. The temporary prosperity of France attracted large numbers of new settlers to that country. The community of Paris more than doubled in a single decade. Similarly, the Jewish population of the smaller countries of Western Europe—Norway, Sweden, Portugal, even Spain—greatly increased, while fugitives from Russia settled in some numbers in the Far East, forming a chain of fresh communities as far afield as China and Japan. A larger number turned their eyes to Central and South America. From Mexico almost to the Straits of Magellan, Jews penetrated, setting up in due course their synagogues and characteristic institutions all over the continent. Most of them directed their steps to the Argentine, where they reinforced the agricultural colonies established by the charitable Baron de Hirsch, at immense cost, a generation before, as a place of refuge for his persecuted co-religionists in Russia.* By 1950, the number of Jews in the country, which before the war was less than 10,000, had approached 400,000. A faint possibility began to show itself that the glories of Spanish-speaking Jewry, in full eclipse for many centuries past, might at last be revived in the New World.

3.   The most spectacular, and the most important result of the War, as far as the Jewish people was concerned, was the renewal of its political connection with that little strip of land on the eastern littoral of the Mediterranean which had been the cradle of their race. The

*Baron de Hirsch worked through his foundation, the Jewish Colonization Association (JCA), which is still responsible for the colonies in the Argentine.

nineteenth century had witnessed a rationalization of the old Messianic conception. The efflorescence of the national idea throughout Europe could not but color the outlook of Jewish theorists, some of whom, as they watched contemporary developments in Flanders, Italy, and the Balkan States, began to think vaguely of the revival of an autonomous Jewish nationality. Moreover, the growing security of the Near East, and especially the benevolent interest which the European powers were taking in Palestinian affairs, rendered possible the development of a more systematic, self-dependent settlement. Philanthropists, Jewish and Gentile, elaborated schemes for diverting the pauper Jewish population of Jerusalem and other towns into productive work on the soil; and the Alliance Israélite opened an agricultural school near Jaffa. Rabbis of undisputed orthodoxy began to teach that Messianic deliverance was not to be the prelude to the rebirth of a Jewish Palestine, but must be preceded by it.

The new conception found its first prophet in a German thinker, Moses Hess, who had been through the whole gamut of assimilation. Returning in a premature old age to his own people, he pointed out in his *Rome and Jerusalem* (1862) the insubstantiality of the ideal of emancipation as an end in itself; and he suggested that the reconstitution of a political nationality in Palestine was the only solution to the indubitable problems of the Jew.

His views attracted little attention until twenty years after, when the Russian reaction made a radical alteration in the attitude of many leaders of Russian Jewish thought, who now despaired of the solution of the Jewish problem along the lines hitherto followed. In the following year, Leo Pinsker, a physician of Odessa, published a brochure, *Auto-Emancipation,* in which he demonstrated that the Jews, the Russian Jews at least, were nourishing an illusion in hoping ever to identify themselves completely with the peoples among whom they lived. Accordingly, he suggested the creation of a national homeland, preferably in Palestine, as the only expedient which could restore their dignity even in the Diaspora. He was not alone in holding such views, and a number of societies called *Hovevei Zion* (Lovers of Zion) were established, principally in Eastern Europe, to carry them into effect.

Meanwhile, an eddy of the stream of imigration from Russia, which had been opened up in that fatal year, had reached Palestine. While *Auto-Emancipation* was in the press, a number of young university students and others had formed an association under the name BILU (the initials of the Hebrew verse "O House of Jacob, come ye and let us go": Isaiah ii. 5) and set out for Jaffa. Subsequently, under the auspices of the *Hovevei Zion,* a few agricultural colonies were founded in the coastal plain of Judaea. The work was embarked upon hastily, and was inadequately supported; but, thanks to the constant and munificent assistance of Baron Edmond de Rothschild of Paris, the settlements managed to establish themselves on a firm basis.

Hardly aware of all this, a strikingly handsome Viennese journalist named Theodor Herzl, was following the case of Alfred Dreyfus in Paris, in 1894. He had been brought up in a completely assimilated environment. But

the Dreyfus Case convinced him that he had been wrong
in his previous views. Anti-Jewish prejudice, as it was now
manifesting itself, was not merely religious in origin. It
was racial, as far as it was anything. The only key to the
endless problem was therefore for the Jews to reorganize
themselves as a nation, with an autonomous center of their
own. Carried away by his feelings, Herzl wrote at high
pressure his famous *Judenstaat,* in which he elaborated
these ideas. This was the first step in the launching of the
Zionist movement, with its object (as it was ultimately
defined) of "securing for the Jewish people a home in
Palestine guaranteed by public law." Into this, Herzl
threw himself with all the fervor and self-devotion of one
of the ancient prophets. His magnetic personality gained
him many adherents all over the world, particularly in
Eastern Europe, where the traditional devotion to Palestine
was still overwhelmingly strong.

In 1897, there was held at Basle the first of a series of
periodical Zionist Congresses, to discuss how the new
presentation of the eternally old striving of the Jewish
people might be brought to fruition. Herzl, thus encouraged, felt himself authorized to enter into official negotiations in order to put his scheme into effect. With
indomitable courage he obtained audiences with the various potentates of Europe, from the German Kaiser to the
Pope, whom he endeavored with varying success to interest. He had an official interview with the Sultan, with
whom negotiations were carried on in 1901-2, with the
object of obtaining a charter for Palestine. It is said that
he might have succeeded, had he consented to use his in-

fluence to silence the outcry in Europe and America
against the Armenian atrocities. Whether this was the
case or not, the negotiations broke down. The British
government, however, was so far impressed that it offered
Herzl for colonization purposes, first a tract of land in the
Peninsula of Sinai, between Palestine and Egypt; and
then, when this was found unsuitable, a stretch of territory in Uganda, in British East Africa. However, it soon
became patent that no land could possibly have the same
appeal in the eyes of the Jewish masses as that of their
fathers, and that they were not likely to make the necessary
sacrifices on behalf of any other. Accordingly, after long
and acrimonious discussions, the offer was declined. It had
nevertheless served its purpose by demonstrating to the
world that, in the opinion of responsible European statesmen, Zionism was a factor to be reckoned with. When,
shortly after, Herzl died, worn out by his labors, at the
early age of forty-four, the movement which he had
created, or rather revitalized, was a living and
indestructible force.

One of the first positive achievements of Zionism had
been the creation of two financial institutions—the Jewish
Colonial Trust and the Jewish National Fund—for carrying on its work. Neither, indeed, obtained more than a
fraction of the money needed for its purpose as Herzl had
conceived it. Nevertheless, through their medium and
under the inspiration of the new ideal, the settlement of
the Jews on the soil of Palestine progressed quietly. The
whole country became dotted with agricultural colonies,
where the labor and technical skill of Jewish farmers was

once more making the land of their fathers, desolate and
neglected for many centuries, to flow with milk and
honey. Among the sand-dunes near Jaffa, a Jewish township sprang up named (with obvious biblical rem-
iniscence) Tel-Aviv, or the Mound of Spring; and a
Jewish school of arts and crafts was established at Jerusalem. Thanks largely to the exertions of one man, Eliezer
ben Jehudah, the language spoken by the colonists was
Hebrew—biblical Hebrew, as it had been spoken by
David and Isaiah, and enriched by the medieval poets and
philosophers, adapted to the needs of the day.

Simultaneously, in Russia, the Hebrew cultural revival
threw up a small number of writers of real genius. Noteworthy among these was Asher Ginzberg (better known
by his pen-name of Ahad ha-Am—"One of the People"),
a forceful essayist, the apostle of "cultural" as opposed to
"political" Zionism. The latter's literary supremacy was
challenged only by Hayim Nahman Bialik, probably the
greatest Hebrew poet since Judah ha-Levi, who was stimulated to his most poignant work by the Kishinev pogrom
of 1903.

The entry of Turkey into the European War in 1914
elevated the Zionist movement into a political pawn of
the first importance to the Franco-British bloc, who desired to counteract the bad impression which their alliance
with the arch-tyrant, Russia, had created in Jewish circles, particularly in the United States of America. On
November 2, 1917 Arthur James (subsequently Lord) Balfour, as British Foreign Secretary, issued a declaration
which stated that the Government viewed with favor the

establishment in Palestine of a national home for the Jewish people, and would use their best endeavors to facilitate the achievement of this object. It can hardly have been anticipated at the time that the debacle of the Turkish forces in Palestine was so near. Within six weeks, the Crescent ceased to wave over Jerusalem, for the first time since the period of the Crusades. The realization of the Zionist ideal, which two months before had seemed a distant dream, now appeared on the verge of actuality.

At the Peace Conference which assembled in Paris, no opportunity was given the Allied Powers to forget the pledges which they had made in the heat of the struggle. Moreover, though none of the victors felt inclined to relinquish their hold on any territory which they had conquered, the era of naked annexation was over. Instead, the system was evolved of "mandates" under the League of Nations, assigned to some interested power, not in its own interest, but in that of humanity. By the San Remo Conference of April 1920, that for Palestine was assigned to Great Britain, to be administered according to the terms of the Balfour Declaration. This arrangement was formally confirmed three years later, by the Council of the League of Nations; and arrangements were made for the establishment of a "Jewish Agency for Palestine," which ultimately came into being in 1929, comprising non-Zionist as well as Zionist elements, to represent world Jewry in its relations with the Palestinian government. Thus, for the first time for 1900 years, the political connection of the Jewish people with the land of their fathers was formally recognized. Hebrew was admitted as one of the official

languages of the country; and a prominent English Jew—
Sir Herbert Samuel, who had held a number of important
political appointments, culminating in that of Home
Secretary—was sent out as first High Commissioner.

One difficulty, perhaps, had been overlooked in this
period of enthusiasm. The Arab population of Palestine
was not numerous; they were for the most part on a very
low grade of civilization; they had shamefully neglected
the country, allowing large parts of it to degenerate into an
uncultivated waste. But their sense of local patriotism became immensely stimulated when they found others interested. Just before the San Remo Conference, anti-Jewish
riots had taken place in Jerusalem, resulting in the loss of
a number of lives; and, in 1921, there was a recurrence in
Jaffa, with even more deplorable results. Sir Herbert
Samuel demonstrated his impartiality by neglecting the
section which he might have been expected to favor; and
severe restrictions were placed upon Jewish immigration.
In 1929, in consequence of an absurd rumor that a plan
was on foot to dispossess the Arabs of the Mosque of
Omar, on the ancient Temple site, another series of anti-
Jewish riots took place, with devastating effect, throughout
the country.

Notwithstanding this, the positive achievements of the
experiment were far from negligible. In spite of the
vexatious limitations imposed, immigrants arrived in the
country in a steady trickle from every corner of the Jewish
world, from New York to Bokhara. The Jewish population, which in 1918 had numbered only 58,000 in a total
of 800,000, had risen within fifteen years to about 200,000.

Fresh Jewish suburbs sprang up outside the walls of Jerusalem. Tel-Aviv, the first Jewish city, developed with
amazing rapidity, until by 1933 it comprised some 60,000
souls. Considerable tracts of land were acquired, especially
in the Valley of Jezreel, by the Jewish National Fund.
New colonies were established here and there throughout
the country. Bands of *Halutzim,* or pioneers, were recruited in the Diaspora to perform the manual labor—
tilling the fields, building, road-making; and visitors used
to European valuations were amazed to meet among them
many University men and women, who had graduated
brilliantly in various abstruse subjects, and were masters of
half a dozen languages. Modern methods of agriculture
were introduced. Hills were once more rendered fertile by
the construction of terraces. The orange-growing industry
attained impressive proportions. Throughout the country,
work of afforestation was executed, swamps drained, and
malaria stamped out.

The earliest enterprise of importance carried out after
the British occupation, was the establishment in Jerusalem
of a University, the foundation stone of which was laid
before the cannon had ceased to mutter, and which was
formally opened in 1925. The medium of instruction was,
of course, Hebrew, which had obtained general currency
for all purposes throughout the new settlement, and which
now entered upon a fresh period of productivity. Newspapers, periodicals, novels, plays, poems, translations, works
of erudition, poured out in a steady stream from a dozen
different presses. A Hebrew theatre was established which
attained an international significance. It was a literary and

practical revival of a dormant language unique in history. Palestine had once again assumed its place in the scheme of Jewish life.

5.   The overthrow of the old order in Central and Eastern Europe, the final completion of Jewish emancipation in every important country of the world, the creation of the League of Nations with its solemn function of safeguarding the rights of minorities, led to a universal hope that the upheaval of 1914-1918, notwithstanding the sacrifices which it had involved and the disorders by which it had been followed, would usher in a millennial era of true freedom and equality for Jewry as a whole. Russia, however, still constituted a perpetual problem. It is true that the Revolution had emancipated the Jews, fully and without reservations. They were officially recognized as constituting a separate nationality, with its own language and institutions. Persons of Jewish birth, though in no case Jewish by conviction or in practice, were beginning to play a part of importance in Russian life; and one, Leon Trotsky, was among the outstanding figures in the new regime. Ambitious schemes were started, with lavish help from America, for creating vast Jewish agricultural colonies in the Ukraine, the Crimea, and Siberia, on a scale which rivalled, if it did not exceed, contemporary experiments in Palestine. It was hoped that an autonomous Jewish republic would ultimately be created as one of the constituents of the Soviet Union.

Yet in practice, the Soviet system was even more disastrous to Jewish life than its Czarist precursor had been.

The vast majority of Russian Jewry had been middle-men and small traders—an integral, though humble, part of that bourgeoisie against which the Bolshevik revolution had been directed. In a Republic of workmen and peasants, it was nearly as difficult for them to find a place as it had been ten centuries previous under the feudal regime. A number were taken into the government service, now opened to them for the first time, absorbed in the factories, or settled on the soil—a process necessarily slow, difficult, and expensive. A large proportion were left absolutely destitute; as unassimilable economically under the new form of government as they had been politically under the old. It was small compensation to be accorded equality of rights and opportunity when all channels of livelihood were closed.

Similarly, on the spiritual side, Judaism suffered, with all other faiths, in the campaign against religion. Synagogues were closed down or converted into clubs; public religious teaching was prohibited; obstacles were placed in the way even of the fundamental rite of circumcision. Zionism was condemned as a bourgeois movement, its adherents being subjected to merciless persecution and sent to Siberia. There was, of course, no bar from either side against intermarriage, which went on at an alarming pace; and, with no logical tie remaining in Judaism, assimilation in the completest sense became rampant.

Though the effects of Bolshevism on Jewish life in Russia were fatal, abroad the Jew was stigmatized as though he were exclusively responsible for the new scheme of things. The fact that the Soviet government, deserted by or mistrusting the tools of the old regime, recruited a large proportion of its civil service and of its diplomatic corps from persons of Jewish origin, gave the latter a disproportionate prominence. Moreover, Karl Marx, the prophet of Communism, happened to be of Jewish blood, though baptized in childhood and brought up as a Christian. Hence there was another excuse for identifying the Jew, already unpopular, with the dreaded system which threatened to undermine the foundations of the established order. It was seriously alleged that there was a universal understanding between Zionism, Bolshevism, and High Finance (all of them aspects of a hypothetical "Jewish International!") to secure the domination of the world; and a ridiculous farrago of nonsense, *The Protocols of the Learned Elders of Zion,* which purported to give an account of the proceedings of the Congress recently held in order to bring about this object, ran through edition after edition in every language. Even the discovery that this egregious production was, in fact, an adaptation of a work written to satirize Napoleon III, three quarters of a century before, did not entirely shake credence in it.

Throughout the world, even in England and America, there were signs of reaction. More serious by far was the condition of affairs in Central and Eastern Europe. Though the wave of pogroms was checked, acts of violence were perpetrated almost daily. The Roumanian Government remained profoundly anti-Jewish, notwithstanding its solemn pledges. In Poland, the Jews were excluded methodically from government employment, and squeezed out of the state monopolies. Attempts were made,

and sometimes enforced by governmental action, to restrict
the number of Jewish students in the Universities in proportion to the numerical importance of the Jewish population; and student riots became the order of the day. More
than one country, in defiance of the Minority Treaties, reduced Jewish traders to the verge of ruin by enforcing
Sunday closing, even in the case of those who had already
lost one day's business activity on Saturday. The crisis
which began to paralyze economic life throughout the
world in 1930, affected the Jewish middle-man to a disproportionate extent; and pauperization began to set in on an
alarming scale.

6.   Most amazing of all was the course of events in
Germany. Though at last German Jewry was fully emancipated, in fact as well as in theory, anti-Semitism was
attaining wilder extremities than ever before. Jewish pre-
eminence, in one field or another of national life, was
spoken of, and attacked, as Jewish "predominance." The
fact that some individuals had been able to accommodate
themselves to changing economic conditions aggrieved
those who were less fortunate. It was alleged that they
had established a stranglehold on German life, from industry on the one hand, to journalism on the other. The
new currents which they had introduced in thought, in
literature, and in drama, were stigmatized as poisonous and
deleterious. Even Albert Einstein, one of the most eminent
contemporary thinkers, drew upon himself a continual
stream of obloquy by reason of his race.

With the momentary amelioration of general conditions,

the anti-Jewish outcry was muffled. The recurrence of the economic crisis renewed it. The National Socialist, or pseudo-Fascist movement, founded by Adolf Hitler, made up for its lack of a constructive program by laying the responsibility for every ill which was besetting the country on the Jews; and one of the cardinal points of the policy of the new party was their expulsion, or at least disenfranchisement.

In 1933, Adolf Hitler became the Chancellor of the German Empire. A reign of terror immediately set in for the Jews, who seemed about to be reduced to a position worse by far than that of their co-religionists in Russia in the dark days before the War. They were thrust out wholesale, without compunction, from government and municipal offices, from the universities, from the professions, even from private employment. Physicians and lawyers were authorized to practice only in proportion to the numbers of the Jewish population. Their businesses were boycotted, with official sanction and encouragement. They were forced to relinquish their association with the great economic organizations which they had created; with the museums which they had established; with the Academies which they had made famous. A journalistic campaign of unheard-of virulence was let loose against them, even in those organs of opinion which they had formerly controlled. Scholars, writers, scientists, of international fame, who had built up Germany's reputation, whose discoveries had enabled her to withstand a world in arms, and whose prestige had assisted in rehabilitating her in the eyes of Europe, were reduced to beggary, or driven into exile. For the first time in history, the persecution extended not merely to those who professed the Jewish religion, but to all, however unimpeachable in their orthodoxy, in whose veins any Jewish blood was to be traced. Scenes reminiscent of the Middle Ages were enacted throughout the country; and the frontiers of barbarism were thrust forward at a stroke from the Vistula to the Rhine. Another hour of crisis in the checkered history of German Jewry had arrived. But the people who had survived the Crusades could survive National Socialism; and, in the long run, the reaction reflected, not on its victims, but on those responsible for its perpetration.

The latest Diaspora was more striking in its way than anything of the sort that had preceded it in human history. Within little more than a year, upwards of seventy thousand German Jews had left the country. The majority were not artisans or merchants, as might normally have been expected, but professional men—University professors, physicians, surgeons, lawyers, art-experts, writers, journalists: in many instances men of international reputation, who had given up their best years and devotion to Germany's service. By the end of 1933 there can have been few countries in the world where some famous German-Jewish scientist or scholar was not at work. But it was, unhappily, a period of intense economic depression, when every nation was erecting barriers against those who might compete in the labour market against native-born citizens. The process of readjustment was therefore peculiarly painful.

BOOK SIX

CATASTROPHE AND RESURRECTION

CXXXI.
CATASTROPHE

1.   At this stage a remarkable phenomenon became apparent. The development of a Jewish Palestine had been regarded by emancipated western Jewry as a quixotic, semi-charitable undertaking, which might perhaps contribute towards the reestablishment of Jewish self-respect and the restoration of a Jewish culture, but could never play a really important part in solving the physical problems of the Jewish people.

But, by a providential coincidence, Palestine had escaped the depression; it was indeed experiencing (thanks to the impetus given by Jewish Practical idealism) a minor 'boom'. So far was this the case that the gates were being opened to immigration on a larger scale than ever before. Accordingly, it was to Palestine that many dispossessed German Jews now went—including even large numbers who had previously been sternly anti-Zionistic in their views. It was the only country which was able to absorb them, or their hardly more fortunate Polish and eastern European co-religionists, on a large scale. In 1934 the Jewish immigration into the country was about 42,000, and in 1935 reached the record figure of 62,000. Within three years, over 35,000 German refugees had landed; and the figures did not show any sign of diminishing. By the close of 1939, the total Jewish population of the country, which at the time of the Balfour Declaration had been some 60,000, approached 500,000; and Tel Aviv was one of the most modern cities in the Middle East, with nearly 150,000 inhabitants. Of the Palestinian Jewish population, some 15 per cent, distributed in 270 rural centers with a total population of 143,000, were engaged in agriculture, 40,000 of them living in workers' colonies. The wild chimera which twenty years before had been ridiculed by hard-headed business men and experienced philanthropists was now the one bright spot on the Jewish horizon. No longer was it possible to talk of the Zionist experiment; it had become a reality. Palestine was not, indeed, Jewish; but, for the first time for fifteen centuries and more, there was a Jewish Palestine again.

Though these mighty achievements could not be annulled, the promise of this period was not destined to be sustained to the full. In April, 1936, there was a new Arab outbreak, differing from those which had preceded it in its duration, its cohesion, and the fact that it was in great measure due to foreign intrigue—particularly on the part of Fascist Italy, anxious to pose as the protector of Islam and to embarrass England in the Near East. A general strike was proclaimed, to be intensified by non-cooperation with the government and a boycott of the Jews. For many months organized gangster warfare was waged on Palestinian Jewry, with armed attacks against colonies, highway ambushes in the country and bomb outrages in the towns, and wholesale murder even of Arabs of more moderate opinions. Notwithstanding the overwhelming temptation to reciprocate vio-

lence for violence, the Jewish leaders managed to impress
on their followers with rare exceptions, a policy of non-
reprisal; and the pent-up feelings of the *Yishuv*[1] found
characteristic expression in the establishment during this
period of new colonies in the most dangerous areas and the
creation of a port at Tel Aviv to remedy the dislocation
caused by the inactivity at Jaffa.

As soon as order was superficially reestablished, a Royal
Commission was sent to Palestine to inquire into the cause
of the unrest. It reported that it was unable to see how the
problems involved could be solved on the basis of the Mandate, and suggested that the difficulty should be met by
dividing the country into two sovereign states, Arab and
Jewish. The idea of a sovereign state, however small, into
which immigration would be untrammelled and which,
therefore, might contribute solidly to the solution of the appalling refugee problem, had some obvious attractions, notwithstanding the fact that the fantastic frontier implied a
Zionism without Zion. Accordingly, at their meetings at
Zurich in August, 1937 (though only after long and bitter
criticism), the Zionist Congress and subsequently the Jewish
Agency authorized negotiations with the British Government along the lines of the proposed compromise, in the
hope that details might be drastically modified. Partition
was, however, unanimously rejected by the leaders of the
Arab malcontents; further disturbances broke out, and were
only suppressed after a systematic military effort; and in the
end the idea of partition was abandoned and an entirely
new policy announced in a White Paper issued in London

[1] The term now applied generally to the Jewish settlement in Palestine.

in May, 1939. This set a maximum of 75,000 for future Jewish immigration into Palestine, to be spread over a period of five years, and intimated that, if possible, the British administration would be withdrawn in 1949 and the country left independent (though bound to Great Britain by treaty), with its Jews a perpetual minority. It was thus that matters stood when, that summer, the Holy Land came under a grimmer menace. However much Imperial policy or local difficulties may have made this decision seem necessary, it was a far, far cry from the golden promise of the Balfour Declaration.

2.   When the Nazis first came into power, they had insisted that their anti-Semitic doctrine was a matter of internal concern and application only. But, as he proceeded from one success of diplomacy or bluster to the other, Hitler discovered that, by fostering or playing on local anti-Jewish prejudices and posing as the champion of Europe against a mythical entity which he termed International Jewry, it was possible to create a pro-German party in other states which espoused totalitarian doctrines and, though otherwise hyper-nationalist, was inclined to look sympathetically on German aspirations. Prejudice was naturally intensified by the influx of refugees, domestic persecution thus indirectly serving a diplomatic end. Official and semiofficial organizations of the Reich now began to carry on an unceasing propaganda against the Jews abroad as well as at home; and under the stimulus not only of German example but also (as afterwards became plain) of German subsidies, the peril spread with alarming rapidity to other countries. Even in

the traditional homes of liberalism in western Europe and beyond the Atlantic there was a menacing growth of anti-Semitism, using the new vocabulary and a new technique, and organized in parties such as the Cagoulards in France (where the premiership of the Jew, Léon Blum, in 1936-1937 and again in 1938 exacerbated the parties of the Right), the British Union of Fascists in England, the Rexists in Belgium, the Silver Shirts and similar bodies in America—all at one in exploiting elementary anti-Jewish prejudice for remoter political objects, and ultimately in a lack of loyalty to their country.

In central and eastern Europe the reaction went beyond the realm of theory. To states less developed mechanically and economically, the fact that the new doctrine had been embraced by "enlightened" Germany, and her political triumphs since the change, stamped it with something more than respectability. In Roumania, where the Minority Treaty had been flouted from the outset, violence became more and more usual and restrictions more and more galling, until at the end of 1936 Octavian Goga formed a professedly anti-Semitic government which set about emulating the German example forthwith; and although it remained in office for only seven weeks (December, 1936—February, 1937) and a momentary alleviation followed, the new doctrines were by now solidly established, as subsequent events were to show. Once the Nazi Magyar collaboration began in 1938, reactionary Hungary saw the introduction of restrictive racial legislation on the lines of the Nuremberg Laws. In Poland, though intense anti-German feeling prevailed, the Endek party introduced Nazi methods and ideology into public life; economic distress was increased by administrative discrimination; and the idea that the Jews, however long established, did not constitute part of the Polish people made such headway that the Government began to discuss mass-emigration—if only an outlet could be found—in terms not far removed from deportation. But most deplorable were developments in Italy, which since 1870 had become the classical land of Jewish Emancipation, and where Jewish equality had been more of a political and social reality than anywhere else in the world. Fascism had originally shown no trace of anti-Semitism, except inasmuch as it is implicit in any hyper-nationalist state; Jews had, in fact, played an important part in the movement from the beginning, and Benito Mussolini had condemned Jew-baiting and racialism in biting terms. But, immediately the military alliance with Germany was concluded in 1938, the handful of 50,000 Italian Jews was offered up on the totalitarian altar.

More tragic still, of necessity, was the lot of the Jews in those countries which actually came under Nazi rule. In March, 1938, Hitler's legions marched into Austria, and the greed, fanaticism, and ebullience of his followers were turned against that country's 200,000 Jews, mostly concentrated in the highly-cultured community of Vienna; the cloak of legalism was now abandoned, and there were no gradations to soften the blow. The Nuremberg Laws and the rest of the new German anti-Jewish code were enforced overnight. Prominent Jews, beginning with the head of the House of Rothschild, were arrested wholesale for no reason other than that they were Jews, brutally maltreated and thrust into concentration camps from which many never returned. Jewish businesses were looted, closed, or confiscated. Synagogues were turned into offices for the Nazi armed guards, whose principal occupation was Jew-baiting of the most elementary and degrading character. The consulates of those few countries the gates of which were not entirely closed to Jews were beset by long lines of pitiful refugees. To the east, thousands were driven over the frontiers of states unwilling to receive them, and many met their death as they wandered hopelessly in no-man's-land or drifted down the Danube in over-crowded boats which were not allowed to put to shore. Suicides rose to an appalling level.

In Germany itself, conditions had progressively deteriorated during the "Cold Pogrom," which had lasted without interruption since 1933. Nevertheless, the Jews had somehow managed to reestablish an impoverished group-life, isolated economically as well as socially, and ultimately dependent on the few businesses that had managed to survive the perpetual boycott and the capital of the handful who were still well-to-do. Something of a spiritual and intellectual revival had resulted from persecution; and the educational system organized for children who were not admitted to ordinary schools, the self-contained cultural life which had now grown up to meet the requirements of men and women now excluded from a normal expression, the orchestras and dramatic performances in which artists dismissed from their employment served the needs of a public forbidden access to concert-halls and theatres, had demonstrated an amazing power of adaptation and resilience.

Though elaborate new humiliations were introduced from time to time, though the more virile elements continued to emigrate, though what was left of the community was increasingly impoverished and increasingly aged, it seemed that something firm, durable, and admirable had been established amid the ruins. But for this very reason the new German-Jewish life was doomed to destruction, with tragic and brutal suddenness.

In October, 1938, the German Government suddenly deported over the eastern frontier some 12,000 Jews of Polish origin. Nearly 5,000 of them were trapped in a no-man's-land near Zbonszyn, where they were herded under sickening conditions while diplomatic conversations dragged on concerning their fate. Among the sufferers were an elderly couple named Grynszpan, who had lived in Hanover for more than thirty years. Their seventeen-year-old son, Herschel, who was in Paris, was half demented by what he heard, and as a reprisal shot and fatally wounded one of the Secretaries of the German Embassy, Ernst vom Rath. This provided the Nazi propaganda machine with a superb pretext to carry a long-premeditated scheme into effect. With hardly a single exception, all of the 600 synagogues in the country—including ancient buildings which had formerly been regarded as national monuments—were gutted. Almost every Jewish business house was sacked. A billion marks' worth of Jewish property was wantonly destroyed. Thousands of Jewish homes were raided, and some 30,000 individuals—not excepting rabbis, however aged—were flung into concentration camps, where they were treated with incredible barbarity. There were hundreds—perhaps

thousands—of deaths. The authorities looked on these
scenes of violence, which outdid in scale any Russian
pogrom or any medieval massacre, not merely impassively,
but approvingly; and, as a legal punishment for the deed
of their unbalanced co-religionist in Paris, a fine of a billion
marks (one-fifth of their property, at a lavish estimate) was
imposed on the Jews of the Reich. It was, moreover, ordered
that all Jewish businesses should be transferred forthwith
into "Aryan" hands, the Jews, however, first making good
at their own expense the damage to their property. German
Jewry was wantonly, deliberately, and irrevocably smashed.

Henceforth there was obviously no conceivability of a
future for Jews in Germany. Prisoners were released from
the concentration camps only on condition that they emigrated forthwith; threats, violence, and pressure were exerted on others; in no case was there any ultimate possibility of remaining. Conditions for the *émigrés* had by now
become worse than ever by reason of the fact that, what
with exchange manipulation, special "flight" taxation, and
so on, they were now able to take with them in currency
value only some 5 per cent of the property they had saved
from the debacle, so that even the well-to-do could look forward to nothing but a life of penury. But necessity overwhelmed all normal conditions. The tragic scenes of the
past few years were multiplied and intensified. Few countries would now open their gates. Refugee-laden vessels,
seeking a port where they might discharge their cargo of
misery, became familiar on the maritime highways of the
world; and tens of thousands went to places (such as
Shanghai) where for the moment a visa was unnecessary or

there was no immigration control, simply because they were admitted. On the initiative of the American Government, an international conference on refugees had met at Evian in the summer of 1938, but there was little practical outcome other than the clarification of what was already so tragically clear, that no country welcomed these enforced wanderers. Very few governments made any constructive contribution to the solution of the problem. Thanks indeed to the practical idealism and organizing ability of Henrietta Szold (1860-1945: creator of the American women's Zionist organization, "Hadassah," which had done so much splendid welfare work), arrangements were made for transferring many children from central Europe to a new life on the soil of Palestine; and the country continued to absorb a limited number of adults, not all of whom, however, entered legally. The United States on its side adopted a somewhat more liberal policy than hitherto, enabling many immigrants to anticipate the normal date of entry; while Great Britain allowed herself to be used as a half-way house for refugees whose ultimate destination was assured.

By the summer of 1939, one-half of the former Jewish population of the Greater Reich had left the country. Yet, no sooner was some progress made towards a solution of the problem than it was intensified by fresh complications. The 5,000 Jews of Memel shared the lot of those of Germany when it was summarily annexed in the autumn of 1938. In Danzig the Nazi administration made existence impossible for 10,000 more, notwithstanding the nominal authority of the League of Nations. Czechoslovakia had been almost the only "Succession State" where the rights of

minorities had been respected and Jewish equality existed
in fact as well as theory. In 1938-1939, with the disintegra-
tion of the country, the erection of Slovakia into a Nazi
puppet-state, the annexation of large areas by Hungary and
the absorption of the former Bohemia into the Reich, another 350,000 Jews—including some of the oldest and proud-
est communities of the Diaspora—were thrown into the
vortex. By the autumn of 1939, areas which had formerly
housed upwards of 2,500,000 Jews—more than one-quarter
of the entire Jewish population of Europe—were under the
rule or the direct influence of Nazi anti-Semitism.

3.   On September 1st, 1939, the German forces invaded Poland, and the second World War in a generation
began. Within a few weeks, the country had been overrun,
save for the zone occupied by the Russians, in which (as
shortly after in the Baltic States of Lithuania, Latvia, and
Estonia) the Soviet order was introduced. The German-
occupied area contained upwards of 2,000,000 Jews—in the
main poverty-stricken but imbued with unbounded vitality
and deep loyalty to Jewish tradition and values. They were
exposed forthwith to a systematic campaign of oppression.
It was simple in a country under martial law to impose
crushing fines, to carry out wholesale executions, to institute
compulsory labor service, or to demand a supply of Jewish
girls for the military brothels. But all this was incidental.
There was hardly a town or village throughout the country
in which Jews were not butchered at this period by the
German soldiery, sometimes in fantastic numbers. The food
ration allotted to Jews later on was barely sufficient to main-

tain life, being only one-half of what was allowed to Polish Christians, and a quarter of that enjoyed by Teutons. Shortly after the conquest of the country, the wearing of a Badge of Shame to distinguish Jew from non-Jew was instituted (November, 1939), as prescribed in the Middle Ages but never enforced in Europe since the period of the French Revolution. In the following year, the Ghetto, too, was reintroduced as a formal institution legally enforced. The largest, holding even at the outset upwards of 350,000 souls, was that of Warsaw, inaugurated in the autumn of 1940. This was surrounded by an eight-foot wall of concrete with several massive gates—a gloomy city within the city; there was a similar walled enclosure at Lodz, while in a dozen other cities there were segregated areas, cut off by electrically-charged wire fences. In the Middle Ages, egress from the Jewish quarter was allowed except at night; now, it was entirely forbidden without special permission, under pain of death for a second offense. The institution was, however, only a temporary expedient.

The astounding German military triumphs in the course of 1940-1941 made the Nazi Government completely indifferent to what was left of neutral opinion. The outrages now became more and more callous, spreading from Poland throughout Europe. In all the occupied countries, the leaders of anti-Semitic propaganda in recent years were seen, after the German invasion, in their true colors, as traitors who did their utmost to weaken the armies in the field and to undermine public confidence. They then became omnipotent in the countries which they had betrayed. Forthwith, nineteenth century Emancipation was reversed, the

Nuremberg Laws or their equivalents were introduced, collective fines were imposed, Jewish business and fortunes were sequestered, racial teaching was introduced into the schools, and the efficacy of the work of anti-Semitism was taken as an index of loyalty to the New Order in Europe. The ground was thus prepared for the reign of terror, under immediate Nazi direction. Much the same pattern was followed everywhere. The sporadic violence at the time of the invasion was succeeded by a period of restrained oppression, during which, though restrictive legislation was put into force, there seemed some prospect of the reestablishment of an ordered existence. Then, by degrees sufficiently gradual to prevent an explosion of public opinion, the thumbscrew was tightened. The wearing of the Jewish Badge of Shame, now generally in the form of an armlet or a patch of the traditional yellow hue bearing the Shield of David and the word "Jew," became universal throughout occupied Europe, being extended to Germany and Bohemia (with Moravia) in September, 1941, and even into France and other western lands in the summer of the following year. (Later, this mark of degradation was applied to other "inferior" races.) As in eastern Europe, Jews were assigned special ration cards, implying an allowance far below subsistence level. Deadlier still, they were deported from certain cities or areas, raids were made on their homes and institutions, and concentration camps were established, so that life became a perpetual nightmare.

The idea of concentrating the Jews in a special reservation in eastern Europe had meanwhile grown upon the German Government, who now regarded it as a zone whither those of all countries could be dispatched, regardless of their antecedents or of their fate. In October, 1941, the deportations from Germany began, the example being imitated elsewhere shortly afterwards. In the following March, orders were issued for the rate to be forced up to the level of 100,-000 monthly. Thus, the "Jewish Problem" would be solved within a very short time, once for all. Wherever the German authority prevailed, Jews were ruthlessly rounded up for dispatch, being allowed to take with them at the most nothing but a handful of personal necessities. From every direction, trains of sealed cattle-trucks, densely packed with miserable humanity, rumbled over the railroads towards eastern Europe, in the stifling heat of summer or the deadly frosts of winter. In an appallingly high number of cases, to be sent on the journey was itself equivalent to a death-warrant. Yet those who died thus were more fortunate than those who survived to meet the terrible fate that awaited them at the end.

For before long, the conception of a Jewish reservation was abandoned in favor of a new, incredible idea. In the summer of 1941 plans were made for the "final solution" of the Jewish question in Europe by the extermination of the Jews; and in the following January the process began, under the direction of a special section of the gestapo, the German secret police. In the course of the next few months, reports began to penetrate to the outside world of the horrors of the death-camps at Majdanek, Belzec, Treblinka, Oswiecim (Auschwitz), and elsewhere, in which Jewish deportees, first from Poland and then from all over Europe, were being exterminated by the thousands and scores of thousands—by shooting, by injections, and above all, by poison gas. It is hardly possible for the human mind to grasp the scale or the heartless deliberation of the atrocities which took place, in the twentieth century, at the hands of ostensibly civilized human beings; nor can any written account, however conservatively phrased, appear even remotely plausible. It was computed that at Oswiecim and the adjacent camp of Brzezinka (Birkenau) alone, more than 1,750,000 Jews from various countries were murdered in the two years ending in April, 1944, and at Majdanek nearly 1,500,000. Thirty-one thousand, including 13,000 brought from Hungary, were shot in the Kamienitcz-Podolski region. In some places, according to the reports which subsequently circulated, pious Jews of the old school perplexed their butchers by dancing to meet their death, in token of their perfect submission to the Divine will. When the Nazis were driven out of Poland, the scene of horror was transferred to the concentration camps on German soil, especially Dachau, Bergen-Belsen, and Buchenwald, which attained ghastly notoriety throughout the civilized world. Here, appalling numbers of Jews and non-Jews alike were herded together in circumstances that made death by hunger or in the gas-chamber a happy release. On May 15th, 1942, a law was passed by the Slovak "parliament" providing for the expatriation of all Jews; and by December 75,000 of them had been conveyed to Poland to meet their fate. On the night of July 12th of the same year, a great round-up began in France, 28,000 men, women, and children from Paris alone being herded in concentration camps near the capital in readiness for deportation. In all, some 120,000 Jews were deported from that country, where

Jewish rights had first been specifically proclaimed in Europe. No more than 5,000 of them returned. The handful of highly-assimilated Jews of Norway, who could not by any stretch of the imagination be considered a "problem" or even an irritant, were attacked by the traitor, Vidkun Quisling, with an energy which would have been ludicrous had its consequences not been so tragic; for all remaining in the country were arrested and deported—many for work in the Silesian coal-mines—their property, of course, being confiscated.

The centuries-long tranquillity of the Jews in Holland and the general sympathy of the Dutch population proved no safeguard: for all Jews who could be traced were ultimately rounded up to meet their fate, a handful only surviving. In no western land were their sufferings less justifiable, or so intense. In Amsterdam, the Portuguese synagogue only was left undamaged, but despite their different historic background its members suffered with their co-religionists. From Belgium, liberated somewhat earlier, at least 30,000 Jews out of 80,000 were deported. Hungary, so long as it remained an independent associated power, retained a modicum of humanity (though little more) in executing its anti-Semitic policy, at least as regards its native community—the eastern European element had been ruthlessly thrust back across the frontiers. But when, after an attempt to conclude a separate peace, the puppet Arrow Cross Government was set up in October, 1944, that country, too, was drawn into the vortex; a pogrom on a major scale was staged in Budapest, and the deportees in the next two months numbered scores of thousands. (Fortunately, deliverance took place before the disaster had become comprehensive.) After Roumania was converted into a totalitarian state and allied herself with Germany (June, 1940), a determined onslaught was made on her Jews. Not only were restrictive laws put into force, on the Nuremberg model, but there was in addition an outburst of unbridled physical violence of fantastic horror. Even this was outdone when the Roumanian forces occupied Bessarabia and Bukovina; here, something like one-third of the entire population was exterminated. All told, in the autumn of 1941, it is believed that the Roumanians were responsible for the massacre of 100,000 Russian and native Jews: subsequently, some 130,000 were deported, under the conditions that had become commonplace, to the newly-annexed territories beyond the River Dniester.

It was Jews of a different type and with a different background who were encountered by the Nazi forces when they broke through to the Mediterranean, but this did not affect their fate: indeed, they were among the worst sufferers. The Jugoslav Jews were almost exterminated, in circumstances of exceptional barbarity, the Croatian Fascists (Ustachi) vying with the Moslems of Bosnia in their bloodlust, and a reward being given for every fugitive handed over to the authorities. There was barely a single survivor of the very ancient Jewish community of the island of Crete, and only a handful from that of Rhodes. The same was the case in Salonica, once the greatest Jewish center of the Mediterranean world, almost all of whose members were deported to a tragic fate.

In Italy—still to some extent a free ally—it was impossible

for the essentially kindly population to imitate Nazi bestiali-
ties, however painfully they adopted the anti-Semitic code.
Hence, even though the restrictive legislation became more
and more harsh, it was an oasis of relative humanity in a
hate-filled world. But, after the abortive attempt to overthrow Fascism in July, 1943, Italy from Rome northwards
became in effect a German-occupied country, and repression
began in full force as everywhere else in Europe. The only
areas (other than Russia) which were not overwhelmed by
the disaster were indomitable England, the neutral havens
of Switzerland, Sweden, European Turkey, and Portugal,
and Finland, which remained democratic even though a
German satellite.

Only in one land was popular opposition in any way
effective. When in the spring of 1940 Denmark was occupied, the people resolutely refused to enforce any discrimi-
natory regulations; and it is said that the king threatened
to wear the Badge of Shame himself if it were imposed on
his Jewish subjects. Three years later, when the Germans
took over the administration of the country, an anti-Jewish
campaign was immediately opened. The Danish patriots
were already prepared; and almost the whole of the incon-
siderable community were ferried in all manner of flimsy
craft over to Sweden, where they were hospitably received.
For once, the Nazi beast had the prey snatched from his
jaws. No country, indeed, lacked courageous citizens who
showed active sympathy—only thus was a Jewish remnant
able to survive clandestinely in some of the occupied areas.
Occasionally, there were demonstrations against the deportations; and to flaunt the Jewish Badge was a recognized

patriotic gesture in France, Belgium, and Holland. In the last-named country, moreover, a general strike took place in February, 1941, in an attempt, temporarily successful, to prevent the mass deportations. Even in Germany, collusion or craft made it possible for a handful to survive in some places. There are some who risked their own lives to help the hunted to escape, or took charge of the children when the parents were deported to an unknown fate. Frequently, the lead was taken by priests and nuns, following the example set by the Vatican itself. Yet even in such circumstances some persons were unable to suppress their proselytizing zeal, or considered it their duty to bring up their charges in the religion with which they were themselves familiar. The losses to the Jewish people by infant conversion in this period, throughout Europe, were comparable only to those at the time of the Forced Conversions of the fifteenth century in the Iberian Peninsula.

In June, 1941, Germany had attacked Russia. The initial arena of struggle included most of the former Pale of Settlement, where Jews were thickly established, comprising great aggregations such as those of Odessa and Kiev. All told, this area had contained some two-thirds of the 3,000,-000 Jews of the Soviet Republics, in addition to something like 1,500,000 in the part of Poland occupied by the Russians two years earlier and in the Baltic States. The tenacity of the Russian resistance gave the excuse for terrific devastation in these areas. The onslaught developed into a campaign of extermination. Of the former Jewish populations, only a minority survived, cowering in the ruins or fighting in the partisan ranks or transferred in time to a safer area.

Simon Dubnow, the octogenarian historian of Jewish martyrdom, was among a group shot in the market-place at Riga immediately after the German capture of the city.

Meanwhile, the tragedy of Polish Jewry was moving to its climax. Conditions in the congested Warsaw Ghetto, the only center of real importance now surviving in the country, became worse and worse with every week that passed. Yet still, Hebraic values were able to reassert themselves. Cultural life flourished as before. An educational system was set up. A theater continued to function. What was most remarkable, secret Zionist activities continued; and under the eyes of the German authorities, Jews made collections for work in Palestine, and young men and women prepared themselves as best they could in the hope of emigration.

This spirit of resilience was itself provocative. On July 22nd, 1942, orders were issued for the deportation towards the death-camps of all the Warsaw Jews, without distinction of age or sex, save for certain potentially useful categories who were given a reprieve. They were to be allowed to take with them fifteen kilograms only of personal effects: resistance was punishable by death. The round-up began forthwith, and continued at the rate of some 4,500 daily. By September, the official number of those deported was some 250,000, probably few of whom now survived; and in the following October, only 40,000 ration cards were issued for distribution in the Ghetto. In April, when orders were given for a large contingent of the survivors to report, they refused to obey. There followed one of the most tragic, most amazing episodes of the entire war. On the night of April 18th-19th (it happened to be Passover Eve) German police and S.S. detachments attacked the Ghetto with the support of artillery. The surviving population, inspired by the underground Jewish fighting organization, fought desperately in its defense with weapons smuggled in from outside. It was no haphazard episode. There was a co-ordinated command, and an organized medical service; contact was maintained with the Polish underground movement; women and girls operated machine-guns, and suicide squads broke through the German lines or blew up tanks with improvised grenades. More than once in the early stages the German troops were driven back, but fire was ultimately used to achieve what rifles and artillery could not. When the central region was at last overwhelmed, resistance continued in the outlying streets; when this was at last suppressed, a few stalwarts held out in the cellars and sewers. It was only at the end of May that the last embers of revolt were stamped out. The survivors—some 20,000—were rounded up and sent to the death camps, Warsaw being now *judenrein*. The three thousand years of Jewish history know of no episode more heroic.

With the need for a place of refuge more acute than ever before, and no alternative haven possible, Palestine assumed a greater importance than ever in the eyes of oppressed Jewry, given moral strength to face the future only by the hope of Zion. Yet the British Government adhered pedantically even now to the policy of the White Paper of 1939. Those who had escaped from the hell of central Europe, and made their way over the mountains and across the deserts, found themselves refused permission to enter the land of their hopes. Unscrupulous ship-owners and captains, sailing under the improbable flags of Central or South American republics, preyed upon the misery of the fugitives, promising to convey them to the Holy Land if they were extravagantly reimbursed. In such circumstances, disaster became a commonplace. A case which became notorious was that of the "S.S. Struma," which lay off Constantinople for three months with nearly 800 Roumanian refugees crammed aboard—the Roumanian Government callously alleging that they had lost all rights by leaving illegally, the British refusing to admit them to Palestine, the Turks not allowing them to land. On February 23rd, 1942, the ramshackle vessel put to sea with its cargo of human misery. On the following night it sank, with only a single survivor.

From the beginning, the Zionist representatives had clamored to be allowed to recruit a Jewish army, so that the flag of Judah could be unfurled in the field against Israel's enemies. This elementary concession was not granted for fear of arousing Arab resentment. Nevertheless, Jews fought in exceptionally great numbers in the Allied ranks. It was the only war in modern history in which Jews were to be found only on one side, the total number of those under arms rising ultimately to well over 1,000,000. Moreover, in occupied Europe, the patriotic movements which continued resistance to the Germans in the dark years from 1940 onwards were composed to a disproportionate extent of Jews, both in the partisan groups and in the ranks of the "free" forces overseas. (In Poland and France at least, there were specific Jewish divisions of the underground movement and the partisans.) Meanwhile, a Palestinian contingent—in fact overwhelmingly Jewish in composition—was raised in the

Holy Land; at first only for para-military duties, though
this was not the case afterwards. Jewish assault troops as
well as Jewish transport and pioneers did good work in the
British campaigns in Abyssinia, northern Africa, Greece,
and Italy, and redemption was brought to many ancient
communities by these muscular kinsmen in khaki, wearing
the Shield of David on their shoulders and obeying Hebrew
words of command.

From the winter of 1942-1943, the tide of battle began to
recede along the Eastern Front. During the course of the
next two years, the Russians reoccupied the zone of former
dense Jewish settlement, with the centers which had contributed so greatly to Jewish cultural life during the past
century. Among the inhabitants who greeted the entering
columns there were hardly any Jews. A few survived, lurking in the cellars, concealed by their neighbors, or fighting
with the irregulars; a few more returned from the surrounding countryside when the German menace had definitely passed. But they were a mere handful all told. The
cities where as many as one-tenth of the former Jewish
population had survived were in a minority. Indeed, as the
Germans retreated before the victorious armies, they exterminated the remaining Jews wherever they could, rather
than allow them to be liberated.

When the roar of the cannon had ceased, in the spring of
1945, it was possible for stricken Jewry to assess the extent
of its disaster. The forebodings of the past five years were
outdone by the reality. Of Poland's former 3,350,000 Jews,
it was estimated that fewer than 55,000 were left in the
country; another quarter of a million had been able to find

refuge in Russia; the rest (save for a few thousands scattered through the world) were dead. Czechoslovakia had before the war some 360,000 Jews; only 40,000 were left. Of Roumania's million, there were now no more than 320,000; and Roumania had fared relatively well, owing to the speed of the Russian advance. Jugoslavia's 75,000 were reduced by almost nine-tenths; the 75,000 formerly in Greece in about the same ratio; Holland's 150,000 by at least four-fifths. Happy were the lands such as Hungary, or France, where as much as one-half of the former Jewish population was left. In the whole of Bohemia and Moravia, only two rabbis remained. Many ancient Jewish centers were obliterated. At Frankfort, only 160 Jews could now be found among the ruins. Of the 56,000 Jews of Salonica, once a preponderantly Jewish city, barely 2,000 could be mustered. The throbbing Jewish life of Vilna, with 54,000 souls in 1931, was represented on its liberation by only 600 survivors. If in due course others ventured out from their hiding-places, it was not in numbers such as to qualify the general picture. Since 1939, perhaps as many as 6,000,000—certainly well over 4,000,000—Jews had perished out of the 9,000,000 who once lived in the lands through which the Nazi fury had swept—between one-quarter and one-third of the entire Jewish population of the world.

It was incomparably the greatest disaster in Jewish life; the greatest disaster, perhaps, in the life of any people since the dawn of history. The great catastrophes of the Dark Ages had embraced one or two countries only at a time; this raged simultaneously from the Arctic Ocean to the southern shores of the Mediterranean, from the Atlantic to the Volga. Nearly one-half of the world's Jews were simultaneously affected; at least twenty times as many persons had perished as in any other comparable period in their people's history. It is difficult for the mind to grasp, or pen to convey, the magnitude of the catastrophe.

Thus in 1945 Jewry prepared to face the future. It was a future utterly unlike the past. The European phase, which had prevailed in Jewish history for the past thousand years, had come to a violent end. The future lay preponderantly with the newest and the oldest havens of Jewish life—with the five million Jews of America, and the Jews of Palestine.

XXXII. THE STATE OF ISRAEL

1.   The scale and the range of the disaster that overtook the Jewish people in the course of this hideous decade
left only one conceivable solution to its agonizing problem:
of this fact, those who remained were now almost unanimously convinced. Morally incapable of return to the ruined
homes where their kindred had been slaughtered, even if
they were not faced with the hostility of their neighbors,
physically unable to enter countries of greater opportunity
because of stringent immigration laws, they could see no
conceivable future except in Palestine, and the Palestinian
Yishuv was able and eager to succor them.

But, even now, the administration kept the gates of the
country stubbornly closed to all but a mere trickle. The
great armies, still stationed in the country as an aftermath
of the war, were now employed with the assistance of
ludicrously strong naval forces in the despicable task of
preventing the arrival of the "illegal" immigrants, who now
began to be smuggled through from Europe in increasing

numbers. This policy, however, defeated its own object, for it made the establishment of a wholly autonomous Jewish area seem absolutely necessary, even in the eyes of many who were not Zionists in the full sense, not as a political or philosophical gesture, but for the fundamental purpose of saving life and maintaining hope. The overwhelming majority of American Jewry had become convinced of this during the past few years; and it was indeed due, to a great extent, to its unswerving support in the political field as well as in the concrete sense that the amazing triumph of the ensuing period was to be achieved.

For Palestinian Jewry for its part could not admit that any earthly power could overrule their right and duty to give refuge in the land—their special relation to which, constantly reiterated in the Bible, had been recognized by the concert of nations—to their broken kinsmen who had survived miraculously from the crematoria. That horrible climax to the traditional quietism had drastically affected the Jewish mentality, and now led to an unprecedented revulsion of feeling. Armed clashes between the British forces and the Jewish population, now in great part trained for battle, became more and more frequent. Extremist groups—the National Military Organization (*Irgun Zevai Leumi*) and the more radical fighters for the Freedom of Israel (*Lohamei Heruth Israel,* sometimes known after their founder as the Stern Group), were strengthened by these happenings and embarked on a systematic terrorist campaign (not restricted to Palestine) reminiscent of the Sinn Feiners in Ireland twenty years before, or of their own ancestors, the *sicarii,* in Judaea in Roman times.

The British government was meanwhile pursuing a blundering policy, which seemed consistent only in its determination to thwart, at the risk of any contradictions, the realization even of moderate Zionist hopes. Shortly after the conclusion of the war, the President of the United States had asked the British Government to alleviate Jewish suffering among the "D P's" on the continent of Europe by the issue of 100,000 immigration certificates to Palestine forthwith. Rather than comply, the British Foreign Minister, Ernest Bevin, suggested the appointment of a joint Anglo-American commission of inquiry to investigate the whole question anew (November, 1945). Although a majority of its members did not favor Zionist claims to the full, this body recommended the removal of the restrictions on land-purchase in Palestine imposed by the unfortunate White Paper of 1939 (still in force, notwithstanding its condemnation at the League of Nations) and the immediate admission of the 100,000 Jewish immigrants, as President Truman had proposed. The outright acceptance of the recommendations, as was naturally to be anticipated, would have ended the tension; instead, the British Government made acquiescence conditional on a series of impossible stipulations—including the complete disarming of Palestinian Jewry, which would have left it powerless in the face of the dangers which might become imminent at any moment, and subject it irrevocably to Arab mercies should the Mandatory Power withdraw. Under the stress of the disappointment, the Palestinian disorders became worse. So did the policy of repression. Concentration camps, unhappily reminiscent of those in Europe from which they had escaped, were set up in Cyprus for housing would-be immigrants whom the might of the glorious British navy had intercepted at sea; and on one occasion the world's conscience was even more profoundly shocked, when those aboard one intercepted vessel, the "Exodus," were actually shipped back to blood-soaked Germany.

In the succeeding months, the British cabinet advanced more than one ill-digested plan for a settlement of the problem which had begun to command universal attention and to attract almost universal obloquy or derision. In accordance with what was now become an obsession at Whitehall, all retained as a fundamental condition the drastic restriction of immigration. Hence, even if they had been acceptable to the Arabs (in fact stubbornly and irreconcilably opposed to any scheme which recognized the special status of Jews in Palestine), they could in no circumstances have been agreed to by any responsible Jewish leader. At length, the British Government announced its intention of submitting the issue to the United Nations, it being naturally understood that the decision would be binding. Yet another commission of investigation was appointed, this time international. Once more impartial inquiry proved on the whole favorable to the basic Zionist claims; for (like the Royal Commission of 1937), this body recommended by a majority, not indeed the constitution of Palestine into a Jewish state, but the constitution of a Jewish state in the country, which was to be divided into two autonomous areas, one Jewish and one Arab; there was to be a two-year transitional period, during which the British Government was to remain in control and in the course of which 150,000 Jews were to be admitted. The area assigned to the Jewish state, under this scheme, was to include the Valley of Jezreel, Eastern Galilee, most of the coastal plain (including Haifa as well as Tel Aviv) and the desolate (but in the view of Jewish agricultural experts recoverable) district in the south of the country, the Negev, where several new colonies had been established in recent years and which was now assuming great importance in Jewish eyes. Jerusalem, on the other hand, notwithstanding its long-standing Jewish majority, was to continue to be administered by an international agency; and the rest of the country, including Western Galilee and the whole of the central area, was, like Transjordan, to be Arab.

Notwithstanding the obstructive attitude of the British Government, the General Assembly of the United Nations endorsed the partition scheme, with certain unimportant modifications, by more than the two-thirds majority which was requisite (November 29th, 1947). The Arab States menaced direct action; and murderous attacks took place on defenseless Jews in many parts of the Moslem world. Palestine began to lapse into a state of civil war, the British forces very often actually failing to intervene to stop attacks on Jewish colonies and convoys, though they permitted the British-officered Arab Legion recruited in Transjordan to take a bloody hand. The *Yishuv* on its side organized its defense, frequently even passing over to the counter-offensive. Meanwhile, wholly confident (and, as events were to show, rightly confident) in its new-found strength, it gladly prepared to shoulder the greater task that was now seen to be imminent. Sullenly, the British prepared for withdrawal.

By May 15th, as they announced, the Mandate which had been received twenty-eight years before from the now-defunct League of Nations would be formally relinquished.

That day was a Sabbath. On the previous afternoon, therefore, a proclamation was read publicly in Tel Aviv by the outstanding personality of the *Yishuv*, David Ben-Gurion, Chairman of the Executive of the Jewish Agency and Prime Minister designate. The proclamation declared that at midnight a sovereign Jewish state (later given the name *Israel*) would come into existence in those parts of the country assigned to the Jews by the decision of the United Nations. On May 16th, 1948, Chaim Weizmann was chosen president by the Provisional Council, and on February 16th, 1949, he was formally elected the first President of the State of Israel.

It was obvious that a period of stress and trial lay ahead. The armies of five Arab states were already poised menacingly on the borders. A nation unused to arms for nearly twenty centuries was to be submitted forthwith to the ordeal of battle. But the *Yishuv* had no doubts or hesitations. The age-old yearnings of a people had resulted, by devious and unexpected ways, in an achievement without parallel in human history. The promise of the prophets had been fulfilled. The Jewish State had been reborn.

2.   Already before this, hostilities between the Arab and the Jewish forces had begun. What happened now was among the most remarkable episodes in Jewish history. The spirit of the Maccabees was revived, after over two thousand years, and in the face of even greater difficulties. The em-

bodiment and inspiration of this heroic chapter was David Ben-Gurion who had taken a prominent part in Jewish life in Palestine since he had first come from Russia forty years before, and was now at the head of the Provisional Government. The nucleus of the Jewish forces consisted of the former *Haganah** which had been organized earlier for the safeguarding of the Jewish colonies against Arab attacks and, in more recent years, although declared illegal, had a great although clandestine extension. Its crack corps, known as *Palmach* (abbreviation for *Pelugoth Machaz*—"striking forces") in particular won an imperishable name; while the extremist groups fought under their own commands with a savage desperation which was sometimes an embarrassment. The Arab forces had everything on their side—numbers, equipment, training, position. The Jews had nothing but a fierce devotion, inspired leadership, and the realization that the alternative to victory was not merely defeat, but obliteration.

In April the much-vaunted local Arab "Army of Liberation," with reinforcements from beyond the frontier, was routed near Mishmar ha-Emek by the vastly-outnumbered *Haganah*—the first military victory in Jewish annals since Bar Kochba. This was the prelude to a number of local successes. Tiberias fell to the Jewish forces on April 18th. A few days later the control of the great seaport town of Haifa, with its large Arab population, was secured. On May 10th, Safed, the ancient city of the mystics, was captured, the panic-stricken defenders wrongly imagining that they were being attacked by a greatly superior army. Two

*The Hebrew word for "defense."

days later, Jaffa surrendered after many assaults to forces
operating from Tel Aviv. Thus by the time of the Declaration of Independence, the Jewish forces were in complete
control of much of the area allotted to them.

Simultaneously with the British evacuation, however, a
concerted assault began by the regular armies of five Arab
states, who expected a rapid victory against ill-armed and
peace-loving opponents. In the south, the Egyptians occupied Gaza and approached within twenty-two miles of Tel
Aviv; in the center, Transjordan's Arab Legion, under
British officers, beleaguered and bombarded the Jewish section of Jerusalem and interrupted all communication between this area and the temporary capital. This they endeavored to isolate also from the north by breaking
through the narrow coastal strip, where the Iraq forces
actually claimed the capture of Nathanya. In Galilee, the
Syrians and Lebanese threatened to overwhelm the area of
Jewish settlement by weight of numbers. But almost everywhere the Jewish strongpoints held out. A brilliant counter-
offensive in the north cleared the enemy from almost the
whole of the historic borders of Palestine in this direction.

By now it was obvious that the new state could not be
overwhelmed by force of arms, as had been anticipated. The
United Nations representatives, endeavoring to reestablish
peace, negotiated a series of truces from June onwards, but
they did not last for long. In every case, on the resumption
of hostilities, there were further amazing Israel triumphs.
The newly-organized navy and air force came into action:
enemy capitals were attacked from the air; the flagship of
the Egyptian fleet was sunk; the Arab cities of Lydda,

Ramleh, and Beersheba were captured; Egyptian territory was invaded by a force which but for British intervention might have pressed on to the Nile delta. In March a mobile Israel column reached Eilat on the Gulf of Akabah, thus establishing a foothold towards the Indian Ocean for the first time in Jewish history since the days of the Monarchy. During much of the intervening period Jewish sections of Jerusalem in the new city outside the walls had been experiencing almost incessant siege and bombardment. A relief column commanded by an American Jew, David Marcus, failed to break through in time to prevent the overwhelming of the Jewish quarter of the Old City by the Arab forces. Jerusalem was cut off from Tel Aviv, and the rare convoys which succeeded in breaking through with provisions did so only at the cost of appallingly heavy casualties. In the summer of 1949, however, a new road was hazardously cut through the Judean hills and relieved the pressure on Jerusalem. The ancient capital, though still subject to attack, was again in touch with the rest of Jewish Palestine. By this time not merely successful defense but overwhelming victory on every front seemed to be well within the bounds of possibility. Owing to the efforts of the representatives of the United Nations, a series of armistice agreements with the Arab states were signed at Rhodes in the first months of 1949 (that with Syria on July 20th), bringing the War of Liberation to a triumphant conclusion. These agreements were supposed to be in anticipation of a permanent peace treaty, which the abashed enemy could not bring himself to face at that time.

The area controlled by the new state comprised the territory allotted to the Jews by the United Nations resolution, plus certain conquered areas originally assigned to the projected Arab state, as well as the Jewish sections of Jerusalem. Gaza to the south was still occupied by the Egyptians while the hill-country north and south of the Holy City, including the whole of ancient Samaria, was incorporated in the newly-renamed kingdom of Jordan. The frontiers of Jordan at more than one point came to within a few miles of the coast and closely hemmed in on three sides the narrow corridor of territory which joined Jerusalem with Tel Aviv. At the outset the Arab authorities had made it known that any person remaining in the areas controlled by the Jews would be regarded as acquiescing in their political pretensions and would have to answer for it. Thus, with the outbreak of hostilities there took place a wholesale evacuation in preparation for a triumphant return. Moreover, panic seized on the population in many other areas, causing here too a general flight. In the subsequent period, while the Arab states refused to open peace negotiations, it was obviously impossible to readmit this potential fifth-column. Thus the striking result that, as would not have been the case had the United Nations Resolutions been complied with by the Arabs, the state of Israel was almost homogeneous in population. There were smaller or larger minorities in various cities, a number of Bedouin in the south, Druze tribesmen on the Carmel, a solid block of population (mainly Christian) in the Nazareth region in Galilee, all of whom now accepted the Israel citizenship, sometimes with enthusiasm. But the population of the country was basically Jewish.

3.   It was a natural consequence of the conceptions of the Hebrew Scriptures and of the tendencies of Jewish life in the Diaspora that the new state was organized forthwith on democratic lines. While hostilities were still in progress, a Parliament had been elected, called by the ancient Hebrew term, *Keneset*. Chaim Weizmann was chosen as President, and Ben-Gurion took office as Prime Minister. On May 11th of that year, the new state was admitted to the United Nations, after having had its independence recognized by a majority of the governments of the world. In the following year the capital was removed from Tel Aviv to Jerusalem, under the shadow of the walls of the ancient city under Arab control; for it was obvious that no city other than Jerusalem could be the capital of the Jewish state.

The creation of the state had been made inevitable because of the desperate necessity of opening a place of refuge where the Jewish "displaced persons" could be at home at last; and it became part of its moral duty to allow free admittance to all who cared to come. On July 5th, 1950, the *Keneset* unanimously passed the Law of the Return which stipulated that every Jew has the right to settle in Israel. But already immigration had begun. Even while the fighting was still in progress large numbers of survivors from the Nazi campaign of extermination were enthusiastically welcomed. Before long the Displaced Persons camps on the continent of Europe were at last virtually cleared of their burden of human misery. The Jews of Iraq, their lives made impossible by the vindictive actions of the government smarting under its defeat, emigrated almost to a man. The ancient Arabized communities of Yemen were seized with a Messianic fervor and were brought into the country *en masse* by a superbly-organized airlift which was given the romantic title "Operation Magic Carpet." The small isolated community of Cochin, in South India, followed their example. From San Nicandro in South Italy there arrived a number of villagers who had become converted to Judaism through their intense study of the Bible. Larger groups came from almost every other country where the position of the Jew was perilous, especially in the Moslem world.

By 1961, the population of Israel, which had stood at 655,000 at the time of the Declaration of Independence, had risen to over 2,000,000, of whom the vast majority were Jews. With the exception of the United States of America, with its 5,300,000 Jews, this was now very likely the largest Jewish community in any country in the entire world, probably exceeding even that of Soviet Russia.

Obviously, the economic strain involved for the new state in absorbing this disproportionate burden was a crushing one. One thing was plain; it was not following its own interest but fulfilling the duty of all the body of Jewry in providing a safe haven at last for the persecuted. It was the clear duty of the Jews of other lands, where they dwelled in freedom and comfort, to collaborate in this great work of *Kibutz Galuyoth*—the Ingathering of the Exiles.

There was indeed to be one unhappy exception. During the heroic moments of the war against Germany, Russian Jewry had been momentarily encouraged by the Soviet government to foster relations again with the communities of the free world. It had been hoped that the former period of tragic isolation which had prevailed for the past twenty years was now ended. But before long the former stringent separation was reimposed, coupled with a determined attempt to suppress the normal manifestations of Jewish life; even tokens of a thorough-going anti-Semitic reaction were not lacking. This was the state of affairs not only as regards the Jews of Russia, but also with the survivors of the other Central and Eastern European countries now brought behind the "Iron Curtain"—in particular Roumania and Hungary, where sizable communities remained. No longer could these once-famous centers of tradition have a share in the glory of Jewish achievement.

But the communities of the other countries of the world willingly played their part in supporting Israel endeavor; especially those of the English-speaking countries, with the United States of America at their head. Through the United Jewish Appeal and through other fund-raising agencies the Jews of the United States collected hundreds of millions of dollars for the settlement of the multitude of Jewish immigrants in Israel. In these fund-raising efforts American Jews rose to unprecedented heights of generosity and devotion toward their brethren in Israel. Not that this could imply any slackening in concern for their domestic interests and for the maintenance of existing institutions; for it was obvious that support for Israel could be based only on a strong and Jewishly-inspired Diaspora. It was not a question of charity, in the old sense; it was the privilege of participation in the most exciting venture of the age.

Too much of the attention and resources of the newly reborn state unfortunately had to be concentrated even now on the problem of physical security. For the surrounding

Arab states, smarting under the disgrace of military defeat in the conflict into which they had so needlessly entered, publicly announced their intention of taking up arms again as soon as possible, in order to blot out the Jewish state. The Egyptians, especially, aspiring under a new republican regime to the leadership of the Arab world, not only encouraged, even organized, destructive raids across the Israel frontier from the Gaza strip to the south, but also piled up armaments, mobilized forces, and made large-scale military preparations with the overt intention of renewing hostilities. The danger ultimately became too acute to be borne any longer and, in November 1956, the Israeli forces crossed the armistice lines and invaded the Sinai Peninsula so as to destroy the military equipment deployed against them. The brief campaign that followed was among the most brilliant in military history. The whole of the Sinai Peninsula was rapidly overrun, the Gaza strip was cut off and occupied, and the navigation of the Gulf of Akaba, long closed to Israel shipping, was freed by the occupation of the Straits of Tiran at its outlet to the Indian Ocean. The final breaking of the Arab blockade and the enforcement of a peace treaty on the most menacing of the Arab states seemed to be imminent when, unfortunately, the English and French governments saw their opportunity to reassert their lost authority in this area and made a landing at the entrance to the Suez Canal. As a result the United Nations took action; paradoxically the Great Powers, trying to establish their former position, and Israel attempting to break out of its illegal blockade, were arraigned together. In consequence the Israeli troops were compelled to withdraw from the area they had occupied, their task uncompleted. But the fruits of victory were not wholly cancelled. Most important was the fact that the new state with its devoted, highly trained citizen army was seen to have a toughness which rendered it a valuable ally and redoubtable foe; even though the Arab states refused to conclude peace, they were now aware that they could not dare to wage war. Moreover, the despatch of United Nations forces to the area of friction made it impossible for the border raids to be renewed; further, the Gulf of Akaba remained open for shipping, with the consequence of a rapid expansion of Israel diplomatic and trade activity in Asia and the prodigious development of the port of Elath and its hinterland. Once again as in the days of Solomon the area seemed about to become a bridge between East and West, drawing and giving inspiration in both directions. In the changed world of the second half of the twentieth century, this could well be part of Israel's function and mission.

XXXIII.
THE SIX DAY WAR

1.   The ostensible triumph over the two Western powers, skillfully exaggerated, much enhanced the prestige of the Egyptian dictator, now able to present his humiliating defeat as a victory. He attempted to assume the leadership of the Afro-Asian countries that were now reasserting themselves, effected a short-lived political union with Syria which threatened Israel on two flanks, and increased rather than diminished his threats against that country. Even the Suez Canal remained closed to Israel shipping, notwithstanding international treaties and the specific promises and undertakings given to her. Nevertheless, conditions were now far improved in some important respects. The brilliant success of the Sinai campaign proved a sharp lesson to the Arab states and made them cautious of provoking further military action—with the result that conditions temporarily became far quieter on the frontiers. Moreover, the presence of the United Nations forces along the armistice lines to the south brought to an end the brutal raids that had been largely responsible for the outbreak of hostilities. Henceforth, the farmers in the border settlements here could do their work of reclaiming and tilling the soil in relative security.

More far-reaching, though at the outset hardly to be anticipated, were the remoter consequences of the opening to Israel navigation of the Gulf of Akaba, the outlet to which at Sharm-el-Sheikh was also now occupied by United Nations forces. This resulted in a noteworthy change in the perspective and even in the geographical balance of the State of Israel. Henceforth it could look effectively south and east as well as west. The vast arid tracts of the Negev, hitherto considered almost impossible for permanent settlement, received an enormous impetus. New colonies were established, new industries developed, new towns created. Water was brought from the north for purposes of irrigation in an ambitious scheme. Those who were formerly familiar with ancient Beersheba as a small Bedouin center in the midst of desolation now saw there an important city, one of the largest in the country, smiling in the midst of its gardens.

The port of Elath was greatly developed and, with the improvement of the road system and railway projects, became potentially one of the most important centers of communications in the country. A Jewish navy and Jewish merchant marine began to ply the Gulf of Akaba and the seas beyond it. As a result, trading as well as diplomatic relations were opened up with the countries bordering on and beyond the Indian Ocean. Among some of the new African states Israel became a relatively important force, her experience in conquering an intractable soil and developing industries where none had existed before being of supreme value to them.

The country at last had the opportunity to take real advantage of its geographical position, constituting as it does in effect a land bridge between the three continents of the Old World. Not only, to be sure, in a material sense. Israel was capable also of acting as a spiritual bridge. Not being historically associated with any tradition of colonial exploitation, it could serve as the channel whereby the best of the culture of the West, of which it was naturally part, could be transmitted to those countries with which it now maintained closer and closer connections. Young colored men and women could now be met constantly on the benches of the Hebrew University or in the kibbutzim, where they familiarized themselves with the methods, standards, and ideals of this young-old country from which they could learn so much. In this sense, the importance and influence of the new Israel far exceeded its dimensions and its population.

To be sure, dangers persisted. The neighboring Arab powers, steadfast in their hostility, managed to secure the general adherence to their policies of the other re-emerging Moslem states of the Mediterranean world, and even of some farther afield, in which the lot of the old, established native Jews rapidly deteriorated. It is probable, however, that this would have occurred before long in any case, as a result of the rising tide of nationalism and anti-Europeanism: the new factor was that there was now a land of refuge in which the fugitives could find a home.

The reluctant withdrawal of the Western powers from the eastern and southern Mediterranean left Israel somewhat isolated in a political and military sense. The consequent necessity for perpetual military vigilance required that a disproportionate amount of the state's resources be spent on armaments. But to this, too, there was another side. The perpetual necessity to stand on the *qui vive* indubitably toughened the fibre of the people. Its youth developed a spirit of unshakable confidence. In the long nightmare of the Diaspora, a characteristic of the Jews as a people had been timidity; now it was remarked that among the Israel youth fear was unknown as a physical fact.

The constant dangers that threatened the new state made it impossible for the communities of the world to abandon the expressions of practical solidarity they had so effectively shown when it had come into being. As a result, Israel helped the Jewish people at large to retain its sense of cohesion even in an age of dwindling religious loyalty. And where this was now in any measure revived, it was bound up with a strong sense of identification with the great Jewish enterprise in the ancient Land of Israel.

2.   In the ensuing years it became more and more evident that the creation of the State of Israel had been in the fullest sense of the term providential. In the course of the nineteenth century, the area of Jewish settlement in the world had increased, this being accompanied generally with an improvement in the economic and political position of the Jews: and they had won legal equality with their fellow citizens at least in the countries of Western Europe and their overseas extensions. It was under these circumstances that they had become established to some extent in the Far East, and had created fresh communities in Central Africa, and that the Jews of the Moslem countries had emerged from their condition of medieval degradation. For the world of the nineteenth century had been a liberal world, which under the influence of Western Europe had set the ideal of

establishing nations on a basis of social uniformity rather than religious conformity.

As the twentieth century advanced, there was a general regression from these conceptions. As we have seen, the new ideologies had cut off a great part of the fecund Jewish communities of Eastern Europe from their co-religionists elsewhere at the time of the rise of communism, at the close of World War I. Now, almost the totality of the exhausted survivors of the Central European communities seemed destined to follow the same path of spiritual suicide. In other regions of the world, in proportion as the European influences and the old traditions of colonialism receded, the Jewish communities—whether semi-autochthonous and long established, or created by recently arrived immigrants from Europe—became weakened, sometimes to the verge of extinction. The new Negro states of Central Africa had no place in their economies and future prospects for the settlers who had formerly prospered there. In the revived Moslem states of the Mediterranean littoral the new nationalism, reinforced by religion, quite apart from the tension created in the Middle East by the Israel-Arab confrontation, made the lot of the Jews more and more precarious. In Algeria, for example, where the native Jews had been the first a century before to become French citizens by virtue of the Loi Crémieux, this privileged position now turned to their disadvantage.

In Communist China, the once-prosperous Jewish communities were now eliminated; while in the other lands of the Far East the withdrawal of English and French rule was proved generally a mortal blow to the Jews. With the exodus of the Jews from Iraq, Yemen, and other Arab lands of Asia, both before and after the establishment of the State and the accompanying hostilities, there seemed to be the prospect that the Jews would be eliminated from the entire Asian continent, apart from Israel. (In this new age of continental strategy, Jewish history too was beginning to be considered on a continental scale, not as hitherto in terms of provinces or countries.) The same was true of a great part—according to some pessimists, all—of the continent of Africa. As for America, the dissolution of the community of Cuba, after the triumph of a new Leftist regime in 1959, gave a grim warning of what might happen elsewhere in the region in similar circumstances; while some observers thought that they could discern in some areas of Latin America, especially those where refugee Nazi leaders had been allowed to establish themselves, the precursory signs of the development of an anti-Semitic movement of the Nazi type.*

3.   In the middle decades of the twentieth century, the communities of free Europe gradually regained a measure of cohesion and solidity, although not to be compared with

* In 1961, Adolf Eichmann, the Nazi functionary who had principally organized Hitler's attempt to apply the "Final Solution" to the Jews of Europe, and was thus directly responsible for the deaths of hundreds of thousands if not millions of persons, was traced in Argentina, audaciously arrested, and brought to Israel. Here he was given—by Jewish judges in a Jewish court, in proceedings carried out in the Hebrew language—an impeccably fair trial, such as none of his countless victims had known, for his indescribable record of ill-doing. The whole world had its attention riveted to the revelation, under conditions of strictest justice, of the horrors of which the Nazi regime had been responsible, and of the tenacity and lofty purpose of the resuscitated Jewish State. He was condemned to death and executed.

the state of affairs that had existed before the great disaster. On the other hand, the changed conditions of the Moslem world, as regards both the Jews and Western influences generally, resulted in the virtual completion of the liquidation of the ancient Jewish communities of North Africa and significant parts of Asia: these two continents, where formerly a significant proportion of the Jewish people had been established from times immemorial, now became to a great extent *judenrein*—"free of Jews" in the Nazi phrase. The emigrants, if they did not go to Israel with its ever open door, tended to gravitate to France, where in these years the new Sephardi influx resuscitated Jewish life in many ancient centers and not only doubled, but to some extent changed the character of, French Jewry. The whole Jewish world was affected to some extent by this new migration, fresh Sephardi centers now being established not only in European lands but also throughout the English-speaking world and in South America. Even in Spain there seemed to be signs of a change of atmosphere and a limited Jewish revival.

On the other hand, the Russian enigma continued. While in Communist Hungary and Roumania the Jews were still able to maintain a certain degree of independent communal and religious life, in the U.S.S.R. itself the prejudices against Jewish religious training or observance, coupled with an increasing opposition to any manifestations of Zionist feeling, became progressively more marked. Whether this was effective in stifling Jewish feeling was problematical: in the 1960's, the outside world heard with amazement that thousands or tens of thousands of young Jews gathered on the occasion of the traditional feast of the Rejoicing of the Law

[Simhat Torah] outside the Moscow synagogue to dance and sing Hebrew songs, the police being unable or unwilling to intervene. The enigma thus remained.

4.   The former Muscovite Empire had changed its constitution and its economy since the days before the Revolution of 1917, but its essential nature was not much altered. This continued to be manifested in Russia's policy in the Middle East, where it was now strenuously continuing its efforts to establish a foothold by encouraging the spread of communism and by the lavish supply of arms to the Arab states. For these there was only one main use—the cancellation of the humiliation they had undergone in the past and the annihilation (no less) of the State of Israel, whose existence they still refused to recognize and whose obliteration from the map was one of their main ambitions, as they incessantly proclaimed to the world. The principal enemy of Israel in this was the adroit demagogue Gamal Abdel Nasser, dictator of Egypt, who had set himself up as the leader and mouthpiece of the Arab world and attempted to justify his claims by being the instrument for the destruction of Israel. For some time his offensive was confined to words, owing to the salutary presence of the United Nations force in the Gaza Strip and at the entrance to the Gulf of Akaba, as has been recounted; though he still illegally barred goods or shipping destined for Israel from passage through the Suez Canal, supposed by law to be open to the goods and shipping of all nations, in peace and war. Meanwhile, to the north terrorist raids were periodically made on Israel territory over the Syrian border, there were frequent clashes in the supposedly demilitarized zone on Jewish farm-workers,

The Six Day War 433

and occasionally even bombardment of Israel villages from the higher ground in Syrian hands—all this provoking now and again organized but brief retaliatory raids by the Jewish defense forces.

Thus encouraged, in the spring of 1967 Nasser suddenly demanded the withdrawal of the United Nations observers stationed in the Gaza Strip, who for the past nineteen years had ensured tranquillity in the south of the country. Almost immediately after this insolent demand was complied with, he secured the evacuation of Sharm-el-Sheikh, at the head of the Gulf of Akaba. This was followed by the statement that no Israel shipping would henceforth be permitted passage through the Straits—a menace clearly contrary to international law, like the blockade of the Suez Canal, and in effect an act of war. Meanwhile, there were more and more menacing concentrations of troops on the Israel borders, and King Hussein of Jordan, backed by other Arab states, made a military pact with Egypt.

The die was cast. The Arab leaders not only gloried in the prospect of a war, but made it clear that it would be a war of annihilation, in which the Jewish state would be wiped out and its inhabitants butchered.

Israel prepared for the inevitable conflict. Levi Eshkol, Prime Minister since 1963 in succession to the veteran David Ben-Gurion, formed a coalition government. Not only Ben-Gurion but also Menahem Beigin, the underground leader in Mandate days, joined the government, while the victor of Sinai, Moshe Dayan, became Minister of Defense.

On June 5th hostilities began. The Egyptians, the major enemy, moved armored columns northwards in the hope of slicing the country in two and linking up with Jordan, and there was heavy shelling and bombing of Israel towns and villages. On the Israeli side the reaction was incredibly swift and extraordinarily efficient. All the major Arab airports were massively and scientifically bombed, and within a matter of hours the Egyptian air force had been effectively destroyed, even before it left the ground. The same took place on a smaller scale in the other neighboring Arab lands. The Israel land forces could now advance without interference from the air, which they did with model efficiency. In the Sinai desert, where the Jewish people had seen its birth, there took place the greatest tank battle as yet known in history, resulting in an overwhelming victory. Within a couple of days, the Egyptian army in the field had been virtually wiped out, and Israel troops had established themselves all along the Suez Canal. Simultaneously, a task force had reached and occupied Sharm-el-Sheikh, and the Gulf of Akaba was again freely open to shipping. On the night of June 8th, the Israeli naval forces struck simultaneously at enemy shipping in the harbors of Alexandria and Port Said.

At the outset of hostilities, King Hussein of Jordan had been informally promised immunity by the Israel authorities except in self-defense. Nevertheless, almost simultaneously with the opening of hostilities to the south, the New City of Jerusalem was heavily attacked by the Jordanians with artillery and machine-gun fire, nearly 1,000 private homes being hit and a large number of civilian casualties inflicted. The Israel reply was as decisive as it was short. Within less than three days, the entire Arab-occupied territory of the historic Palestine on the west bank of the Jordan had been occupied. The greatest triumph of the whole campaign was completed when, on Wednesday, June 7th, the old walled city of Jerusalem—the true Jerusalem, from which Jews had been utterly excluded for nearly twenty years, and in which they had been subject to insult and humiliation for a hundred times as long—was taken by Israel paratroopers. It was almost the greatest military triumph in Jewish history of all time: not since the Roman triumph nearly two thousand years before had Jews controlled the city which Judaism had made sacred and famous. That day, amid scenes of indescribable emotion and elation, the conquerors went to pray, each in his own fashion, before the Western Wall, the solitary relic still standing of the ancient Temple.

Now attention was turned toward Syria, and after particularly bitter fighting the northern enemy was ejected from the strong positions constructed along the frontier, from which the Israel border settlements had been harassed for so long. Perhaps the campaign would have finished with the occupation of the enemy capitals—an achievement perfectly within the ability of the tough and now confident Israel troops—had not the Security Council of the United Nations demanded a cease fire. But the hostilities ended with the Israel forces everywhere triumphant, and in control not only of the entire Palestinian territory west of the Jordan, including both the Gaza Strip and the former legendary capital of their people, but of territory well beyond this, both south and north. The Six Day War had been perhaps the most brilliant campaign in military history, even outdoing the Sinai campaign of 1957: the Israel army had shown itself the best fighting force in the world—and the more so since it was a citizen army intent not on conquest but on self-protection.

While all this was happening, an unprecedented wave of expression of solidarity spread throughout the Jews of the free world. All elements—Zionist and non-Zionist, young and old, religious and irreligious—demonstrated their sympathy with their brethren in the Land of Israel in body and soul, in moral support and material contributions. The shattered unity of the Jewish people seemed to be reconstituted in this spontaneous expression of feeling which showed in a positive fashion the place that Israel had come to play in their lives: the realization that if the State was now overwhelmed (and at one time this seemed probable enough) every Jew everywhere would be affected, Judaism as a religion would suffer a blow that might be mortal, the heritage of Jewish history would become meaningless.

Yet more amazing was what had become manifest in Israel itself in these critical days. Here was a people that within a generation had become a balanced state, had restored its nationhood, its language, its unity, had brought into being out of the raw material of pedlars and shopkeepers and students a martial youth ready to defend its country as well as to rebuild it. This indomitable people had risen from its greatest disaster to snatch from the jaws of destiny its supreme victory. Our generation is too near to appreciate even now the scale of the achievement or the miracle of the rebirth.

SUGGESTIONS FOR FURTHER STUDY

(PB: available in a paperback edition)

ABRAHAMS, I. *Jewish Life in the Middle Ages.* 2d ed. London, 1932.

ADLER, E. N. *Jewish Travellers.* New York and London, 1967.

AGUS, J. *Evolution of Jewish Thought.* New York and London, 1960.

BAER, YITZHAK. *A History of the Jews in Christian Spain.* 2 vols. Philadelphia, 1961, 1966.

BARON, S. W. *The Jewish Community.* 3 vols. Philadelphia, 1942.

————. *A Social and Religious History of the Jews.* 2d ed., rev. New York and Philadelphia, 1952 *et seq.*

BEVAN, E. R., and SINGER, C. J., eds. *The Legacy of Israel.* New York and London, 1927.

BICKERMAN, ELIAS. *From Ezra to the Last of the Maccabees.* New York, 1962 (PB).

BRIGHT, JOHN. *A History of Israel.* New York, 1959; London, 1960.

DUBNOV, S. M. *History of the Jews in Russia and Poland.* 3 vols. Philadelphia, 1916.

ELBOGEN, I. *A Century of Jewish Life.* Philadelphia, 1944.

FINKELSTEIN, L., ed. *The Jews: Their History, Culture, and Religion.* 2 vols. 3d ed. New York, 1960.

GOITEIN, S. *Jews and Arabs: Their Contacts Through the Ages.* New York, 1955 (PB).

GRAYZEL, S. *The Church and the Jews in the XIIIth Century.* New York and London, 1967.

GREGOROVIUS, F. *The Ghetto and the Jews of Rome.* New York, 1966 (PB).

HERTZBERG, ARTHUR. *The Zionist Idea.* New York, 1966 (PB).

HERZL, THEODOR. *Diaries of Theodor Herzl.* Edited by Marvin Lowenthal. New York, n.d. (PB).

HILBURG, RAUL. *Destruction of the European Jews.* Chicago and London, 1961 (PB).

HUSIK, I. *A History of Medieval Jewish Philosophy.* Philadelphia, New York, and London, 1941 (PB).

JACOBS, J. *Jewish Contributions to Civilization.* Philadelphia, 1919.

Jewish Encyclopedia (for individual topics). 12 vols. New York and London, 1901.

Jewish Social Studies (for individual topics). New York, 1939 *et seq.*

The Jews of Czechoslovakia. Philadelphia, 1968

JOSEPHUS, FLAVIUS. *Jerusalem and Rome.* Edited by N. N. Glatzer. New York and London, 1960 (PB).

KAUFMANN, Y. *Religion of Israel.* Edited by M. Greenberg. Chicago, 1960; London, 1961.

LEBESON, ANITA. *Jewish Pioneers in America, 1492–1848.* New York, 1931.

LEON, HARRY J. *The Jews of Ancient Rome.* Philadelphia, 1960.

MANN, J. *The Jews in Egypt and Palestine Under the Fatimids.* 2 vols. London, 1921.

MARCUS, J. R. *Early American Jewry.* 2 vols. Philadelphia, 1951.

———. *The Jew in the Medieval World.* New York, 1938 (PB).

MARGOLIS, M. L., and MARX, A. *A History of the Jewish People.* Philadelphia and New York, 1927 (PB).

MOORE, GEORGE F. *Judaism in the First Centuries of the Christian Era.* 3 vols. Cambridge, Mass., 1927–30.

NETANYAHU, B., gen. ed. *The World History of the Jewish People.* 2 vols. New Brunswick, N.J., and London, 1965, 1966.

NEUMANN, A. A. *The Jews of Spain.* 2 vols. Philadelphia, 1942.

PARKES, JAMES. *Anti-Semitism.* New York, 1964; London, 1965.

———. *The Conflict of the Church and the Synagogue.* New York, 1966 (PB).

PHILIPSON, D. *The Reform Movement in Judaism.* rev. ed. New York, 1967

ROTH, CECIL. *History of the Jews in England.* 3d ed. New York and London, 1967.

———. *History of the Jews in Italy.* Philadelphia, 1946.

———. *History of the Marranos.* Philadelphia and New York, 1941 (PB).

———. *The Jewish Contribution to Civilization.* New York, 1939; London, 1945.

———. *The Jews in the Renaissance.* Philadelphia, 1959 (PB).

———. *Life of Menasseh ben Israel.* Philadelphia, 1934.

SACHAR, HOWARD M. *The Course of Modern Jewish History.* Cleveland and New York, 1958 (PB).

SAMUEL, MAURICE. *The Great Hatred.* New York, 1940.

SCHAPPES, M. U. *A Documentary History of the Jews in the U.S.* New York, 1950.

SCHECHTER, S. *Studies in Judaism.* 3 vols. Philadelphia, 1924.

SCHOLEM, G. G. *Major Trends in Jewish Mysticism.* 3d rev. ed., New York, 1961 (PB).

SCHÜRER, EMIL. *A History of the Jewish People in the Time of Jesus.* Edited by N. N. Glatzer. New York, 1961 (PB).

SCHWARZ, L. W., ed. *Great Ages and Ideas of the Jewish People.* New York, 1956.

STRACK, H. L. *Introduction to the Talmud and Midrash.* Philadelphia, 1931 (PB).

TCHERIKOVER, VICTOR. *Hellenistic Civilization and the Jews.* Philadelphia, 1959.

WAXMAN, M. *A History of Jewish Literature.* 6 vols. 2d ed., rev. New York, 1960.

WEIZMANN, CHAIM. *Trial and Error.* New York and London, 1949 (PB).

WISCHNITZER, MARK. *History of Jewish Crafts & Guilds.* New York, 1965.

———. *To Dwell in Safety: Jewish Migration Since 1800.* Philadelphia, 1949.

ZBOROWSKI, M., and HERZOG, E. *Life Is With People.* New York, 1962 (PB).

INDEX

Abba the Tall, 128, 201
Abd-ur-Rahman I, 159
Abd-ur-Rahman III, 159
Abijah, King of Judah, 38
Abomination of Desolation, 73, 88
Abrabanel, Don Isaac, 228, 240
Abraham, 4, 8
Abraham ibn Ezra, 171
Abramovitch, Solomon (*see* Mendele Mocher Seforim)
Absalom, Son of David, 23 f.
Abulafia, Samuel, 218
Achad Ha'am, 373
Achaemenids, Empire of, 61
Acra, 72, 79
Adiabene, Royal House of, 120
Aelia Capitolina, 115
Africa, Jews in, relations with, 426, 429 f.
Agobard, Archbishop of Lyons, 166
Agrippa, Son of Aristobulus, 102
Agrippa II, 103, 112
Ahab, King of Israel, 32, 48
Ahaz, King of Judah, 40
Ahaziah, King of Israel, 32
Ahaziah, King of Judah, 38
Akibah ben Joseph, 114 f., 126
Alaric, 144
Aleikhem, Shalom (*see* Rabinovitz, Shalom), 340
Alenu, the, 201
Alexander of Macedon, 70
Alexander I, 334
Alexander II, 335, 351
Alexandria, 90 f., 102, 136
Ali, Mehemet, 345

Aliens Immigration Act, 355
Alfonso the Wise, 178
Alfonso VI, 187
Alliance Israélite Universelle, 346
Al-Mohades, Berber tribes, 163, 187
Al-Moravides, Berber tribes, 162
Alsace, Jews of, 214
Amalekites, 18, 21
Amalfi, 191
Amalgamated Clothing Workers of America, 362
Amaziah, King of Judah, 39
American Jewish Committee, 361
Ammonites, 17, 21
Amon, King of Judah, 42
Amoraim, 130, 152
Amorites, 3
Amos, 34, 49 f.
Amsterdam, Jews in, 299
Amulo, Archbishop of Lyons, 166
Anan ben David, 153
Andalusia, 162, 170
Anjou, house of, 186
Anthony, Mark, 94
Antigonus, Son of Aristobulus, 94
Antioch, 106
Antiochus the Great, 70 ff.
Antiochus VII, 79 f.
Antipas, Son of Herod, 99
Antipater, the Idumaean, 93
Anti-Semitism, in Germany, 347, in France, 349; in Russia, 351 ff., 365
Aphek, 17
Apocrypha, 89
Appollonius, 72

439

Index

Index 451

DATE DUE